Coleridge:
Lectures on Shakespeare
(1811–1819)

Coleridge: Lectures on Shakespeare (1811–1819)

Edited by
Adam Roberts

EDINBURGH
University Press

Edinburgh University Press is one of the leading university presses in the UK. We publish academic books and journals in our selected subject areas across the humanities and social sciences, combining cutting-edge scholarship with high editorial and production values to produce academic works of lasting importance. For more information visit our website: edinburghuniversitypress.com

Edinburgh University Press Ltd
The Tun – Holyrood Road
12(2f) Jackson's Entry
Edinburgh EH8 8PJ

Typeset in 11/12.5 Baskerville by
Servis Filmsetting Ltd, Stockport, Cheshire,
printed and bound in Great Britain by
CPI Group (UK) Ltd, Croydon CR0 4YY

A CIP record for this book is available from the British Library

ISBN 978 1 4744 1378 7 (hardback)
ISBN 978 1 4744 1379 4 (webready PDF)
ISBN 978 1 4744 1380 0 (epub)

Contents

CONTENTS

Introduction

Coleridge as Lecturer

The purpose of this edition is to present those of Coleridge's Shakespeare lectures as have come down to us. Not that there have been any shortage of prior editions of Coleridge's Shakespearian criticism, since what he had to say is not only central to any understanding of Coleridge as a critic, it proved immensely influential in the development of Shakespearean studies, and continues to exercise influence to this day. Nonetheless, a scholar, student or reader desirous to read what Coleridge actually said may well find themselves frustrated. Minimising that frustration is the present edition's aim.

Between 1808 and 1819 Coleridge delivered something like a hundred lectures on literature, education and philosophy – we aren't sure of the exact number, but it's approximately that. The majority of these were literary-critical, and the majority of *those* concerned Shakespeare, the subject of the present volume. But the largest majority of all, where these lectures are concerned, must be filed under the category 'lost'. Much of Coleridge's lecturing was extemporised. He tended to work from only scrappy notes, if any, together with volumes in which he had scribbled marginalia, and then spoke on and around his matter. Nor did he ever write up this material in finished form after the lecture was given. Charles Robert Leslie later recalled:

I had frequent opportunities of seeing and hearing Coleridge ... [His] lectures were, unfortunately, extemporaneous. He now and then took up scraps of paper on which he had noted the leading points of his subject, and he had books about him for quotation. On turning to one of these (a work of his own), he said, 'As this is a secret which I confided to the public a year or two ago, and which, to do the public justice, has been very faithfully kept, I may be permitted to read you a passage from it.' His voice was deep and musical, and his words followed each other in an unbroken flow, yet free from monotony. There was indeed a peculiar charm in his utterance. His pronunciation was remarkably correct: in some respects pedantically so. He gave the full sound of the *l* in *talk*, and *should* and *would*.[1]

Coleridge lectured for two reasons: for money and for reputation, although the need for money was the more pressing of these motivations. For much of 1804 and 1805 he had lived in the Mediterranean, landing a job in Malta in which he worked for the British governor of the island as 'Acting Public Secretary'. He was also in receipt of a generous annuity from Josiah Wedgwood of £150, but this he remitted to his wife who was raising their children, and from whom he was by this time effectively separated. Whilst in Malta he was financially secure, but in 1806 he returned to England, arriving in August, by his own reckoning 'shirtless & almost penniless'.[2] The need to earn was urgent. Coleridge's first recourse was his pen, and accordingly he tried to scratch together journalistic commissions. This, though, proved harder than he had hoped, and he looked for other opportunities. In a letter to Sara Coleridge of 16 September 1806, he wrote:

> I have had an application from the R. Institution for a Course of Lectures which I am much disposed to accept, both for money and reputation . . . I shall quit Town and trust to be at Keswick on Monday Sept. 29th. If I finally accept the Lectures, I must return by the midst of November.[3]

The Royal Institution of Great Britain had been founded in 1799 by a group of leading scientists, amongst whom was Humphry Davy, and was dedicated to 'the diffusion of knowledge'.[4] Davy was a friend of Coleridge and it seems the invitation to lecture came from him. Although Coleridge on this occasion declined for reasons of ill health, his letters of 1806 and 1807 are full of speculation about the earning potential of a course of lectures on the fine arts, estimates ranging from £120 to £400, either as a flat fee or an annual salary. Davy repeated the invitation several times, and Coleridge eventually accepted it, delivering between January and June 1808 a course of twenty lectures on 'the Principles of Poetry', plus an extra lecture on education.

[1]   Tom Taylor (ed.), *Autobiographical Recollections by the Late Charles Robert Leslie* (2 vols, London: John Murray, 1860), 1:47. The 'work of his own' must have been the *Biographia Literaria*.

[2]   Coleridge letter to Robert Southey, 20 August 1808 in Ernest Leslie Griggs (ed.), *The Collected Letters of Samuel Taylor Coleridge* (6 vols, Oxford: Oxford University Press, 1956–71), 2:1177.

[3]   Griggs, *Collected Letters*, 2:1181.

[4]   It still exists: http://www.rigb.org/.

Coleridge was no neophyte where lecturing was concerned. On the contrary: he was an experienced preacher (a consideration discussed below) and in 1795 had delivered six lectures on 'Revealed Religion' in Bristol. Still, with the 'Lectures on Literature' he was embarking upon something new, and it is clear that he learned and improved as he went along. Events, however, conspired to interrupt his progress. Illness and despondency, in part related to Coleridge's opium addiction, compelled him to withdraw during the middle of the 1808 course and he was absent for almost two months. Unfortunately 'no reports of what Coleridge came to regard as the main lectures of this course, the series on Shakespeare, are known to us'.[5] Reaction to this first course of lectures was mixed, the amount earned was apparently less than he had hoped, and Coleridge does not seem to have been keen to repeat the experiment. Instead, once the lecture course was completed, he devoted his energies to producing his periodical *The Friend*, again with hopes of making money. This was supposed to be a weekly journal, wholly authored by Coleridge himself, but the twenty-eight issues that were published between June 1809 and March 1810 emerged irregularly, and the whole project proved unsustainable.

During this time Coleridge was mostly living in the Lake District with his old friend and former collaborator Wordsworth; but his spirits were low, his health bad, and he was often stupefied by alcohol and opium. In March 1810 Sara Hutchinson, sister to Wordsworth's wife Mary and the woman for whom, as 'Asra', Coleridge nursed an all-consuming, hopeless love, left the Wordsworths' house to live with her brother and a friend on a remote Welsh farm. Coleridge felt himself, in Richard Holmes words, 'stung to death' by her departure. Over the months that followed his despair curdled. When Sara didn't write or otherwise contact him, he began (rather unfairly) to feel himself utterly abandoned. His letters from this period record his 'depression of spirits, little less than absolute Despondency', and mourn, not unangrily, Asra's 'cruel neglect & contemptuous silence ever since.'[6] In October 1810, Coleridge accepted a lift down to London in the coach of a mutual friend called Basil Montagu. It proved a traumatic journey. Montagu tactlessly reportedly that Wordsworth had said a number of disobliging things about Coleridge's character and personal failings. Coleridge was hurt and shaken, and a breach opened in the friendship between the two poets. With the earnest intervention

[5]   R. A. Foakes, 'Introduction', *Samuel Taylor Coleridge Lectures 1808–1819: On Literature* (Princeton: Princeton University Press/London: Routledge, 1987), 1:19.
[6]   Richard Holmes, *Coleridge: Darker Reflections* (London: Harper Collins, 1998), 192; Griggs, *Collected Letters* 3:287.

of mutual friends some sort of peace between Wordsworth and Coleridge was eventually engineered, although subsequent meetings between the two men achieved only a superficial rapprochement.

1810, in other words, marks a sort of threshold in Coleridge's life. The immediate consequence was to exacerbate Coleridge's proneness to depression, and narcotic indulgence. He stayed with friends, the Morgans, in Hammersmith, but, to quote Richard Holmes again, 'his stay there was not always tranquil':

> There were drunken scenes, periods of extreme depression and a return of his nightmares and screaming fits. Several times Coleridge fled away to temporary lodgings around Fleet Street fearful that he was 'depressing' their spirits with his behaviour . . . But the Morgans – kindhearted, unshockable, deeply convinced of Coleridge's fundamental genius – were proof against these 'habits' and aberrations. In every case Morgan hurried back into London, tracked Coleridge down, and prevailed upon him to return.[7]

In 1811 Coleridge contributed some articles to journals, but the work was irregular and poorly paid, and he turned again to the idea of a course of public lectures. By October 1811, with the Morgan's help, he organised a new series of lectures, finding a suitable venue and publishing a prospectus that announced 'A Course of Lectures on Shakespeare and Milton in Illustration of the Principles of Poetry'. The subscription rates were listed as: 'single tickets for the whole course, 2 Guineas, or 3 Guineas with the privilege of introducing a lady'.

Coleridge delivered seventeen lectures between November 1811 and January 1812, of which ten have been, for want of a better word, preserved. These form the bulk of the present volume. The surviving lectures cover either general criticism or specific Shakespeare plays; none of Coleridge's opinions on Milton (from this course) have come down to us. This series was considerably more successful than the 1808–9 one had been. Although Coleridge worried that attendance was 'scanty', his friend Henry Crabb Robinson records audiences of 150, which is a pretty healthy number for an undertaking like this. Newspapers reported 'several Fashionables' as being in attendance, although most of the audience was probably made up of figures from the London literary world. Charles Lamb, Crabb Robinson and Godwin attended all the lectures; Hazlitt, Campbell and Humphry

---

[7]   Holmes, *Coleridge: Darker Reflections*, 221.

Davy attended some of them. 'Those who are known to have attended one or more of the 1811–12 course', Foakes notes, 'included Aaron Burr, Mary Russell Mitford, Samuel Rogers and Lord Byron.'[8]

The course was deemed a success, in terms of both money and reception, and Coleridge immediately planned and delivered another: six lectures on 'the Drama of the Greek, French, English and Spanish stage' followed at a venue off St James's Square, in London, between May and June 1812. Although this series appears not to have been so successful as the previous one,[9] Coleridge nonetheless tried again later the same year, with twelve lectures 'on the Belle Letters' at the Surrey Institution delivered between November 1812 and January 1813. Of these last two courses, almost nothing has survived.

Coleridge continued living with the Morgans. When money troubles forced John Morgan abroad in August 1813, Coleridge attempted to raise funds to help his friend. This involved amongst other things delivering a course of eight lectures on 'Shakespeare and Education' in Bristol, October–November 1813. Of this course very little has come down to us; and nothing at all remains of his overlapping series on 'Milton and Poetry' given in 'Mangeon's Hotel' at Clifton, near Bristol, in November 1813, and which may have run to four lectures. Coleridge was something of a local celebrity, and indeed was (and remains) one of the West Country's most famous sons, so it made commercial sense to offer lectures to a Bristolian audience. Still in Bristol, Coleridge went on to deliver a course of six lectures on Milton and Cervantes at the White Lion in the city centre in 1814; and in the same venue in the same year and indeterminate number of lectures on the French Revolution (almost nothing from either course survives).

---

[8] Foakes, *Lectures 1808–1819*, 1:159. Holmes notes two important absentees: 'the seventeen year-old John Keats, who had just begun attending surgical lectures at St Thomas's Hospital, across the river by Westminster Bridge; and the nineteen-year old Percy Bysshe Shelley, who had just eloped with his first wife Harriet to Edinburgh' (*Coleridge: Darker Reflections*, 267). There are fascinating consonances between the developing aesthetic thinking of Keats and Shelley and points Coleridge made in these lectures, which implies either that the two men found out about the content through other means than immediate attendance, or else that they developed similar lines of thought independently.

[9] Foakes records that 'attendance fell away' by the last lecture: 'indications are that Coleridge failed to obtain anything like the number of subscribers he had hoped for'. He also quotes Wordsworth's scorn, expressed in letters to friends, at this time when the breach between the two men was at its most severe: 'Coleridge is to commence a course of six Lectures, One Guinea the course upon the Drama. This is a most odious way of picking up money and scattering about his own & his friend's thoughts' (Foakes, *Lectures 1808–1819*, 1:418–20).

After this Coleridge withdrew from lecturing for several years, concentrating during 1815–17 on writing and publishing the *Biographia Literaria*,[10] along with various other projects. He returned to lecturing with an ambitious concurrent double set of lectures in 1818–19. At the London Philosophical Society he gave fourteen lectures on 'the principles of Judgement, Culture and European Literature', which series overlapped for a time with a separate set of six lectures on Shakespeare at the Crown and Anchor pub off the Strand. Five of these six make up the bulk of the remainder of the present volume. When the courses were running in parallel, Coleridge lectured at the Philosophical Society on Mondays and the Crown and Anchor on Thursdays.

> On Monday evening, Mr. Coleridge commenced a course of weekly biographical and historical lectures on the most important revolutions in the belief and opinions of mankind and on Thursday another course, on six selected plays of Shakspeare. These lectures are delivered at the Crown and Anchor Tavern in the Strand. That of Monday was principally introductory, shewing the progressive state of civilization, and the consequently improved state of human reason. Mr C. denied that true philosophy had any existence before the days of Pythagoras, and entered largely into a view of ancient history, as illustrative of the subject. There was much novelty in the manner in which he handled this branch of his theory. We can at present afford no more than this brief notice, which may, however, direct the lovers of science and inquiry where they may reap information in an uncommon, if not an unique way.[11]

In 1819 Coleridge gave another seven lectures at the Crown and Anchor – alternating again with a series of Philosophical lectures – on 'Shakespeare, Milton, Dante, Spenser, Ariosto and Cervantes'. These series proved to be his last, and records of it are scrappy. The only text relevant to the present volume is a portion of the third lecture, on *Troilus and Cressida*. This, combined with a proportion of the 1818–19 series and ten lectures of the 1811–12, forms the content of this volume. The principles according to which these lectures have been reproduced here are discussed below.

---

[10] S. T. Coleridge, *Biographia Literaria, or Biographical Sketches of My Literary Life and Opinions* (2 vols, London: Rest Fenner, 1817).

[11] Anon, 'Mr Coleridge's Lectures', *Literary Gazette* (19 December 1818), 808.

Coleridge was by no means the only person giving lectures at this time, although he probably was the most prominent figure on the London circuit. There was, for instance, an appetite for theological instruction: for example, *A Course of Lectures, containing a Description and Systematic Arrangement of the several Branches of Divinity; accompanied with an Account, both of the principal Authors, and of the Progress which has been made at different Periods in Theological Learning*, by Herbert Marsh, D.D. F.R.S. Margaret Professor of Divinity at Cambridge (these lectures were collected in volume form, 1809). Others were more technical in purpose, such as Robert Mitchell Meadows' *Three Lectures on Engraving, Delivered at the Surrey Institution in the Year 1809* (published in book form in 1811). George Campbell lectured on 'Ecclesiastical History' at Marischal College in 1806; Dr Collyer lectured on 'Scripture Doctrine' and 'Scripture Fact' in 1817; and the Rev. Ezekiel Blomfield's *Lectures on the Philosophy of History* were published posthumously in 1819. There are many other examples, not least the hugely successful lectures by Humphry Davy on scientific matters at the Royal Institution from 1801 onwards. As noted above, Davy was a friend of Coleridge, and instrumental in persuading him to offer public lectures. By 1819, the *New Annual Register* could say

> the establishment of various institutions for lectures on liter-ature and science, may be regarded as one of the signs and consequences, as well as one of the causes of a more general prevalence of miscellaneous knowledge on almost every subject, than existed among our ancestors. Among the subjects of these lectures, none have been more engaging and popular than the belles lettres.[12]

Shakespeare was a popular topic. Radical firebrand John Thelwall lectured in 1817–18 at an institution in Lincoln's Inn Fields on Shakespeare and Dr Johnson. Two other Shakespearian series are especially pertinent to Coleridge's own lecturing, one course deliv-ered in London and one on the Continent. The former was offered by Coleridge's one-time friend William Hazlitt, whose published crit-icism and essays had established him as the key radical critic of his generation. Hazlitt's *Characters of Shakespear's Plays* (1817), though based on variously published essays rather than on lectures, remains (alongside Schlegel and Coleridge) one of the key Romantic interven-tions into Shakespearian criticism. But Hazlitt also lectured. His first course, on Philosophy, was offered in 1812 at the Russell Institution.

---

[12]   Anon, 'Part III', *The New Annual Register for the Year 1818* (1819), 144.

In 1818 he gave talks on 'the English Poets, from Chaucer to the present day' at the Surrey Institution. These were then published as *Lectures on the English Poets* (1818), followed by a collection of his drama criticism, *A View of the English Stage* (1818), and a second edition of *Characters of Shakespear's Plays*. A little while later Hazlitt again lectured on Elizabethan drama, publishing this course as *Lectures on the Dramatic Literature of the Age of Elizabeth* (1820). The interactions and respective merits of Coleridge and Hazlitt are discussed below.

The 'Continental' lectures referred to are those on drama, with a special emphasis on Shakespeare, delivered by August Wilhelm Schlegel in Berlin in 1801 and again in 1804, which were written-up and published as *Über dramatische Kunst und Litteratur* in three volumes (Heidelberg: Mohr & Zimmer, 1809–11). Coleridge read these lectures in German, although it is a little unclear at exactly what point in his own career as a lecturer he did so. Since there are clear parallels between what Schlegel and Coleridge say about the nature of Shakespeare's genius, the organic nature of artistic merit and other things, and since plagiary is sometimes attributed to Coleridge in this matter, this timing is more important than it might otherwise be, and is discussed in greater detail below. Midway through Coleridge's own career as a lecturer, an English translation of Schlegel's lectures by John Black was published in London, under the title *A Course of Lectures on Dramatic Art and Literature*.[13]

Contemporary opinions as to the skill with which Coleridge's delivered his lectures vary. Foakes records Crabb Robinson's opinion, based on attending the whole course, that Coleridge was 'quite dazzling' as a lecturer:

> 'Coleridge's digressions are not the worst part of his lectures' . . . another who attended one lecture was delighted by Coleridge's eloquence . . . what Mary Russell Mitford called the 'electric power of [his] genius' . . . James Gillman said of them 'in his lectures he was brilliant, fluent and rapid; his words seemed to flow as from a person repeating with grace and energy some delightful poem'.

Others were much less positive. Byron parodied him in 'The Blues: a Literary Eclogue' (1823) as the shambolic lecturer Scamp, whose lectures were:

---

[13] John Black, *A Course of Lectures on Dramatic Art and Literature* (2 vols, London: Baldwin, Cradock and Joy, 1815).

> such a palaver!
> I'd inoculate sooner my wife with the slaver
> Of a dog when gone rabid, than listen two hours
> To the torrent of trash which around him he pours,
> Pump'd up with such effort, disgorged with such labour.[14]

Some argued that the lectures were harming Coleridge's reputation. In 1821 Richard Farmer publicly made the case for a proper scholarly edition of Shakespeare's works, and identified Coleridge as one of only two men living with the competence to undertake such a task (the other was Professor John Wilson). 'Unfortunately', Farmer continues, Coleridge 'could do nothing unless by fits and starts ... incapable of continuous labour he allowed his wide Shaksperian knowledge and high enthusiasm to evaporate in fitful outbursts of fantastic eulogy.'[15] The anonymous satirical poem *Sortes Horatianae* (1814) includes some lively mockery of the Lake school, including this eight-line dig at Coleridge:

> Coleridge* should mount some rock's o'erjutting height,
> And tell his tale in accents of delight;
> Fancy his seat 'Apollo's forked hill,'
> The high tribunal of poetic skill;
> Or Surrey's chair, in which he toil'd in vain,
> While tittering students mocked the tragic strain;
> And think the winds that round would gently blow
> Teem'd with the praises of the crowd below.

The 'Apollo's hill' reference is to Pope (the *Epistle to Arbuthnot*, where the toadlike Bufo is 'Proud as Apollo on his forked hill') and the 'Surrey's chair' is a reference to Coleridge's London lectures. Here is the appended footnote:

> *Mr. Coleridge is well known as having produced, at divers times, a dainty volume of Poetics, and a Play, which will be honorably mentioned hereafter.––He is also a Lecturer, at the Surrey Institution, on Poetry and 'les Belles Lettres.' With no very prominent talents, either natural or acquired, for a public Speaker, he endeavours to supply the absence of propriety with pathos, but seldom succeeds in interesting the feelings of his

---

[14] Lord George Gordon Byron, 'The Blues: a Literary Eclogue', *The Liberal* 3 (1821), 4.
[15] Richard Farmer, *An Essay on the Learning of Shakespeare* (London: T. H. Rodd, 1821), 100.

auditors, till he has completely overwhelmed his own; as the following anecdote will prove:

In the course of his lecture, one evening, he had wandered from the subject matter to the story of two lovers—in the moon! So completely absorbed was he in their imaginary distresses, that he failed to observe its effect upon his hearers, until bending from his desk to make a last appeal, he saw, as well as he could through eyes suffused with tears, that they were literally laughing at him.

Constitit et lacrymans.[16]

The Latin is *Aeneid* 1:459, and describes what happened when Aeneas retold the story of the fall of Troy: 'he stopped, and began weeping'. The reference to the Surrey Institution situates this anecdote during Coleridge's 1812–13 series on 'Belles Lettres' delivered in that location, and concerning which almost nothing else is known. It is impossible to guess, from the Prospectus to this series, at which point in which lecture Coleridge might have wandered from his brief to a tear-jerking discussion of two lovers in the moon. Still, and although this is presented to us in order to mock its subject, I'd say there's genuine pathos in the picture of Coleridge, moved to tears by his own extempore lecturing, suddenly realising that his audience was literally laughing at him.

Coleridge's tears index both emotional sensitivity and a less attractive tendency towards self-pity, two qualities that, of course, have a great deal in common. They also, in a way, mark the disparity between the two contexts in terms of which his Shakespeare lectures have often been discussed: that is to say, the gap between Coleridge's often miserable personal circumstances on the one hand, and on the other the greatness he explores in the figure of Shakespeare. The distance between these two things is of the kind that can strike a certain kind of person as comic, or at least as an opportunity to try and diminish the lecturer. And it *is* easy to feel superior to Coleridge, an impulse it is wise for a modern critic or reader to resist. The very magnitude of Shakespeare's genius, as Coleridge represents it, can retort back upon the explicator. For Samuel Schoenbaum there is a tacit element of wishful thinking, if not quite projection, about the Shakespeare Coleridge built:

---

[16] *Sortes Horatianae: a Poetical Review of Poetical Talent, with Notes* (London: T. Hamilton, 1814), 89.

Amid the wreckage of his private life, the Lake Poet formulated an ideal image of transcendent genius . . . Shakespeare was a patriot. He loved children and nature, and respected kings, physicians, and priests. He possessed an exquisite sense of beauty. If gross passages occur in his plays, the age is accountable; anyway, they contain not a single vicious sentiment. At all times he kept to the high road of life: 'with him there were no innocent adulteries; he never rendered that amiable which religion and reason taught us to detest; he never clothed vice in the garb of virtue.' Although endowed with all manly powers, and indeed more than a man, Shakespeare yet had 'all the feelings, the sensibility, the purity, innocence and delicacy of an affectionate girl of eighteen.'[17]

It is hard to disagree with Schoenbaum that 'the gigantic, myriad-minded persona that emerges from [Coleridge's] scattered remarks . . . bears little resemblance even to an extraordinary mortal occupied, as most mortals must be, with the bread and cheese of daily life'. Nonetheless the way Schoenbaum works tacitly to emphasise the disparity between two posited extremes, of Coleridge's inadequacies on the one hand, and the hyperbolic excess of his version of Shakespeare on the other, can be challenged. As for the latter, it seems to me that, compared with later critical hyperbole, even unto the present day – for instance, Harold's Bloom's claim that Shakespeare single-handedly invented the modern human – Coleridge's praise seems measured.[18] And as for the former, the gap that we should measure is not between the two historical personages of Shakespeare on the one hand and Coleridge on the other, but rather the dimensions of the Shakespeare Coleridge generated out of his own potent imaginative engagement, a Shakespeare himself centrally interested in the disjunction of the failings of external action and the greatness of internal capacity. Coleridge's critical imagination makes a Shakespeare who is himself radically defined by the genius of his imagination – not an artist carefully copying external reality, like a Dutch painter, but an artist re-making reality in the crucible of his own divinely fired mind. He is

Proteus, who now flowed a river; now raged a fire; now roared a lion—he assumes all changes, but still in the stream, in the fire, in the beast, it is not only resemblance, but it is the Divinity

[17] Samuel Schoenbaum, *Shakespeare's Lives* (Oxford: Clarendon Press, 1970), 183.
[18] See Harold Bloom, *Shakespeare: The Invention of the Human* (New York: Riverhead Books, 1998). It makes sense to situate Bloom in the tradition of Shakespearian scholarship that begins with Coleridge.

that appears in it, and assumes the character. (1811–12 series, lecture 3)

It is, of course, an intensely Romantic conception of Shakespeare. Indeed, we can go further, and call it the central statement of Romantic Shakespearianism. But saying so does not limit its application. On the contrary, and to the extent that we are all still living in a markedly post-Romantic cultural and social moment, and working with a Romantic Bard, saying so only reaffirms its relevance.

Schlegel and Coleridge

The question of the relationship between Coleridge's version of Shakespeare and Schlegel's chronologically prior statement of several equivalent positions is a vexed one. At what point did Coleridge first become aware of the German critic's *Über dramatische Kunst und Litteratur*? Does Coleridge's advocacy of those positions amount to plagiary?

Certainly Schlegel cannot be overlooked in any account of the influential Romantic reappraisal of Shakespeare's reputation. René Wellek notes that although Schlegel lectured on a very wide range of literary, dramatic and philosophical questions, Shakespeare was 'the center of [his] critical interests, the author to whom he devoted more effort and time than to any other'. This included translating seventeen plays into German, and repeatedly writing and lecturing on Shakespeare from 1791 onward.

> The leading motif of Schlegel's discussion, even very early, is Shakespeare's conscious artistry, the opposition to the view of Shakespeare as a mere force of nature, the praise of Shakespeare's works as miracles of harmony and composition ... There is an inner unity in [a Shakespearean] play; every detail is then defended as contributing to this final effect.[19]

This, of course, is also the central thrust of Coleridge's critical position. Repeatedly in the lectures he attacks the eighteenth-century notion of Shakespeare as a mere 'child of nature', an untutored genius whose plays are shapeless mixtures of splendour and foolishness.[20] Schlegel dismisses the idea that Shakespeare should be judged according to the

---

[19] René Wellek, *A History of Modern Criticism: 1750–1950. 2: The Romantic Age* (London: Lowe and Brydon, 1955), 64.

[20] 'Along with Schlegel, it is Coleridge who first repudiates the notion of Shakespeare as a child of nature, a rudely untutored genius. In Coleridge, as in the Germans,

classical unities; so does Coleridge. Schlegel repudiates the received wisdom that Shakespeare was a 'genius who lacked judgement' by insisting the former term necessarily includes the latter. Coleridge argues something very similar. Schlegel praises Shakespeare's 'organic form' ('organische Form'), opposed to the more mechanical art of lesser creators; Coleridge appropriates this concept and makes it a centrepiece of his account of Shakespeare, dedicating (it seems) his December 1812 Lecture on *Romeo and Juliet* and *Hamlet* to unpicking the confusion of 'mechanical regularity with organic form', and attributing the idea to 'a Continental Critic'.[21] In a broader sense, several key pieces of Coleridgean critical terminology, relevant to his account of Shakespeare and also to his larger critical project, derive from or are developed out of German thought, especially from Schelling, Schlegel and Kant. To mention only a few: Imagination, Esemplasy; distinctions between symbol and allegory, between classical and modern and various others.

Is it fair, though, to call this plagiary? Coleridge was sufficiently aware of the possibility of this charge to include a specific rebuttal in his notes for the third lecture of his 1818–19 course, on *Hamlet*:

> *Hamlet* was the Play, or rather Hamlet himself was the character, in the intuition and exposition of which I first made my turn for philosophical criticism, and especially for insight into the genius of Shakespeare, *noticed* first among my Acquaintances, as Sir G. Beaumont will bear witness, and as Mr Wordsworth knows . . . long before Schlegel had given at Vienna the Lectures on Shakespeare, which he afterwards published, I had given Eighteen Lectures on the same subject *substantially* the same, proceeding from the same, the *very* same, point of view, and deducing the same conclusions, as far as I either then or now agree with him.

Sir George Beaumont, 7th Baronet and patron of the arts, is invoked here as a sort of character witness, and the 'eighteen lectures' refers to the fact that Coleridge's first course of lectures, 1808–9, preceded that 1809–11 publication of Schlegel's *Über dramatische Kunst und Litteratur*. Coleridge goes on to say:

---

the Shakespeare who warbled his native woodnotes wild gives way to the deliberate master' (Schoenbaum, *Shakespeare's Lives*, 183).

[21] Foakes, *Lectures 1808–1819*, 1:495. For a more detailed account of this matter, see John Neubauer, 'Organicist Poetics as Romantic Heritage?', in Angela Esterhammer (ed.), *Romantic Poetry* (Amsterdam/Philadelphia: John Benjamins, 2002), 491–508.

Even in detail the coincidence of Schlegel with my Lectures was so extra-ordinary, that all at a later period who heard the same *words* (taken from my Royal Institution Notes) concluded a borrowing on my part from Schlegel—Mr. Hazlitt, whose hatred of me is in such an inverse ratio to my zealous Kindness towards him . . . Mr Hazlitt himself replied to an assertion of my plagiarism from Schlegel in these words;—'That is a Lie; for I myself heard the very same character of Hamlet from Coleridge before he went to Germany, and when he had neither read nor could read a page of German.' Now Hazlitt was on a visit to my Cottage at Nether Stowey, Somerset, in the summer of the year 1798, in the September of which (see my *Literary Life*) I first was out of sight of the Shores of Great Britain.[22]

Wellek, as it happens, is disinclined to give Coleridge the benefit of the doubt where the issue of plagiary is concerned;[23] although, he does at least concede that Coleridge was not 'a mere echo of the Germans with no originality and no independence', since he 'combines the ideas he derived from Germany in a personal way'. A more nuanced account of the way Coleridge mediated his influences – up to and including outright theft – can be found in Thomas McFarland's *Coleridge and the Pantheist Tradition* (1969).[24] More scathing is Norman Fruman's *Coleridge, the Damaged Archangel* (1972), a book which takes Coleridge's indulgence in plagiary as axiomatic, and discusses his indebtedness to Schlegel's Shakespearian writings as symptomatic of a life-defining pattern of intellectual dishonesty, all of which are

[22] This opening passage was probably not delivered as part of the lecture, at least not as phrased here. It is written in the edition of Shakespeare (Samuel Ayscough (ed.), *The Dramatic Works of William Shakespeare* (2 vols, London: John Stockdale, 1807), 2:999–1000) and dated 'Recorded by me, S. T. Coleridge, Jan 7, 1819, Highgate'. It expresses Coleridge's anger at a report implying the plagiary he here denies, carried in the *Morning Chronicle* (29 December 1819).

[23] 'He himself acknowledges that he read Schlegel late in 1811 and certainly after 1811 Coleridge's Shakespear lectures draw heavily on Schlegel. Coleridge even took the volumes with him into the 1811–12 lectures and asked for them again for the 1813–14 lectures. The later lectures do not tread on the same ground, probably because Schlegel had been translated by John Black in 1815 and could thus be known to his audience' (Wellek, *A History of Modern Criticism*, 155–6). In fact Wellek believes, although he cannot prove it, that Coleridge was reading Schlegel's Shakespearian criticism throughout the 1800s, going back perhaps as far as 1797.

[24] Thomas McFarland, *Coleridge and the Pantheist Tradition* (Oxford: Clarendon Press, 1969). See in particular Chapter 1 'The Problem of Coleridge's Plagiarisms' and the section 'Coleridge's Indebtedness to A. W. Schlegel' (251–61). See also G. N. G. Orsini, 'Coleridge and Schlegel Reconsidered', *Comparative Literature*, 16:2 (1964), 97–118.

manifestations of 'an internally consistent pattern of act and motive'.[25] Fruman's book is as much polemical as it is scholarly, and has divided Coleridgeans. I don't really have space to enter in to any detailed discussion of the larger question of how plagiary impacts our sense of Coleridge as a writer and thinker. Alongside the Shakespeare lectures, the other Coleridgean work most haunted by accusations of intellectual theft is the *Biographia Literaria*. In a recent edition of that work I argued that plagiary and originality, both of which are manifestly present, actualise the main thesis of the book itself: namely, the way all art derives from the interplay of copied 'fancy' and original 'imagination'. That, in other words, questions of influence and individuality, of derivativeness and new-mintedness, are not only the subject but the form of the *Biographia*. Fancy is explicitly a mode of plagiary, just as imagination is explicitly a mode of wholly original thought, and the two coexist less as a dialectic and more an antinomy.[26] But it would be difficult to make a similar argument where the Shakespeare lectures are concerned. Here Coleridge has little to say about (for example) Shakespeare's treatment of his source material, in part because one of the assumptions made here is that Shakespeare drew not from art, and not even from life, but from his own imagination, a by-definition unplagiarisable idiom.

But there is another sense in which Fruman's critique intersects with what Coleridge says in these lectures, in which it embodies precisely a mode of imaginative engagement with character that Coleridge himself set in motion. *Coleridge, the Damaged Archangel* figures – as its very title suggests – as the account of a great man who was brought down by one fatal flaw of character.

> Intellectual dishonesty in a man of genius seems bizarre, as does petty greed in a man of great wealth. Yet compulsive acquisition of reputation or power derives from overmastering personal needs, the ultimate sources of which are always obscure. The broad outlines of Coleridge's profoundest intellectual aspirations are clear enough: above all he was driven by a desire to achieve a reputation for dazzling creative gifts and universal knowledge. In ways ... destructive of his peace of mind, he presented to the world, both in his private correspondence and in his public utterances, a personal portrait of childlike innocence and severe

---

[25] Norman Fruman, *Coleridge, the Damaged Archangel* (New York: G. Braziller, 1971), 415. Fruman's discussion of the Lectures on Shakespeare is pp. 141–61.

[26] See Adam Roberts (ed.), *Coleridge: Biographia Literaria* (Edinburgh: Edinburgh University Press, 2014), cxxxiv–cxliii.

moral rigor. His letters in later life can be positively embarrassing, as when he writes, 'I have never knowingly or intentionally
been guilty of a dishonorable transaction, but have in all things
that respect my neighbor been more sinned against than sinning,'
or, 'I know the meaning of the word Envy only by the interpretation given in the Dictionaries . . .' Not many men could bring
themselves to write, even if they believed it true, 'I can trace in
my heart no envy, no malice, & no revenge,' or refer to their
'constitutional indifference to praise.'[27]

It is a compelling piece of psychological portraiture, this. To say so
is not to accept, uncritically, the fundamental accuracy of Fruman's
version of Coleridge (indeed several critics have taken issue with
aspects of Fruman's case). But it perhaps connects with the Lectures
on Shakespeare in ways Fruman might not have intended. After all,
the merit of Shakespeare's portrait of *Macbeth* does not depend upon
the absolute accuracy of the play's portrayal of the historical Scottish
king. And in one respect, Fruman is working within Coleridge's own,
original and influential model of how Shakespeare constructed his
characters: the way one potent flaw generates dramatic insight into an
exceptional individual.

    This emphasis on a 'tragic flaw', of course, is not an idea invented
out of whole cloth by Coleridge. There was throughout the eighteenth century much discussion of Aristotle's ἁμαρτία as, in effect, a
'tragic flaw' of character (although there are no usages of the precise
phrase 'tragic flaw' before the twentieth century). The usage in this
context, however, was complicated by *hamartia*'s appearance in the
Greek New Testament as a word for sin.[28] Coleridge is little interested in Shakespeare's characters as 'sinners'; but he is very interested
in the way that Shakespearian psychological portraiture embodies

---

[27] Fruman, *Damaged Archangel*, 56.

[28] See for example Romans 5: 12, Romans 3: 20. This usage has very little, if anything, to
do with the way Aristotle uses the term in the *Poetics*. 'It is the height of irony that the
idea of the tragic flaw should have had its origin in the Aristotelian notion of *hamartia*.
Whatever this problematic word may be taken to mean, it has nothing to do with such
ideas as fault, vice, guilt, moral deficiency, or the like. Hamartia is a morally neutral
non-normative term, derived from the verb *hamartano*, meaning "to miss the mark",
"to fall short of an objective". And by extension: to reach one destination rather than
the intended one; to make a mistake, not in the sense of a moral failure, but in the
non-judgmental sense of taking one thing for another, taking something for its opposite. Hamartia may betoken an error of discernment due to ignorance, to the lack of an
essential piece of information. Finally, hamartia may be viewed simply as an act which,
for whatever reason, ends in failure rather than success' (Jules Brody, 'Fate, Philology,
Freud', *Philosophy and Literature*, 38.1 (2014): 23).

a sense of the moral life distorted by the pressure of some inward topography or obsession, what he calls a 'predominant passion'. It is this, as Coleridge sees it, that articulates Shakespeare's apprehension of human existence as fundamentally *moral* existence. Peter Hoheisel puts it well:

> in essence Coleridge admires Shakespeare for his grasp of moral reality in human reality. Shakespeare is not a moralist in the sense of someone who moralizes, gives an opinion on the rightness or wrongness of an action; rather he grasps the consequences of any distortion in what it means to be a whole human being in a controlling idea related to a mental faculty in the characters. Usually he finds a moral imbalance, some psychological distortion, in the mind of the main character. And this imbalance symbolizes an eternal truth about a fault in human nature. As a psychological critic, Coleridge is not primarily concerned about interaction between characters, or an analysis of their motivations and desires for its own sake, but with the permanent psychological truth about the eternal condition of human nature which each character portrays. To the core Coleridge is a metaphysician who believes in an eternal human nature expressed in varying conditions, not an empirical psychological critic who is concerned with describing the dynamics of human interaction in Shakespeare's plays. He sees Shakespeare as not essentially concerned with simply showing how people react to different situations and people, but with creating types whose basic interest and artistic viability consist in how well they incarnate the permanent moral condition of mankind. Just as Kant treated each subject in relation to the mental faculty to which it pertained, so Coleridge sees each play in relation to the mental state of the characters, representing either a moral balance or imbalance. Thus Coleridge finds Shakespeare often creating characters in which an intellectual or moral faculty is in 'morbid excess.' For example he sees Hamlet as showing the need to maintain a healthy balance between 'outward objects' and 'inward thoughts—a due balance between the real and the imaginary world.'[29]

I quote Hoheisel at some length, because he puts his finger on something crucial about the way Coleridge's version of Shakespeare fed into nineteenth-century, and through them into modern, terms of

---

[29]　Peter Hoheisel, 'Coleridge on Shakespeare: Method amid the Rhetoric', *Studies in Romanticism*, 13:1 (1974), 21–2.

critical debate. 'In speaking of the Dramas of Shakespeare,' Coleridge says in the fourth of the 1811–12 lectures, 'I shall be inclined to pursue a *psychological*, rather than a historical, mode of reasoning.' One of the most influential later versions of this approach was A. C. Bradley's *Shakespearian Tragedy* (1904); but even when 'character-based' criticism fell out of favour with the coming of deconstruction in the later twentieth century the notion persisted that Shakespeare actualises psychological richness and acuity via a sense of the way the lines of force of single ideas can bend subjectivity out of shape.[30] It is not, as Timothy Corrigan notes, that he is 'part psychological critic and part moral critic concerned on the one hand with psychological accuracy and on the other with philosophical truth'. Rather Coleridge grasps that

> human psychology is a ratio or interaction of intellect and morality. The one does not belong to the realm of psychology and the other to the realm of metaphysics: the tension between the two, rather, is what accounts for psychological completeness in both real persons and fictional characters.[31]

It is partly for this reason that Coleridge's most influential readings of character have tended to concentrate on the morally ambiguous, or the straightforwardly villainous, amongst Shakespeare's creations:

> Coleridge lectured on a limited range of plays, and is best known for his commentary on *Hamlet* with its brilliant account of the character as inhibited from action by a habit of introspection . . . Like this one, other formulations by Coleridge have remained a

[30] George Watson considers it 'absurd' that 'Coleridge should be described as a character-critic, an ancestor of A C Bradley'. Coleridge, Watson insists, had no interest in 'character-analysis': 'Bradley's style of criticism was based on an assumption that Shakespearian characters are as naturalistic as the characters of nineteenth-century novels; and if there is one species of literature Coleridge is not interested in, it is the novel' (George Watson, *The Literary Critics: a Study of English Descriptive Criticism*, 2nd edn (London: Chatto and Windus, 1986), 113–14). Noting Watson's argument here, I might also register my considered disagreement with pretty much every part of it. Coleridge was centrally interested in subjectivity and its representation, in what we might nowadays call the psychodynamics of individual life. If that's not an interest in character, I don't know what is. Of course there is much more to an interest in Shakespeare's characters than the identification of 'naturalistic' traits à la novel; but Bradley himself was not so naif as to treat Shakespeare's characters as if they were written by George Eliot or Zola. And besides, calling Coleridge – a man who reviewed Gothic novels for the press, who lectured on Cervantes and who wrote detailed marginalia praising Defoe, Fielding and many others – *uninterested in the novel* is a very strange thing to do.

[31] Timothy Corrigan, 'Coleridge's Shakespearian Criticism', *Coleridge, Language and Criticism* (Athens: University of Georgia Press, 1982), 99.

challenge to interpreters of the tragedies ever since, notably his incisive account of Iago's 'passionless character, all *will* in intellect', whose soliloquys express 'the motive hunting of a motiveless malignity.' He dismissed the common stage treatment of the Weird Sisters as comic witches with broomsticks, and recognized their mysterious 'grotesqueness mingled with terror'; he also rejected the hitherto common idea of Lady Macbeth as a monster lacking any conscience, seeing her rather as showing 'constant effort' in the play to '*bully* conscience'. His comments on King Lear show a subtle appreciation of Edmund as potentially admirable, and one whose circumstances, his bastardy, being sent abroad for education, and his humiliation by his father in the opening scene prevent his villainy from 'passing into utter *monstrosity*.'[32]

For Coleridge, Hamlet's 'problem' is not that he is a quasi-novelistic individual, tragically flawed, but rather that his interiority is so much stronger and more compelling than his connection with the exterior world:

> What was the point to which Shakespeare directed himself? He meant to portray a person, in whose view the external world, and all its incidents and objects, were comparatively dim, and of no interest in themselves, and which began to interest only, when they were reflected in the mirror of his mind. Hamlet beheld external objects in the same way that a man of vivid imagination, who shuts his eyes, sees what has previously made an impression on his organs.
>
> Shakespeare places him in the most stimulating circumstances that a human being can be placed in. He is the heir apparent of a throne; his father dies suspiciously; his mother excludes him from the throne by marrying his uncle. This is not enough; but the Ghost of the murdered father is introduced, to assure the son that he was put to death by his own brother. What is the result? Endless reasoning and urging–perpetual solicitation of the mind to act, but as constant an escape from action; ceaseless reproaches of himself for his sloth, while the whole energy of his resolution passes away in those reproaches. This, too, not from cowardice, for he is made one of the bravest of his time–not

---

[32] R. A. Foakes, 'The Critical Reception of Shakespeare's Tragedies', in Claire McEachern (ed.), *The Cambridge Companion to Shakespearian Tragedy* (Cambridge: Cambridge University Press, 2002), 229–30.

from want of forethought or quickness of apprehension, for he sees through the very souls of all who surround him, but merely from that aversion to action, which prevails among such as have a world in themselves. (1811–12 series, Lecture 12)

There is nothing like this in Schlegel, which positions the matter outside the logic of plagiary. Indeed, one reason why there is nothing like this in Schlegel is that there is so much of Coleridge *in* it. Richard Holmes considers the 1812 Hamlet lecture 'the focus and highlight of the entire series', noting that Crabb Robinson 'immediately hailed it as "perhaps his very best", and recognized the deliberately autobiographical theme of introversion and inaction. "Somebody said to me, this is a Satire on himself; No, I said, it is an Elegy".'[33] Holmes also records that 'towards the end of his life, Coleridge would mildly claim, "I have a smack of Hamlet myself, if I may say so".' Coleridge's critique is both an acute imaginative entry into the logic of Shakespeare's character, and a projection of Coleridge's own 'world-in-himself' onto the fabric of the play. In its own way, and of course at a far less sophisticated level than Shakespeare, this is the mode of characterisation implicit in Fruman's 'damaged archangel' version of Coleridge himself.

Hazlitt and Coleridge

It can be said, with little prospect of counter-argument, that the two most important critics working in England during the eighteen-teens were Hazlitt and Coleridge. Both lectured on Shakespeare and literature more generally. Both advanced readings and aesthetic theories that had a shaping effect upon Shakespearean criticism (and criticism more generally) through the nineteenth and twentieth centuries, and both are still relevant today. Matthew Scott gives some sense of the difference in their methods, beginning with Coleridge:

His method of lecturing and mode of organizing his material, combined with a naturally extempore cast of mind, ensures that Coleridge's line of argument is often difficult to follow and that much of what is distinct and valuable about these extraordinary contributions to literary aesthetics is thrown up by the apparently arbitrary association of ideas when material previously worked out in notes is suddenly brought to bear upon an unexpected sequence of thoughts. And although they approach

[33] Holmes, *Coleridge: Darker Reflections*, 281–6.

Coleridge's in their importance to the history of literary criticism, the more conventional lectures of his contemporary William Hazlitt give us some impression of how unusual Coleridge's must have seemed to his audiences. Where Hazlitt tends to follow a common theme through each course, proceeding in roughly chronological manner with obvious teleological purpose, Coleridge is disorganized but dazzling and difficult, and never afraid of the most daring or expansive claims.[34]

When Hazlitt first met Coleridge in 1798 he reported 'I could not have been more delighted if I had heard the music of the spheres.'[35] For several years the two were friends. By the time of the lectures, though, relations had deteriorated. Hazlitt attended at least some of the 1811–12 series, and in conversation with Charles Lamb, John Rickman and George Dyer afterwards said that he 'did not think Coleridge at all competent to the task he had undertaken of lecturing on Shakespeare'. (His companions disagreed: 'Dyer thought that Coleridge was the fittest man for a Lecturer he had ever known: he was constantly lecturing when in company, only he did it better.')[36] As the decade progressed, Hazlitt only grew more hostile. Coleridge's judgement in 1819, scribbled on the flyleaf of a copy of *Christabel, Kubla Khan, The Vision of Sleep* (1816), characterises Hazlitt as:

Unhappy man! I understand that when one of his Faction had declared in a pamphlet ('Hypocrisy unveiled') the Christabel *'the most obscene poem in the English Language'* he shrugged himself up with a sort of sensual orgasm of enjoyment, and exclaimed–How he'll stare! (i.e. meaning me) Curse him! I hate him.–When I reflect on such things, and know that to be real which otherwise I could not have believed possible, it is an unspeakable Comfort to me that I can with my whole heart obey the divine precept, Matth: V. 43, 44, 45, 46.–[37]

---

34 Matthew Scott, 'Coleridge's Lectures 1808–1819: On Literature', in Frederick Burwick (ed.), *The Oxford Handbook of Samuel Taylor Coleridge* (Oxford: Oxford University Press, 2009), 185–203; 189.
35 William Hazlitt, 'My First Acquaintance with Poets', *The Liberal* 3 (1823), 26.
36 Foakes, *Lectures 1808–1819*, 1:233.
37 Quoted in John Beer, 'Coleridge, Hazlitt and Christabel', *Review of English Studies*, 37:145 (1986), 40. The anonymously authored Hazlitt ally pamphlet *Hypocrisy unveiled, and Calumny detected: in a review of Blackwood's Magazine* (1818) denigrated *Blackwood's* because it 'has praised Byron's *Parisina*, and Coleridge's *Christabel*, poems which sin as heinously against Purity and decency as it is well possible to imagine'. Beer's article quotes from other Coleridge letters in which he characterised Hazlitt's animosity towards him as 'pure malignity' and 'frantic hatred'.

The Biblical reference is to Christ's command to love your enemies, which adds a slightly priggish flavour to this note. And if Hazlitt really did hate Coleridge, it didn't stop him concluding his 1818 lecture 'On the Living Poets' by describing Coleridge as 'the only person I ever knew who answered to the idea of a man of genius'. Still, he was often critical, and sometimes very hostile.

Critical disinterestedness encourages us to rise above local feuds and spats; but critics are human beings and it is only natural to feel the tug of allegiance one way or the other. Since many anglophone literary critics of the last few generations have been left-leaning liberals (I say so with no mocking intent; I'm one such myself) partiality has sometimes expressed itself in a preference for Hazlitt, perceived as left-leaning and liberal, over a Coleridge who had, by this point in his career, abandoned his youthful radical and reinvented himself as a Church and State Tory.[38] A palpable sense of affiliation informs at least some critical accounts of Coleridge's and Hazlitt's lecture series as rival modes of interpreting Shakespeare, which in turn pressures us to choose sides. For example, in two books – *Shakespeare and the English Romantic Imagination*[39] and *Shakespearean Constitutions: Politics, Theatre, Criticism 1730–1830*[40] – Jonathan Bate mounts a vigorous defence of Hazlitt as not only the more politically sympathetic reader of Shakespeare, but the better critic too. Hazlitt not only thought theatre was 'political'

> but argued that behind the show of power and kingly glory in plays like Henry VIII, there was a subversive critique of monarchy. It was Hazlitt who was first to offer a negative reading of that most popular of Shakespearean kings, Henry V: 'Henry, because he did not know how to govern his own kingdom, determined to make war upon his neighbours. Because his own title to the crown was doubtful, he laid claim to that of France. Because he did not know how to exercise the enormous power, which had just dropped into his hands, to any one good purpose, he immediately undertook (a cheap and obvious resource of sovereignty) to do all the mischief he could.' Coleridge thought

---

[38] This puts the matter rather crudely. Some kind of realignment in Coleridge's political and ideological centre-of-gravity had indeed taken place, although it was a more complex process, with many more threads of connection to his youthful views, than is commonly understood. For an intelligent discussion of this matter, see Pamela Edwards, *The Statesman's Science: History, Nature, and Law in the Political Thought of Samuel Taylor Coleridge* (New York: Columbia University Press, 2004).

[39] Oxford: Oxford University Press, 1986.

[40] Oxford: Oxford University Press, 1989.

very differently about Shakespeare's kings. Hazlitt wrote in 1819 of how 'Mr Coleridge, in his late Lectures, contend[ed] that not to fall down in prostration of soul before the abstract majesty of kings as it is seen in the diminished perspective of centuries, argues an inherent littleness of mind.'[41]

It is, perhaps, a little unfair to represent Coleridge not by his own words, but via Hazlitt's hostile prism. But the larger point is one reiterated by several other critics: namely, that Coleridge's political commitment to authority and kingship vitiates his Shakespearian criticism:

> Coleridge has his cake and eats it too as far as Shakespeare's politics are concerned: one moment the Bard is an anti-Jacobin, the next he stands serenely above the cut and thrust of faction, being credited in the same lecture with having 'no sectarian character of Politician or religion' despite writing 'in an age of political & religious heat'. Hazlitt, who was lecturing to a very different, predominantly Dissenting audience at the Surrey Institution, read the *Courier* report and wrote a reply in the pro-radical *Yellow Dwarf*. He chid Coleridge with his own former Jacobinism, reminding him of the *Conciones ad Populum*. But he also produced a counter-reading of *The Tempest*, which takes the form of an ironic amplification of Coleridge's comparison with modern France. Hazlitt reads Caliban as the legitimate ruler of the isle and Prospero as the usurper: Prospero is therefore the Jacobin, or the Bonaparte, and Caliban the Bourbon, 'the Louis XVIII of the enchanted island in *The Tempest*'. The initial purpose of this is to ridicule Coleridge's version of Caliban, but Hazlitt cannot resist pursuing his reading: 'Caliban is so far from being a prototype of modern Jacobinism, that he is strictly the legitimate sovereign of the isle, and Prospero and the rest are usurpers, who have ousted him from his hereditary jurisdiction ... "This island's mine, by Sycorax my mother"; and he complains bitterly of the artifices used by his new friends to cajole him out of it.' If we are to speak of usurpation, does it not come from the court rather than the native, not from Caliban but from 'those finished Court-practitioners, Sebastian and Antonio'? 'Were they Jacobins like Caliban, or legitimate personages, like Mr Coleridge? Did they

---

[41] This and the following is quoted from Jonathan Bate's review of Foakes's Bollingen edition of Coleridge's *Lectures on Literature*; Jonathan Bate, 'Shakespeare and the Literary Police', *London Review of Books*, 10:17 (1988), 26–7.

belong to the new school or the old? That is the question: but it is
a question which our lay-preacher will take care not to answer.'
Hazlitt has brilliantly turned the argument, and the play is seen
in new light as an attack on legitimacy. For Hazlitt, Prospero is
like all absolute rulers in that he relies on arbitrary power and
the forcible repression of opposition. Furthermore, contained
within the claim that Caliban is the real owner of the island is a
reading in terms of colonial exploitation – the play thus becomes
an exemplary text for abolitionists. Out of Coleridge's passing
remark, Hazlitt has created the kind of *Tempest* that has been
rediscovered in the 1980s.

There are powerful points here, although there is also, perhaps, an
inevitable whiff of self-congratulation occasioned by a critic of the
late twentieth century claiming Hazlitt as a cultural materialist *avant
la lettre*. We ought, surely, to be very wary of believing that the
evolution of Coleridge's own political sympathies, since it removes
him from the sort of views of which we tend to approve, is to be
deplored as a personal *and critical* failing. At the very least, it requires
a degree of myopia to arraign Coleridge for personal and political
failings whilst elevating Hazlitt – a man who hero-worshipped the ur-
fascist Napoleon, a lifelong misogynist with a history of sexual assault
against women – as a poster-boy for progressive ideas.

The best book on Hazlitt I know is David Bromwich's 1983 study,
Hazlitt: the Mind of a Critic. Comparing Hazlitt and Coleridge, Bromwich
identifies four key differences between the two men, several of which
are relevant to a reading of the Shakespeare lectures. First:

> To Coleridge, poetry's greatness is that it frees us from belief
> and practice by showing us a thing completely organized, beau-
> tiful in conformity to its own law, and therefore free of any
> rhetorical motive. To Hazlitt, its greatness is that it makes new
> channels for belief and practice, or immeasurably deepens the
> existing ones.[42]

Bromwich argues that Coleridge's celebrated phrase from the
Biographia, 'the willing suspension of disbelief', has no Hazlittian
equivalent; and that where Coleridge seeks to enforce a strict distinction between art and rhetoric, Hazlitt sees the two as always inter-
twined – most especially in Shakespeare. The second of Bromwich's

---

[42]   David Bromwich's *Hazlitt: the Mind of a Critic* (Oxford: Oxford University Press, 1983),
       231. The subsequent material quoted from Bromwich's book is all to be found in pages
       231–6.

distinctions is between Coleridge's commitment to a 'clerisy', a spe-
cially trained caste of critics and teachers, as a means of preserving
great culture, where Hazlitt 'inherits the Johnsonian feeling about
the common reader's taste and judgements as the only measure of
"duration" in literature'. Coleridge's naked hostility to the new demo-
graphic of 'the reading public' is expressed both in the 1811–12 lectures and in the *Biographia*. And the Shakespeare lectures several times
denigrate the vogue for going to the theatre to see the latest celebrity
actor *in* Shakespeare, rather than going to see Shakespeare's work
itself, an early attack upon what is now called 'celebrity culture'. That
said, I suspect that Bromwich's third distinction – that

> Coleridge views the mind of the poet, or the text of a poem, as
> the staging ground for a reconciliation of opposites. Hazlitt sees
> no reason why opposites should be reconciled, and never leads
> us to expect this as a formal property of a great work.

– is a little misleading. Hazlitt is surely not quite so Manichean as all
that; and although Coleridge often declares that an organic unity is
the acme of great art, such unity is the reach by which our grasp is
inevitably exceeded rather than any practical template for literature
as such. Coleridge certainly reveres Shakespeare as artist; but he does
not consider him perfect. Indeed, it is the tension between the idea
of unity and its actualisation that powers Shakespeare's masterpieces
as far as Coleridge is concerned. The gap between Hamlet's inner
and outer worlds is one example of this. Finally Bromwich argues
that 'Coleridge's thinking about literature revolves around an idea
of the symbol.' If we take symbol in a capacious enough manner
(Bromwich, usefully, makes the connection with Auerbach) then this
is hard to deny; except that we mistake Coleridge's investment in this
notion if we think of a symbol as a simplification of life. Something
the reverse is true, in fact. Life, for Coleridge, is often banal; where
the idealism of Shakespeare is multifarious, vivid, potent, complex
and compelling.

The Shakespeare of the Lectures

One thing the comparison with Hazlitt brings out is the *oddity* of
Coleridge's Shakespearian lectures – of all his lectures, in fact. The
largest constituency for Coleridge's prose, today, is probably located
within the university sector, and students (and the professors who
teach them) have come to expect certain things from an academic lecture: a degree of comprehensiveness, a coherent structure, an accessible

and engaging delivery in which key points are reinforced by modified repetition and summary in paratextual material such as handouts and PowerPoint displays. From a very great number of guides as to what constitutes effective lecturing in an academic context, I select one, more or less at random – from Stanford University's online 'Teaching Commons' Resources page. To lecture well, according to this site, the lecturer should amongst other things do the following:

> Outline clear objectives for your lecture – both what students should know after the lecture and why it is important.
> Develop a lecture outline and any audiovisuals.
> Limit the main points in a lecture to five or fewer.
> Create effective visuals, analogies, demonstrations, and examples to reinforce the main points.
> Share your outline with students.
> Emphasize your objectives and key points in the beginning, as you get to them, and as a summary at the end.
> Integrate visuals, multimedia, discussion, active learning strategies, small-group techniques, and peer instruction.
> Plan for diverse learners. Use verbal, visual, and kinesthetic approaches such as hands-on exercises and simulations.[43]

Good advice, all; but a checklist of pretty much all the things Coleridge does *not* do in his Shakespeare lectures. His lectures on *Hamlet* and *The Tempest* (say) do not provide an overview of the play, do not situate either text in its time or in a broader critical debate, do not work methodically through a small number of closely related points. Instead Coleridge isolates a few key scenes or speeches, almost always from the opening Acts, and expatiates upon a series of sometimes only obliquely connected points related to them. Nor has the seeming immethodical and rhapsodic bent in Coleridge's approach gone unnoticed.

> When Henry Crabb Robinson wrote that Coleridge's 'pretended lectures are immethodical rhapsodies, moral, metaphysical, and literary, abounding in brilliant thoughts, fine flashes of rhetoric, ingenious paradoxes, occasionally profound and salutary truths,' but not 'an instructive course of readings on any one subject a man can wish to fix his attention on,' he described a manner of presentation which continues to vex Coleridge's readers as it did at least one of his auditors. Far from developing a full body of

---

[43] https://teachingcommons.stanford.edu/resources/teaching-resources/teaching-strate gies/checklist-effective-lecturing. Accessed December 2015.

Shakespearean criticism, Coleridge did not even give a detailed critique of any one play.[44]

This is Peter Hoheisel's summary, which he lays down in order to argue against it: 'contrary to Robinson, there is a method amid the rhetoric, and that method, to put it in a Coleridgean way, is to illuminate certain central principles which contain endless potentiality for development.' For Coleridge a Shakespearean play 'is "romantic poetry revealing itself in the drama" and its structure develops from an internal logic. External rules, such as the classical unities, cannot be imposed on it like a grid'. Coleridge several times insists that Shakespeare is no wild and untutored 'child of nature', that his judgement is fully equal to his genius. 'The dramatic judgement of Shakespeare', as Hohesiel summarises, 'is evidenced in his skilful use of language and imagery, and above all in the profound grasp of eternal human truth which that language and imagery embody.' So for example:

> The images of Shakespeare prove his genius not primarily because they are striking or beautiful or faithfully copy nature, but because they are modified by a predominant passion and because they reduce multitude to unity or succession to an instant. They are the work of genius because they are adequate symbols of the vision. The dramatist creates his images according to his idea; their virtue, again, lies in how well they make us see that idea, not the images for their own sake.

As Coleridge sees it, it is Shakespeare's apprehension of human existence as fundamentally *moral* existence:

> In essence Coleridge admires Shakespeare for his grasp of moral reality in human reality. Shakespeare is not a moralist in the sense of someone who moralizes, gives an opinion on the rightness or wrongness of an action; rather he grasps the consequences of any distortion in what it means to be a whole human being.

This, according to Hoheisel, is why Coleridge tends to limit himself only to the opening sections of plays, because the opening scenes contain everything from which Shakespeare's moral interrogation inevitably develops.[45]

---

[44] Hoheisel, 'Coleridge on Shakespeare', 15. The following quotation is from p. 17.
[45] 'The drama and development of the plays, therefore, is simply the working out, the consequences, the incarnation in event, dialogue, and characterization, of the seminal moral idea which Shakespeare is meditating upon and to which he gives dramatic and

If it seems somehow fair to judge Coleridge-as-lecturer by the norms of contemporary academic praxis, that may be because Coleridge is so closely implicated in the creation of the academy itself, as one of the guiding lights for those who worked to establish the university sector on its present footing. For one thing, the *Biographia Literaria*, or at least certain aspects of it (close-reading most notably) proved foundational for the twentieth-century creation of 'English' as an academic discipline. For another, Coleridge argued for the need of a 'clerisy', an elite group of learned people, a caste of intellectuals and literati tasked with the education of the nation as a whole. It's common enough amongst academics (such as myself) to see in their professional life the practical manifestation of that ideal. The truth, of course, is otherwise. To go back to what Coleridge actually wrote about the 'clerisy':

> The CLERISY of the nation, or national church, in its primary acceptation and original intention, comprehended the learned of all denominations;—the sages and professors of the law and jurisprudence, of medicine and physiology, of music, of military and civil architecture, of the physical sciences, with the mathematical as the common organ of the preceding; in short, all the so called liberal arts and sciences, the possession and application of which constitute the civilization of a country, as well as the Theological. The last was, indeed, placed at the head of all; and of good right did it claim the precedence. But why? Because under the name of Theology, or Divinity, were contained the interpretation of languages; the conservation and tradition of past events; the momentous epochs, and revolutions of the race and nation; the continuation of the records; logic, ethics, and the determination of ethical science, in application to the rights and duties of men in all their various relations, social and civil; and lastly, the ground-knowledge, the prima scientia as it was named, – PHILOSOPHY.[46]

Coleridge is clear that he conceived the duties of the clerisy to be primarily pedagogic: to dispose of

---

artistic expression. Thus because of his conviction that the idea contains the consequences, Coleridge devotes most of his attention to the opening of the play where the idea is established, and practically ignores the rest of the play, to the chagrin of the Henry Crabb Robinsons among his auditors and those subsequent critics who have muttered "incomplete" (though none more critical than S. T. C. himself) in judgement of his effort at analysis' (Hoheisel, 'Coleridge on Shakespeare', 23).

[46] John Colmer (ed.), *Coleridge: On the Constitution of the Church and State* (Princeton: Princeton University Press and London: Routledge, 1976), 46–7.

materials of NATIONAL EDUCATION, *the nisus formativus* of the body politic, the shaping and informing spirit, which, educing or eliciting the latent man in all the natives of the soil, trains them up to be citizens of the country, free subjects of the realm.

'Nisus formativus' means the forming force, the formative urge; and 'educing' (Latin: *educo* 'I lead out, I draw out; I raise up, I erect') a more directive, root-sense of educating. But he is equally clear that this class, as its name makes clear, should be a limb of the church. He has in mind clerics rather than professors.

This is not to deny that one of the ways Coleridge's clerisy idea developed was precisely into the expansion of the university sector, to broaden educational opportunities for the citizenry and to furnish the nation with an intelligentsia. Given the glowing terms in which S. T. C. talks of 'the clerisy', it can be hard for any latter-day inheritor of the mantle – such as myself – to talk objectively about it. But Coleridge did not have people like me in mind when he coined his term. It's not just that I'm not religious, and it's not that I'm part of a university system specifically set apart from the church. It's that what we do (increasingly so, with the introduction of tuition fees) is simply not disseminated into every town and home of the realm. This is one, practical reason why Coleridge models the clerisy on the clergy. The clerisy's job is to educate the nation, practically and morally; and to do that it needs to go into every village, even into every home. Priests already do that. My sense is that Coleridge can't imagine a secular organisation having that same access without it becoming a ghastly secret-police-style invasion of privacy. The 1820s, when Coleridge coined the term, saw especially heated debate in Britain over the establishment of the Metropolitan Police Force, when what was seen as a French-style invasion of state apparatus of law, order and control into private life was fiercely debated and as fiercely opposed.

Now, clearly, a course of lectures on Shakespeare at which attendance costs two guineas (or three with the privilege of introducing a lady) is not calculated to 'educe' on this national, popular scale. But it is well to keep in mind that Coleridge's idea of the ideal educator overlaps to a large degree with his idea of the ideal priest. This in turn leads us to reconsider which paradigm for 'the lecture' he was working from. Not, clearly, any anachronistic or modern-day model of 'effective lecturing'; but from a different model altogether: the sermon.

Coleridge was a preacher before he was anything else. In the early 1790s he preached often, all around the country. He even planned to become a Unitarian minister, until a no-strings-attached annuity from the Wedgwoods enabled him to concentrate on reading, thinking and writing. And the logic of the sermon informs much of what he then goes on to write. His Ancient Mariner, we could say, is a preacher of rare power, and Coleridge's edition of his, in effect, verse–sermon includes in its later iterations a prose gloss elucidating the theological moral. In the middle of his stint as a lecturer-on-Shakespeare, Coleridge published two (of three planned) *Lay Sermons*, addressed to the upper (1816), middle (1817) and – in the unwritten third – working classes, and concerning the contemporary political situation. As R. J. White notes, these political pamphlets

> *were* sermons. They begin with a text, and end with it, in the approved pulpit manner.
>
> Coleridge did it to the manner born. 'Have you ever heard me preach, Charles?' he once asked his friend Lamb. 'N-n-never heard you d-d-do anything else, C-c-coleridge.' He had begun as a young Radical at Bristol in 1795, lecturing at the coffee-house on the Quay on the 'grand political View of Christianity' . . . Next year he was among the Midland Charity Sermons. 'The Sacred may eventually help off the *profane*–and my Sermons spread a sort of sanctity over my sedition.' John Thelwall, who was often in trouble over his Jacobin politics, remarked enviously that Coleridge 'cannot preach very often without travelling from the pulpit to the Tower.' The transition was easy. 'Mount him but upon his darling hobby-horse, "the republic of God's own making", and away he goes, scattering *levelling* sedition and constructive treason.' That he never became a Unitarian minister was not the fault of the Unitarians, but the consequence of Thomas Wedgwood's offer of £150 a year as an endowment for the pursuit of poetry and philosophy for the greater glory of his country, an endowment (Hazlitt tells us) that Coleridge accepted while tying on one of his shoes. All the same, he continued even after 1798 to preach.[47]

A lecture is not, of course, quite the same thing as a sermon. We might say that the latter is designed to establish or reinforce religious faith, where the former is supposed to deepen knowledge of one or other technical, scientific or cultural discourse. Many more sermons are preached to people who already believe than to unbelievers.

---

[47] R. J. White (ed.), *Samuel Taylor Coleridge. Lay Sermons* (Princeton: Princeton University Press and London: Routledge, 1972), xxxiv–xxxv.

Indeed, I'm not sure we would even call attempts to proselytise and convert *sermons*, actually: does a sermon not imply a willing audience? Then again, the phrases 'preaching to the converted' and 'preaching to the choir' exist because of our shared sense of what constitutes a *bad* sermon: a preacher who takes his or her audience for granted, who brings nothing new to the experience. By the same token, we might define a good sermon as one that deepens and enriches an already-existing faith, that makes the auditor consider things from a new light, that makes a portion of lived experience new. The overlap with lectures depends upon which kind we are talking about. We might distinguish between two sorts. An elementary lecture is designed, and if well-delivered is received, as an exercise in apprising an audience of a body of knowledge. From such a lecture an auditor learns something she or he did not know before. This, though, does not really describe what Coleridge is doing in the lectures collected in this volume. Coleridge's performances embody a different approach: one that presumes a certain knowledge of Shakespeare and attempts to inflect that knowledge in new ways, to correct previous errors of emphasis and interpretation and to propose a new way of looking at a shared body of culture. In this respect these lectures, and others like them, have more in common with the logic of the sermon.

I am arguing, in other words, that there is more here than the fact that both sermons and lectures belong to what Robert H. Ellison calls the 'genre of oral literature' – a genre he identifies as both very important to nineteenth-century culture and as generally overlooked by critical study.[48] Of course, it wouldn't do to press the analogy too far. The emphasis in a sermon must be, in one sense, theological; and although Coleridge was committed to a paradigm of literary genius as informed by 'the vision and the faculty divine', his purpose in the Shakespeare lectures was literary-critical rather than religious. Then again, his analysis reverts more often than not to an engagement with specifically moral questions, and Coleridge's ethics cannot be separated from Coleridge's faith.

---

[48] 'I believe we can regard the sermon as a genre of "oral literature". Some scholars have objected to the use of this phrase . . . [as] paradoxical, even oxymoronic. Walter J Ong [calls] "oral literature" a "monstrous" term, arguing that it is "preposterous" to discuss the creative works of an oral culture in terms of a form that is, by definition, written . . . I propose, however, that there is a place for this term in orality-literacy studies, that it may more properly describe genres like the sermon, which, more than any other form of nineteenth-century prose, is characterized by the often uneasy juxtaposition of oral and written traditions' (Robert H. Ellison, *The Victorian Pulpit: Spoken and Written Sermons in Nineteenth-Century Britain* (Selinsgrove, PA: Susquehanna University Press, 1998), 14–15). What Ellison argues of the sermon applies a fortiori for the lecture.

The more relevant parallel is formal. O. C. Edwards' study of the different kinds of sermon that predominated in the long eighteenth century identifies a number of older styles of preaching that persisting through the period – specifically, the Spanish 'concetto' style, the German 'emblematic' and the Puritan 'plain style' sermons – whilst noting newer styles such as the Anglican preaching of Tillotson, the evangelical sermons of the eighteenth-century 'awakenings' and those of Lutheran Pietism, all of which came into fashion.[49] None of these has any close formal affinity with the traditional mode of university lecturing, as old as the Middle Ages: the synoptic and systematic itemisation of terms of knowledge. And when we put it like this it becomes easier to see the ways in which Coleridge's approach takes a quasi-Germanic 'emblematic' approach to its topic, mixed with elements of the 'inspired' Tillotsonian or nonconformist tradition. There may have been reasons other than personal quirk that lead Coleridge to extemporise his lectures rather than reading from a prepared text.

So for example: the second lecture of the 1811–12 series begins with a designedly amusing division of readers into four classes, characterised by their increasing acuity and retention. The lecture as a whole then goes on to make more serious points about the importance of precision in the use of words, the divisions of taste, a definition of poetry and a brief emblematic history of the English stage. The initial four-part distinction is not exactly the text upon which the lecture is then preached, but it does formally embody the shape the lecture then takes. The third lecture from the same series opens with Coleridge's view 'that poetry is no proper antithesis to prose—in the correct opposite of poetry is science, and the correct antithesis of prose is metre', and then develops this idea with a series of meditations upon moral pleasure, metrical form, knowledge and truth to life, bringing in (sermonically) the Bible as poetry and 'religious controversy' as a shaping influence on Shakespeare himself. The fourth lecture devolves, in a manner of speaking, this principle upon itself: it starts by identifying the starting point of Shakespeare's writing life, and goes on to close-read the 'sweet' and organically satisfying imagery of the *Venus and Adonis* and *Rape of Lucrece*. The remaining lectures in this series, at least the ones that we have been able to recover, tend to concentrate on one specific Shakespearian play (for instance Lecture 7 is on *Romeo and Juliet*, Lecture 9 on *The Tempest* and so on) and to do so by

---

[49] O. C. Edwards Jr, 'Varieties of Sermon: A Survey of Preaching in the Long Eighteenth Century', in Joris Van Eijnatten (ed.), *Preaching, Sermon and Cultural Change in the Long Eighteenth-Century* (Leiden/Boston: Brill, 2009), 3–55.

establishing an emblematic point at the beginning, often derived from the opening scenes of the play, elaborating upon it as a way of unlocking the specific excellence of the text under consideration. Sometimes the connection between the one and the other is more intuitive and poetic – more, we could say, organic – than is common in lecturing. So, for example, the sixth lecture of the 1811–12 series opens, rather oddly, with comments on the undesirability of corporal punishment at school. The lecture itself soon moves onto Shakespeare, but the initial emblem animates the whole. This is, in part, because Coleridge's point has to do with the foolishness of trying to apply any mode of procrustean schoolmasterish 'rules' to Shakespeare, an artist whose plays grow like the ideal Rousseau-esque child by a natural genius, not by obedience to the classical unities. And the shadowy figure of the master's stick or cane becomes itself transformed in Coleridge's imagination, to the following conceit:

> The wit of Shakespeare is like the flourishing of a man's stick, when he is walking, in the full flow of animal spirits: it is a sort of overflow of hilarity which disburdens, and seems like a conductor, to distribute a portion of our joy to the surrounding air by carrying it away from us.

Directly following this wonderful image, Coleridge reverts to questions of moral delinquency and moral freedom. The eighth lecture begins with the thought that that 'religion is the Poetry of all mankind', moves from this into a meditation on divine and human love, and then undertakes a reading of *Romeo and Juliet* in a manner that, with considerable nuance and sensitivity, juxtaposes the romantic love shared by that play's deuteragonists with the passion the lover of Shakespeare – such as Coleridge himself – feels for this art. The ninth lecture takes ancient sculpture as its emblem, moving on to a discussion of *The Tempest* as an artefact not of slavish imitation but of 'the imagination', since 'the scheme of his drama does not appeal to any sensuous impression of time and place, but to the imagination'. The twelfth lecture opens with 'the anecdote of John Wilkes, who said of himself that even in the company of ladies, the handsomest man ever created had but ten minutes' advantage of him', and goes on to explore some of Coleridge's most sensitively insightful character-readings of the dynamic between the inner and outer lives of Richard II and Hamlet.

This, then, returns me to the specific rationale for the present edition. Most editions of these lectures have, in effect, reverted back upon a fundamentally literary conception of what, textually speaking, they are. That is to say, previous editions of these lectures have tended to resolve Coleridge's oral performance back into the notes and prompts (such as they were) out of which they were extemporised, augmented by the literary-journalistic and other post hoc memorials of those lectures. Robert H. Ellison's judgement on the 'genre of the sermon', though, applies just as urgently to the genre of the lecture: namely, that it is characterised by the often uneasy juxtaposition of oral *and* written traditions. The present edition seeks, in a small way, to shift the balance back from written to oral, to present a text not only easier to read, but easier, if you should wish, to reënact as orality by reading it aloud.

Rationale of the Present Edition

As noted above, Coleridge almost never lectured from a written-out script, and he himself oversaw no printed collection of his Shakespearian lucubrations. Accordingly there is no 'official' version of the lectures. One main source for this material comes via a contemporary called John Payne Collier (1789–1883), who attended the 1811–12 lectures and made shorthand notes. Collier, the son of a literary father – writer and journalist John Dyer Collier (1762–1825) – doubtless gained entry into the London literary world via his father's many friendships and contacts. He met and dined with Coleridge and Hazlitt, and knew Coleridge's friend Henry Crabb Robinson. He learned shorthand and worked for a time as a reporter. In 1811 he entered Middle Temple and proceeded far enough with his studies to qualify as a barrister, although he was not actually called to the bar until 1829, and in the interim he wrote for the *Times* and *Morning Chronicle*, as his father had also done and did. As R. A. Foakes notes, 'we have Henry Crabb Robinson's word for it that the lectures Coleridge gave in 1811–12 were reported for the *Morning Chronicle* "sometimes by Mr Collier, sometimes by John C. and sometimes by myself".' Foakes thinks that in 1811 Collier was a 'young' and 'uncertain' individual, prone to 'hero-worshipping' and 'overwhelmed in the presence of the genius Coleridge'; and he considers it likely that such an individual 'sought to set down faithfully and accurately what Coleridge said'.[50] At any rate, Collier made shorthand transcriptions of many of Coleridge's seventeen lectures. Then there is a gap of several decades until 1854 when

[50] R. A. Foakes (ed.), *Coleridge on Shakespeare: The Text of the Lectures of 1811–12* (London: Routledge & Kegan Paul, 1971), 2.

Collier, now in his sixties, moved house. As a consequence of this move he chanced upon some (though not all) of the shorthand notes he had made in 1811–12. These he transcribed, making them public first in four brief notes in the journal *Notes and Queries* (July–August 1854), and then in the book *Seven Lectures on Shakespeare and Milton, by the late S. T. Coleridge* (1856). The text recorded in this latter volume, in Foakes' words, was 'accepted into the canon of Coleridge's works, and provides the only substantial record we possess of the lectures he gave on Shakespeare'. This material, reprinted in later books – such as Thomas Ashe's *Coleridge's Lectures and Notes on Shakespeare* (1883), T. M. Raysor's *Coleridge: Shakespearian Criticism* (1930) and the 1960 Everyman edition of *Coleridge on Shakespeare* – is where much of the influence of Coleridge's critical thought on this topic derives.

But there are several problems with this provenance, not the least of which is the untrustworthiness of Collier himself as a literary scholar. He was, not to mince words, a serial and incorrigible forger and embellisher of the material which he published. His most notorious forgery was his claim to have discovered a rare 1632 Folio of Shakespeare that included 117 marginal annotations and emendations by an actor from the Bard's own troop. Collier published these, and vigorously defended their authenticity, although the marginalia are in fact in Collier's own handwriting. Nor is this the only evidence of his unreliability.[51] Yet, despite his various literary delinquencies, there is reason to believe that Collier's shorthand notes of Coleridge's 1811–12 lectures *do* provide a fair record of what Coleridge said. When they can be checked against other sources – Coleridge's own notes and other accounts – they mostly stand up; Collier's more egregious forgeries date from the 1830s. That said, for the 1856 published version Collier rewrote and 'improved', added extra material, guessed at passages he had not fully understood and generally so meddled with his own notes as to severely dilute the authenticity and the worth of his account.

At the other extreme, where textual trustworthiness is concerned, we now have the monumental scholarly achievement of R. A.

---

[51] A detailed account of this, and similar cases, can be found in Arthur Freeman and Janet Ing Freeman's *John Payne Collier: Scholarship and Forgery in the Nineteenth Century* (New Haven, CT: Yale University Press, 2004). Shortly before he died, at the ripe old age of 95, Collier wrote in his journal: 'I am bitterly and most sincerely grieved that in every way I am such a despicable offender, I am ashamed of almost every act of my life' (quoted in Andrew Murphy, *Shakespeare in Print: A History and Chronology of Shakespeare Publishing* (Cambridge: Cambridge University Press, 2003), 201).

Foakes. In his two-volume *Lectures 1808–1819: On Literature*, Foakes prints what few lecture notes Coleridge himself made, transcribes Collier's own shorthand notes and the notes of others who occasionally recorded Coleridge's speaking, and augments this material with a wealth of other sources such as accounts in newspapers, diary entries, letters and memoirs. It is an extraordinarily comprehensive edition, and one of the jewels in the crown of the multi-volume 'Bollingen' *Collected Coleridge*.[52] But the very scrupulousness with which this edition is made entails its own difficulties for the reader. The text proceeds via hiccoughy successions of crossings-out, abbreviations, insertions, oddities and memoranda; whole passages are repeated, often many times. It could hardly be otherwise, of course, given the scrappy, half-revised and variegated nature of the material Foakes is collating.

One need not disrespect Foakes' approach to take issue with it. Two observations in particular are worth making. The first is that by making the reading process so awkward and choppy Foakes ends up producing a text in which the reader, especially the student reader, can have a tough job orienting themself. The second observation is that Foakes' stated aim of 'offer[ing] a more authentic text' of these lectures cannot be supported. Short of travelling by time machine back to 1811 and actually standing in the lecture hall there is no 'authentic' access to these lectures. Neither Collier's shorthand notes nor Coleridge's marginalia grant us magical access to the *ipsissima verba* actually spoken. In one sense, of course, Foakes' approach represents a painstaking fidelity to the textual remains of Coleridge's lectures; in another sense it is a misrepresentation so major as to do real violence to the source material. Even those who disapproved of Coleridge's tendency to digress and ramble agreed with Coleridge's admirers that he was an exceptionally *fluent* speaker. An edition of his Shakespeare lectures ought at the very least, we might think, to reflect that fluency.

Collier's 1856 volume, for all its problems, is at least readable. And it ought to be possible to improve on Collier without sacrificing readability. By comparing his original shorthand notes, written in the lecture hall as Coleridge spoke, against his later printed text, the latter can be brought closer to the former. Where Collier has made an obvious error, misunderstood Coleridge's point or omitted a quotation

---

[52] This is the standard scholarly edition of Coleridge's poetry and prose published under the Bollingen rubric by Princeton at http://press.princeton.edu/catalogs/series/title/collected-works-of-samuel-taylor-coleridge.html. Throughout the text this will be abbreviated to CC.

shoemaker, and can read and write correctly .(for spelling is still of some consequence) he becomes an author.*

The crying ·sin of modern criticism is that it is over-loaded with personality. . If an author commit an error, there is no wish to set him right for the sake of truth, but for the sake of triumph—that the reviewer may show how much wiser, or how much abler he is than the writer. Reviewers are usually people who would have been poets, historians, biographers, &c., if they could : they have

* Here my short-hand note informs me that Coleridge made a quotation from Jeremy Taylor, but from what work, or of what import, does not appear. He observed, that "although Jeremy Taylor wrote only in prose, according to some definitions of poetry he might be considered one of our noblest poets."—J. P. C.

Figure 1   A detail from p. 4 of Collier's *Seven Lectures on Shakespeare and Milton* (1856).

– and where such errors can be confirmed, quotations recovered and so on – the text ought to be amended. In this present edition, at all points the aim has been to reproduce the lectures as lectures, rather than as a mosaic of shorthand notes, newspaper reports and other scraps. For example, in his 1856 version of the first lecture from the 1811–12 series, Collier printed the note shown on Figure 1.

Foakes prints not this, but Collier's transcribed shorthand notes:

shoe maker and co^d. read & write *for spelling was not necessary* he became author. Coleridge here quoted from Bishop Jeremy Taylor, who he observ'd tho' writing in prose might be considered the first of our Poets. The passage related to the subject he was discussing & contained among others the following sentence [m] "the favour of the people is as fickle as the smiles of an infant or the fall of a die" – [n16] After <vigorously> censuring personality Coleridge quoted from (I believe) the Lectures he himself had formerly delivered at the Royal Institution.

He adds a footnote recording that 'the favour ... fall of a die' is quoted from Taylor's Σύμβολον Θεολογικόν (1674), but leaves it at that. I believe it makes more sense to include the actual passage

> I have often heard the question put whether Pope is a great poet, and it has been warmly debated on both sides, some positively maintaining the affirmative, and others dogmatically insisting upon the negative ; but it never occurred to either party to make the necessary preliminary inquiry—What is meant by the words "poet" and "poetry ?" Poetry is not merely invention : if it were, Gulliver's Travels would be poetry ; and before you can arrive at a decision of the question, as to Pope's claim, it is absolutely necessary to ascertain what people intend by the words they use. Harmonious versification no more makes poetry than mere invention makes a poet ; and to both these requisites there is much besides to be added. In morals, politics, and philosophy no useful discussion can be entered upon, unless we begin by explaining and understanding the terms we employ.

Figure 2   Excerpt from Collier's *Seven Lectures.*

Coleridge was quoting, and in the text below I do so. Or again, from the second of the 1811–12 lectures (Figure 2).

The passage in Figure 2 is the 1856 version. Collier's original notes differ from this: 'He illustrated this sentiment further by an allusion to Gulliver's Travels, which I did not exactly comprehend.'

'This sentiment' is the question whether Pope is a good or bad poet. In other words, the version printed of 1856 was Collier's best guess, long after the event. And it wasn't a very good guess. Since we happen to have S. T. C.'s own lecture notes for this paragraph (though, alas, not for the rest of the lecture), we can see precisely in what ways Collier got it wrong. Here's S. T. C.:

I[t] has, I doubt not, occurred to many of my Auditors, as well as to myself, to hear literary when the conversation has turned on literature, to hear it asked—whether we think Mr Pope a great Poet—offence and shock given to many—the dispute follows—the disputants leave off with but a mean opinion of each another—yet never thought that the dispute was strictly preposterous, i.e., began at the wrong end—and that they each should have first ascertained what the other understood by the word *Poetry*. If the veracious Lemuel Gulliver on his return from his celebrated Travels, and previous to his publication, had asked of us mentioned to us the names of two public characters in the country which he had unfortunately heard at an unfortunate alien act had compelled him to leave, and then asked—which of the two we thought the nobler Houynmn, we should most certainly if only we could neigh out the word, answer him by asking him—what is a H.? What do you mean by the word? (CC 5:1 200)

Here, the best editorial option is surely to restore Coleridge's actual point, and to do so in a way that fits tonally and stylistically with the rest of the lecture, rather than reverting suddenly to note form. I appreciate that there is an element of – we could say – the fake antique about this, but it strikes me as the best of the various editorial compromises available.

For scholars interested in the intricacies of Coleridge's career as a lecturer, Foakes' *Lectures 1808–1819: On Literature* is always going to be the edition of choice. But this edition has in mind students, scholars and general readers who wish to 'get at' what Coleridge said about Shakespeare, and to contextualise some of the most famous and enduring critical perspectives on his plays. I have aimed to produce a readable and easily navigable work, as accessible to scholars as students and the general reader. I do not pretend that what follows is the *echt* Coleridge, the actual words actually spoken by Coleridge the lecture hall. Such an actuality is unachievable. But that it can never be achieved does not mean that it cannot be better or worse approximated, and the hope is that this volume approaches closer to that unachievable asymptote than other editions.

Notes on the Text

Texts of the lectures, below, are worked together from Coleridge's own notes, such shorthand transcriptions as exist and, occasionally, from other reports, such as newspaper accounts. Where quoted material that has otherwise gone unreported can, with some certainty, be identified it has been restored. This includes passages from Richard Hooker's *Lawes of Ecclesiastical Polity*, from Coleridge's own *The Friend*, from Pope, from various poets and so on. The overall textual approach of this edition is discussed above.

Inconsistently applied spellings (for instance, 'shew' and 'show', 'pourtray' and 'portray') and play titles (such as *Love's Labour's Lost*, which appears variously as '*Love's Labour lost*', '*Love's Labor Lost*' and '*Love's Labors Lost*'), together with Shakespeare's own name (variously 'Shakespeare', 'Shakspeare', 'Shakspere') have been regularised in favour of the modern form, except when I am quoting from other published work or writers, in which case I have left all spellings as they occur in the original. Occasional instances of consistently used Regency spelling have been retained ('cloathed', 'develope', 'ideot' 'gypsey'). Punctuation and accidentals have also been regularised, and in many cases punctuation-free text has been punctuated by the editor. There is no way of ensuring that this results in text with which Coleridge (himself never very exact when it came to accidentals in his published prose) would have agreed; but neither is the text as printed here likely to be radically different to such an imaginary copy-text. In general, punctuation broadly follows the way it is recorded by Collier and Tomalin, on the understanding that, in howsoever shadowy a form, it reflects the aggregative and on-rushing manner of Coleridge's actual delivery. Where reports are couched in the third person, they are here reframed to the first, to represent what Coleridge would have said in a lecture hall to a present audience.

The 1811–1812 Lectures

The two core sources for the ten lectures to have survived from this course of seventeen are the shorthand note-taking of two individuals: John Collier and 'J Tomalin'.

Lecture 1 and 2 are based on Collier's transcription. Lecture 1 as here printed is augmented at its opening by three pages of Coleridge's own notes (CC 5:1, 185–8). Specifically, the first two paragraphs and the first sentence of the third are Collier; the paragraph that follows Coleridge's note, the remainder Collier augmented with Coleridge's notes where appropriate. There is one sentence in this version of the lecture ('Yet Poetry is better than this' in paragraph 9) which is pure editorial speculation, needful to link Coleridge's notes to Collier's next transcribed paragraph. The beginning of Lecture 2 similarly incorporates Coleridge's notes, adjusting Collier's shorthand records where appropriate: in particular Collier's 'he illustrated this senti-ment further by an allusion to Gulliver's Travels, which I did not exactly comprehend' (CC 5:1, 204) is replaced by S. T. C.'s notes; quotations from Catullus, Plato and Pope are added to the text where Collier's notes indicate such quotation was made. These two lectures are shorter than the remainder of the remainder of the course not because Coleridge spoke for a shorter length of time, but because, as Collier confesses in the preface to his 1856 edition, he only notated portions of the lectures, either because of 'want of facility', or because he was 'frequently so engrossed and absorbed' that his note-taking became interrupted.

Lectures 3, 4 and 5 are based on the transcription made by a certain J. Tomalin. Nothing more is known of this individual, not even his first name (John? Joseph? Jeremiah?). We know that Tomalin made transcripts of eight lectures, but these were all lost by Ernest Hartley Coleridge (on a train journey to Torquay towards the end of the century). All that survives are the texts copied out by James Dykes Campbell much later – in 1888, according to the note Campbell appended to his transcript of Lecture 3 – from Tomalin's original notes. These have been, where appropriate, combined with or modified in the light of Coleridge's own notes, recorded in CC 5:1, 217–68. In Lecture 3, a quotation by Dryden has been substituted for the similar-sounding but untraced quotation Tomalin attributes to 'Webster'. What may be an account of Lecture 4 by Collier has been discovered, and checked against Tomalin's transcription. The account is included in the Appendix.

The remainder of the 1811–12 lectures are based, again, on Collier's notes, which have been checked against such examples of Coleridge's notes as are available.

The 1818–1819 Lectures

Lecture 1: the text combines and regularises Coleridge's MS Notes (recorded in Foakes, *Lectures on Literature*, 2:263–8) with Henry Nelson Coleridge's continuation from *Literary Remains*.[53]

Lecture 2: Foakes records four pages of marginalia from Coleridge's edition of *Richard II*. There is not enough material here reasonably to reconstruct this lecture.

Lecture 3: the text is based on Henry Nelson Coleridge's 'Hamlet' section in *Literary Remains* (1:202–26), checked against and adapted in the light of the marginalia in Coleridge's edition of *Hamlet* (CC 5:2, 293–302). Henry Nelson Coleridge combined this latter material with other Coleridgean notes on Shakespeare very likely not originally part of this lecture, and he certainly expanded and regularised the expression and style of the material he reprinted; but in accordance with the editorial principles of this edition his text has retained in adapted form. The four paragraphs from 'In all the best attested stories of ghosts and visions . . .' to '. . . harrows me with fear and wonder' derive from the notes Coleridge made for the sixth of the '1818 Lectures on European Literature' (CC 5:2, 137–40). It is possible that Coleridge reused this material for the later lecture, although there is no direct evidence that he did. Its presence here is preferred on the basis that we know Coleridge *did* talk about ghosts in the later

---

[53] Henry Nelson Coleridge (ed.), *The Literary Remains of Samuel Taylor Coleridge* (2 vols, London: William Pickering, 1836), 2:95–102.

lecture (the report in the *Champion*, 10 January 1819, says 'we wish that he had given some portion of the time consumed by the almost unintelligible ambiguous apologies for belief in ghosts and goblins, to the elucidation of the yet obscure traits of character of Hamlet'). The notes on *Hamlet* recorded by Foakes do not otherwise include such a discussion, and Coleridge did sometimes reuse material from one lecture to another.

Lecture 4: the text is based on Henry Nelson Coleridge's 'Macbeth' section in *Literary Remains* (2:235–50), the prose being reverted to the capitalisations, spellings and in most cases word-order and expression of the marginalia in Coleridge's edition of *Macbeth* that Foakes argued he used as the basis for this lecture (CC 5:2, 305–10). The second paragraph is based on Coleridge's notes for the second lecture of his 1813 series (CC 5:1, 527–8).

Lecture 5: There not being enough material to reconstruct the whole lecture, this is styled 'a portion': the opening and closing sections are evidently missing. It regularises the notes and more substantial marginalia in Coleridge's edition of *Othello* (CC 5:2, 313–17) with their record in Henry Nelson Coleridge's 'Othello' section in *Literary Remains* (1:255–67).

Lecture 6: the text is based on the 'Lear' section in *Literary Remains* (185–201) and the long note and subsequent marginalia in Coleridge's edition of *Lear* (CC 5:2, 313–17) that he used as a basis for this lecture. The short opening paragraph (not in Foakes) is presumably Henry Nelson Coleridge recording a now-lost marginalium or note. There's no evidence Coleridge opened his 28 January 1819 lecture with this paragraph, but he might have done, and it fits well. The third paragraph is expanded into readable prose from a brief S. T. C. portion of note omitted by Henry Nelson Coleridge. From the account of this lecture in the *Courier* (Monday 1 February 1819) we know that Coleridge began with 'the motives of Edmund's baseness towards his brother' including an analysis of the 'Thou nature art my Goddess' soliloquy (not part of S. T. C.'s marginalia), and that the lecture continued with an 'analysis of the *Fool's* character' that included the phrase 'babbling the food of anguish to the mind of Lear' (identified by the *Courier* as 'the happy expression of Mr. Coleridge himself'), followed by 'elucidations of Lear's character'. The present restoration has taken the marginalia via this summary as a guiding principle.

1819 Lectures
Only one Shakespeare lecture – on *Troilus and Cressida* – is (partially) recoverable from the notes for this series. The text here is taken from

Henry Nelson Coleridge's *Literary Remains*, itself based on Coleridge's notes. This has been altered where appropriate to bring it closer to the two paragraphs quoted from Coleridge's actual lecture recorded in the *New Times* report of 1 March 1819 (CC 2:379–80).

LECTURES ON SHAKESPEARE

Lectures on Shakespeare 1811–1812

Samuel Taylor Coleridge

Venue: the Great Room of the London Philosophical Society, Scot's Corporation Hall, Crane Court, off Fleet Street.

Lecture 1: Monday, 18 November 1811 (On the Principles of Criticism)
Lecture 2: Thursday, 21 November 1811 (On Poetry)
Lecture 3: Monday, 25 November 1811 (On Dramatic Poetry)
Lecture 4: Thursday, 28 November 1811 (*Venus and Adonis, Rape of Lucrece*)
Lecture 5: Monday, 2 December 1811 (*Love's Labour's Lost*)
Lecture 6: Thursday, 5 December 1811 (On Shakespeare's Wit)
Lecture 7: Monday, 9 December 1811 (*Romeo and Juliet*)
Lecture 8: Thursday, 12 December 1811 (*Romeo and Juliet*)
Lecture 9: Monday, 16 December 1811 (*The Tempest*)
[Lecture 10: Thursday, 19 December 1811]
[Lecture 11: Monday, 30 December 1811]
Lecture 12: Thursday, 2 January 1812 (*Richard II, Hamlet*)
[Lecture 13: Thursday, 9 January 1812]
[Lecture 14: Monday, 13 January 1812]
[Lecture 15: Thursday, 16 January 1812]
[Lecture 16: Monday, 20 January 1812]
[Lecture 17: Monday, 27 January 1812]

LECTURE 1

I cannot avoid the acknowledgment of the difficulty of the task I have undertaken; yet I have undertaken it voluntarily, and I shall discharge it to the best of my abilities, requesting those who hear me to allow for deficiencies, and to bear in mind the wide extent of my subject; *inopem me copia fecit.*[54] What I most rely upon is your sympathy; and, as I proceed, I trust that I shall interest you: sympathy and interest are to a lecturer like the sun, the spring and the showers to nature–absolutely necessary to the production of blossoms and fruit.

May I venture to observe that my own life has been employed more in reading and conversation–in collecting and reflecting, than in printing and publishing; for I never felt the desire, so often experienced by others, of becoming an author. It was accident made me an author in the first instance: I was called a poet almost before I knew I could write poetry. Conscious superiority, if indeed it be superior, need not fear to have its self-love or its pride wounded; and contempt, the most absurd and debasing feeling that can actuate the human mind, must be far below the sphere in which lofty intellects live and move and have their being.

On the first examination of a work, especially a work of fiction and fancy, it is right to observe to what feeling or passion it addresses itself. And since passion has been appealed to, we may then, if only we be honest and good (for Poetry and all its sister arts presuppose a state of mind and a cultivation of taste correspondent to them, and cannot at once create it), determine what rank, what comparative estimation, we ought to give to this part of our nature;–whether it is one of those which though permanent in itself is perpetually varying the Objects that gratify it:–such as curiosity which turns with the disgust of satiety from the last novel or romance to devour a fresh one; destined like the former to pass from a dainty into a nuisance;–or a base passion such as we ought, in that shape at least, to exterminate from our heart–such as *envy, under the common mask of Scorn,*[55] or whether

---

[54] 'Copiousness has made me poor'; 'my very wealth has made me a pauper'. Ovid *Metamorphosis* 3:466. Coleridge was fond of quoting this tag, for instance in Griggs, *Collected Letters* 3:126 and *Biographia Literaria*, Chapter 15.

[55] It is more conventional for envy or scorn to be disguised, or 'masked', as positive

they are indeed the worthy and constituent Powers of our nobler Nature, not only permanent in themselves, but always and solely to be gratified by the same outward excellencies, the same in essence, though infinitely varying in form, subject and degree.–Such are our Imagination, our delight from the clear perception of Truth, and our moral sense, including our awe for true greatness, our pity for suffering, and our indignation at wrongs. In short, has the pleasure you have received, had any tendency to make you a better man, or to keep you a good one, or to reward you in part for having been so.

To the essentials of a sound Judgment concerning the comparative merit of poems, this must be sufficient, and might appear easy–but alas! the obstacles are many–and the Prospectus has promised for me that I should discuss them under the name of false criticism, especially in poetry. Now these many be reduced to two classes–

1. Accidental, from particular circumstances of the age and people amongst which we live; or–
2. Permanent, or those at least which as they flow from our common nature, we may safely in every age and in every state of Society which we have known or heard of or have any reason to anticipate.

Under the first head, accidental causes, may be classed–1. The enormous stimulant power of events making the desire to be strongly stimulated almost an appetite in a large majority of the world. 2. Events from taxation and their immediate action on our domestic happiness, from the unexampled influence of opinions on the conduct of young men, have made all men more anxious to know what is going on in the world–have made us a world of Readers. 3. The passion of public speaking, which encourages a too great desire to be understood at the first blush. 4. The prevalence of Reviews, Magazines, Selections and so on, these with Newspapers and *Novels*,[56] constituting nine-tenths of the reading of nine-tenths of the reading Public from their habits as Readers.

Of the last, and of the perusal of them, I will run the risk of asserting, that where the reading of novels prevails as a habit, it occasions

---

quantities (see for instance Arthur Murphy's popular tragedy *Zenobia* (1768) 1:i: 'But I am used/To bear your scorn; your scorn that wounds the deeper,/Masked as it is with pity and esteem'). It is possible that Coleridge here referred to, or perhaps even quoted, his own poem 'Ode on the Departing Year' (1796), where the violence of Revolutionary Terror is described as 'masked hate, and envying scorn'.

[56] Coleridge's notes include the parenthesis: '(here introduce the passage concerning novels)' (CC 5:1, 186). This edition takes this to be the passage 'Of the last . . . faculties' inserted below.

in time the entire destruction, of the powers of the mind: it is such an utter loss to the reader, that it is not so much to be called *pastime* as *kill-time*.[57] It is filling the mind with a little mawkish sensibility, instead of encouraging and cultivating the more noble faculties.

Reviews are pernicious, because the writers decide without any reference to fixed principles, because they are filled with personalities; and, above all, because they teach people rather to judge than to read; they encourage superficiality, and a disposition to adopt the sentiments dictated under the word *We*, than to form opinions of our own. In elder times writers were looked up to almost as intermediate beings, between angels and men. Some time afterwards they were thought venerable teachers; from thence they descended to instructive friends; and now they are deemed rather culprits than benefactors.[58] The first question asked of a person who was reading generally is—'What trash have you there?' I admit that there is some reason for this difference in the estimate; for in these times, if a man fail as a shoe maker, and can read and write correctly—*for spelling is not necessary*—he becomes an author. It is apposite here to quote from Bishop Jeremy Taylor, who, though he wrote only in prose, might yet according to some definitions of poetry be considered one of the first of our Poets.[59]

> When we make books and publish them, and by dedications implore the patronage of some worthy person, I find by experience that we cannot acquire that end, which is pretended to by such addresses; for neither friendship nor power, interest or favour, can give those defences to a book, which it needs: because the evil fortune of books comes from causes discernible indeed, but irremediable; and the breath of the people is like the voice of an exterminating angel, not so killing but so secret. But

---

[57] Coleridge makes this point again in the *Biographia Literaria*: 'to the devotees of the circulating libraries, I dare not compliment their *pass-time*, or rather *kill-time*, with the name of reading' (Chapter 3).

[58] Also reworked in the *Biographia* Chapter 3: 'In times of old, books were as religious oracles; as literature advanced, they next became venerable preceptors; they then descended to the rank of instructive friends; and, as their numbers increased, they sank still lower to that of entertaining companions; and at present they seem degraded into culprits to hold up their hands at the bar of every self-elected, yet not the less peremptory, judge, who chooses to write from humour or interest, from enmity or arrogance.'

[59] In John Payne Collier (ed.), *Seven Lectures on Shakespeare and Milton, by the Late S. T. Coleridge* (London: Chapman and Hall, 1856), Collier omits this quotation and appends the following apologetic footnote: 'Here my short-hand note informs me that Coleridge made a quotation from Jeremy Taylor, but from what work, or of what import, does not appear. He observed, that "although Jeremy Taylor wrote only in prose, according to some definitions of poetry he might be considered one of our noblest poets."—J. P. C.'

that is not all; it is also as contingent as the smiles of an infant, or the fall of a die.[60]

Fifthly, this combining with the increase of cities and therewith the starvation of ordinary gossip produced a substitute for the ever demanding appetite–and instead of the observations about Miss or Mr Such-a-one's dress or behaviour at the village Church or last Ball occasioned a rage for a more dignified gossip about *public* characters.[61]

This is an AGE OF PERSONALITY, an age of literary and political *Gossiping*, when the meanest insects are worshipped with a sort of Egyptian superstition, if only the brainless head be atoned for by the sting of *personal* malignity in the tail! When the most vapid satires have become the objects of a keen public interest purely from the number of contemporary characters *named* in the patch-work notes (which possess, however, the comparative merit of being more poetical than the Text), and because, to increase the stimulus, the author has sagaciously left his own name for whispers and conjectures![62]– an age, when even Sermons are published with a double appendix stuffed with *names*–a generation so transformed from the characteristic reserve of Britons, that from the ephemeral sheet of a London Newspaper to the everlasting Scotch Professorial Quarto,[63] almost every publication exhibits or flatters the epidemic distemper; that the very 'last year's rebuses' in the Lady's Diary, are answered in a serious Elegy '*on my father's death*' with the name and habitat of the elegiac Oedipus subscribed;–and '*other ingenious solutions were likewise given*' to the said *rebuses*–not, as heretofore, by Crito, Philander, A B, Y, &c. but by fifty or sixty plain English sirnames at full length, with their several places of abode![64] An age, when a bashful *Philalethes* or

---

[60] This is from the dedicatory letter to Lord Hatton with which Taylor opens his Σύμβολον Θεολογικόν [Symbolon Theologikon], *Or, A Collection of Polemicall Discourses* (London: R Norton, 1674).

[61] S. T. C.'s own notes here say '–here the Friend &c–' The following paragraph incorporates the relevant passage, from *The Friend* 10 (19 October 1809). Collier's notes of the lecture record the broad outlines of this, but erroneously attribute the passage: 'After vigorously censuring Personality Coleridge quoted from (I believe) the Lectures he had himself formerly delivered at the Royal Institution' (CC 5:1, 190). This whole paragraph was also published in *Biographia Literaria*, Chapter 2.

[62] A reference to the anonymous *The Pursuits of Literature: a Satirical Poem in Four Dialogues*; first published in four volumes 1794–97, afterwards reissued several times in one volume with explanatory notes identifying all the contemporary figures mentioned.

[63] Coleridge means *The Edinburgh Review*.

[64] *The Ladies' Diary* for 1796 asked readers to write poetic riddles fitted to one of ten supplied 'answers' (the ten answers were: Cradle; Eve; Thimble; Bridge; Nail; Pulpit; Lips; Air; Coals; Knot). The journal then printed eleven winning entries, identified by the names of the authors, as well as a list that began 'other separate answers to the

Phileleutheros[65] is as rare on the title-pages and among the signatures of our magazines, as a real name used to be in the days of our shy and notice-shunning grandfathers! When (more exquisite than all) I see an epic poem (Spirits of Maro and Maeonides,[66] make ready to welcome your new compeer!) advertised with the special recommendation, that the said *Epic Poem*[67] contains more than a hundred names of *living* persons!

And lastly (for it would weary you were I to enumerate all the causes from Luxury, Lotteries, and so on) the one consoling cause, though innocently in consequence of its coexistence with the above stated as auxiliary, the greater desire of knowledge, better domestic habits—which yet, combining with the above make a hundred readers where a century ago there was but one, and of every hundred *five* hundred critics!

Yet poetry is better than this. In the words of Richard Hooker, 'her seat is the Bosom of God, her Voice the Harmony of the World: All things in Heaven and Earth do her homage'.[68] It is the language of heaven, and in the exquisite delight we derive from poetry we have, as it were, a type, a foretaste, and a prophecy of the joys of heaven.

Another cause of false criticism is the greater purity of morality in the present age, compared even with the last. Who now will venture to read a number of the *Spectator*, or of the *Tatler*, to his wife and daughters, without first examining it to make sure that it contains no improper sentences unfit for the delicacy of female ears? Even our theatres, the representations at which usually reflect the morals

---

Prize Enigmas, beside those inserted in the supplement, were given by the following ladies and gentleman' with 52 names listed. Finally, after this, the *Diary* included a 'General Answer to the Enigmas', which poem contained all 11 enigma answers. This was called 'An Elegy, by Mr. Job Aryes of Riccall, on the death of his father, our ingenious correspondent, Mr. James Ayres, who was many years Master of the Free-school at Kirby-Mispeton, near Malton'.

[65] 'Philalethes' and 'Phileleutheros' are pseudonyms for notional authors (derived from the Greek words 'lover of truth' and 'lover of freedom' respectively).

[66] Alternative names for Vergil and Homer.

[67] Probably Anne Hamilton's *The Epics of the Ton, or the Glories of the Great World* (1807), in which, as its title implies, a hundred members of fashionable London life are described in mock-heroic couplets. Or perhaps Coleridge has in mind Hannah Cowley's serious epic *The Siege of Acre* (1801), a poem about a recent event in the Napoleonic wars that includes a great many actual people, identified by extracts from contemporary newspapers appended to the edition. 'How exquisite a task to Bards is given', Cowley writes at the beginning of her third book, 'when actual deeds are subjects for the song/When living Beings to the theme belong.'

[68] Richard Hooker, *Of the Lawes of Ecclesiastical Politie* (London: William Stansby, 1594), 1:16.

of the period, have taken a sort of domestic turn, and while the performances at them improved the hearts, they injured the taste of the Auditory.[69] It is a bad cause, but an excellent effect.

Attempts have been made to write systems of Education; but they appear to me something like Greek and Latin grammars put into the hands of boys, before they understand a word of Greek or Latin. Why are you to furnish the means of judging, before you give the capacity to judge? These seem to me to be among the principal *accidental* causes of false criticism.

Among the *permanent* causes, I may notice—

First, the greater delight in being reminded of one's knowledge than of one's ignorance. The reader, who would follow a close reasoner to the summit and absolute principle of any one important subject, has chosen a chamois-hunter for his guide. Our guide will, indeed, take us the shortest way, will save us many a wearisome and perilous wandering, and warn us of many a mock road that had formerly led himself to the brink of chasms and precipices, or at best in an idle circle to the spot from which he started. But he cannot carry us on his shoulders: we must strain our own sinews, as he has strained his; and make firm footing on the smooth rock for ourselves, by the blood of toil from our own feet.[70] Systems have been produced with the avowed object of instructing men how to think; but in my opinion the proper title for such a work ought to be 'A System To Teach Men How to Think Without Thinking.'[71]

Nothing is more essential, nothing can be more important, than in every possible way to cultivate and improve the thinking powers: the mind as much requires exercise as the body, and no man can fully and adequately discharge the duties of whatever station he is placed in without the power of thought.—On man God has not only bestowed gifts, but *the power of giving*: he is not like the creature of a mere created being, born but to die: he has had faculties communicated to him, which, are beneficial to others. Man, in a secondary sense, may be looked upon in part as his own creator, for by the improvement of the faculties bestowed upon him by God, he not only enlarges them, but even creates new ones.

---

[69] That is, audience.

[70] The passage 'The reader, who ... from our own feet' is quoted from *The Friend* 3 (August 1809).

[71] Swiss theologian Jean-Pierre de Crousaz's *Nouvel Essai de Logique* (1712) had been translated into English as *A New Treatise of the Art of Thinking; Or: A Compleat System of Reflections Concerning the Conduct and Improvement of the Mind* (London: Thomas Woodward) in 1724. This version went through many editions.

A second permanent cause of false criticism is the effort, and at first the very painful effort, of *really* thinking—really referring to our own inward experiences;—and the ease with which we accept as a substitute for this, which can alone operate a true conviction, the opinions of those about us—which we have heard or been accustomed to take for granted and so on. I may illustrate this moral imbecility by a case which came within my own knowledge. A friend of mine had observed that he did not think Shakespeare had made Constance, in *King John*, speak the language of nature, when she said on the loss of Arthur,

> Grief fills the room up of my absent child,
> Lies in his bed, walks up and down with me;
> Puts on his pretty looks, repeats his words,
> Remembers me of all his gracious parts,
> Stuffs out his vacant garments with his form:
> Then have I reason to be fond of grief.[72]

Within three months after he had made his remark, my friend died. I called upon his mother, an ignorant though amiable woman, who had scarcely heard the name of Shakespeare, much less read him. Like King Philip in the play, I attempted to console her, and among other things I told her, in the anguish of her sorrow, that she seemed to be *as fond of grief as she had been of her son.*[73] What was her reply? Almost a prose parody on the very language of Shakespeare—the same thoughts in nearly the same words, but with a different arrangement. Yet how many have declared the first *unnatural*, and admired the remote silence of a German Tragedy, consisting of directions to the actors.[74]

As a third permanent cause of false criticism we may notice the vague use of terms. And here I may take the liberty of impressing upon my hearers, the necessity of appropriating them more strictly than in the ordinary transactions of life, which yet because it is ordinary is the master of our feelings and occasions in us a repugnance to the reasoner, who forbids us to use them as we have been accustomed to do. Because Poetry is for every man in his own conceit, and its *glory*

---

[72] *King John*, III, iv, 93–8.
[73] This is what King Philip says in Shakespeare's *King John*, which in turn provokes Constance's reply previously quoted.
[74] Coleridge may be thinking of, for instance, Schiller's *Kabale und Liebe* ('Love and Intrigue', 1784), which follows scenes of poisoning and trauma with the following stage-direction: '(A long and expressive silence should precede this scene)' (*Cabal and Love, a Tragedy. Translated from the German, Etc. In Five Acts* (London: Thomas Boosey, 1796), 100).

that it is so;–but to the Chemist, Geometrician, Anatomist–nay even to every Trader he allows it. This is shown in the word *Taste* and the terms connected with it, as the Sublime, the Beautiful, the Grand, the Majestic, the Picturesque, the Delightful, the Interesting, and the Amusing–what strange work if an author were forced to refer to any one principle all the senses which ignorance or even the subtlety of momentary analogies may have used any one of these terms!

I was one day surveying the fall of the Clyde,[75] and ruminating on what epithet could be best applied to it, and after much deliberation I pitched upon 'majestic' as the proper one. While I was still engaged on it a gentleman and lady came up, neither of whose faces bore much of the stamp of wisdom, and the first words the gentleman uttered were 'It is very majestic.' I was pleased to find a concurrent opinion, and I complimented the person on the choice of his term in warm language: 'Yes, sir,' replied the gentleman, 'I say it is very majestic: it is sublime and it is beautiful, and it is grand and picturesque.'–'Aye', added the lady, 'it is the prettiest thing I ever saw.' I own that I was not a little disconcerted.

You will see, by the terms of my prospectus, that I intend my lectures to be, not only 'in illustration of the principles of poetry,' but to include a statement of the application of those principles, 'as grounds of criticism on the most popular works of later English poets, those of the living included.'[76]

Permit me to conclude by quoting from my journal THE FRIEND: 'As long therefore as I obtrude no unsupported assertions on my readers; and as long as I state my opinions and the evidence which induced or compelled me to adopt them, with calmness and that diffidence in myself, which is by no means incompatible with a firm belief in the justness of the opinions themselves; while I attack no man's private life from any cause, and detract from no man's honours in his public character, from the truth of his doctrines, or the merits of his compositions, without detailing all my reasons and resting the result solely on the arguments adduced; while I moreover explain fully the motives of duty, which influenced me in resolving to institute such investigation; while I confine all asperity of censure, and all expressions of contempt, to gross violations of truth, honour, and decency, to the base corrupter and the detected slanderer; while I write on no

---

[75] Coleridge visited the Clyde in 1803. He had previously used this anecdote in the first lecture of his 1808 series.

[76] Collier appends a note at this point: 'here [Coleridge] laid by his lecture and picked up the prospectus', confirming (as Foakes notes) that he was lecturing from written notes and not extemporising.

subject, which I have not studied with my best attention, on no subject
which my education and acquirements have incapacitated me from
properly understanding; and above all while I approve myself, alike
in praise and in blame, in close reasoning and in impassioned declamation, a steady friend to the two best and surest friends of all men,
Truth and Honesty; I will not fear an accusation of either presumption or arrogance from the good and the wise, I shall pity it from the
weak, and despise it from the wicked.'[77]

---

[77] Quoted from *The Friend* No. 2 (June 1809). Collier's notes say that S. T. C. concluded
the lecture by 'read[ing] a passage from one of his works I rather think his own lectures
at the Royal Institution relative to impartiality to living authors and concluded by
declaring that in pursuing this object he should not fear an accusation of arrogance &
presumption from the good and the wise, he should pity it in the weak and despise it in
the wicked'. Foakes identifies the passage as being from *The Friend* (CC 5:1, 194). The
1856 text of *Seven Lectures* ends with: 'No man can truly apply principles, who displays
the slightest bias in the application of them; and I shall have much greater pleasure in
pointing out the good, than in exposing the bad. I fear no accusation of arrogance from
the amiable and the wise: I shall pity the weak, and despise the malevolent.'

LECTURE 2

Readers may be divided into four classes:[78]

1. Sponges, persons who absorb what they read and return it nearly in the same state only a little dirtied.
2. Sand-glasses, who permit everything to pass away and are content to doze away their time in actual idleness.
3. Strain-bags, who retain only the dregs of what they receive: sensuality and calumny, as, by the bye, the History of the Bible by a Mohawk for the use of the Mohawks containing only the stories of Cain and Abel, the assassination of Eglon, the very fat man, by Ehud a man left-handed, of Sisera asleep by Jael, David and Goliath, Judith and Holophernes, Herod's massacre of the Innocents and the last great conflagration.[79]
4. Great Mogul's diamond tiaras, who are equally rare and valuable.[80]

---

[78] This distinction first appeared in S. T. C.'s third lecture of his 1808 series 'On the Principles of Poetry': 'Sorts of Readers. 1. Spunges that suck up every thing and, when pressed give it out in the same state, only perhaps somewhat dirtier—2. Sand Glasses— or rather the upper Half of the Sand Glass, which in a brief hour assuredly lets out what it has received—& whose reading is only a profitless measurement & dozeing away of Time—. 3. Straining Bags, who get rid of whatever is good & pure, and retain the Dregs.—and this Straining-bag Class is again subdivided into Species of the Sensual, who retain evil for the gratification of their own base Imaginations, & the calumnious, who judge only by defects, & to whose envy a beauty is an eye-sore, a fervent praise respecting an other a near grievance, and the more virulent in its action because the miserable man does not dare confess the Truth to his own Heart—. 4 and lastly, the Great-Moguls Diamond Sieves—which is perhaps going farther for a Simile than its superior Dignity can repay, inasmuch as a common Cullender would have been equally symbolic' (CC 5:1, 65–6). S. T. C. probably derived this fourfold distinction from John Donne, perhaps via Robert Southey, whose Commonplace Book contains the following entry: 'Donne's βιαθάνατος. Readers, Girionides [Southey's slip of the pen for Donne's Gorionides] observes to be of four sorts: spunges, which attract all without distinguishing; hour-glasses, which receive and pour out as fast; bags, which retain only the dregs of the spices, and let the wine escape; and sieves, which retain the best only' (Robert Southey, *Common-place Book. Edited by his Son-in-law, John Wood Warter* (London: Longman, 1849), 3:695).

[79] The Mohawks had a reputation for being the most warlike of the six nations of the Iroquois; hence a Mohawk reading of the Bible would, in strain-bag fashion, retain only the most violent episodes. The Biblical references are, in order: Genesis 4: 8; Judges 3: 15–22; Judges 3: 21; 1 Samuel 17: 23–50; Judith 13; Matthew 2: 16; Revelation 18: 8–9 and Revelation 20: 7–10.

[80] Since 'tiara' in Latin means *turban* rather than *jewelled diadem*, S. T. C. may be taking

Of the various causes which I mentioned as impeding the acquisition of a just Taste in the fine arts in general, but especially in Poetry, the one which more perhaps than any other, bears upon not only the subject of these Lectures, and which alone I can anticipate as likely to occasion perplexity, or misunderstanding, and the feeling of repugnance which arises in all well-constituted minds when paradoxes and seeming Protests against opinions established among men by common suffrages are obtruded on their attention, is *the lax use of general terms*;— or rather the extending this laxity of expression beyond ordinary conversation, in which it is not only natural but a necessary result of that process, by which words are for ever acquiring new shades of meaning. Thus, general terms are confined to one individual sense, such as 'indorsed', given by Milton in the expression—'And elephants *indorsed* with towers.'[81] And vice versa, words originally expressing one particular thing extended to a whole class, as 'Virtue', which at first meant the possession or exertion of manly strength, thence transferred to Fortitude, or the truest and most appropriate Strength, and is now become the class term for moral excellence in all its different species. So far from blaming those who use call a thing beautiful for instance where strictly speaking it should have been called delightful or pleasant, I should think it a mark of pedantry and affectation to labour after a constant precision on occasions where the whole effect we wish to produce is to be produced without it—in short, where our meaning is entirely understood—It was my design therefore only to guard you against the expectation (for habit always breeds expectation) of the same laxity in the investigation of a *philosophic* question;— against the extension of a liberty quite allowable when we are taking things in the gross, to other employments of the understandings, the very essence of which is analytic, which our avowed purpose is to separate, not to blend, to discover what each given object has peculiar to itself, rather than which it has in common with many others—or to speak more accurately, to do the former first, to distinguish subtly in order that we then be able to assimilate truly. I will at once exemplify my position in general, by a fact that at the same time lead me into the main road, on which I am hence forward to travel with no other

the word as an orientalised version of a straining-cloth, as per the 1808 version of the phrase 'Great-Moguls Diamond Sieves' noted above n.25. Alternatively he may indeed have been referring to the 'Moghul diamond' (a famously large jewel dug out of the Golconda mines near Hyderabad) as set in a coronet or papal crown.

81 Milton, *Paradise Regained*, 3:329. The Latin *indorsare* means 'to put on the back' from *dorsum* back.

digressions or deviations, than perhaps to pluck a chance flower from the hedge or neighbouring field.

It has, I doubt not, occurred often to many of my auditors, as well as to myself, when the conversation has turned on literature, to hear it asked –whether we think Mr Pope a great Poet. This is a matter that has been warmly discussed on both sides, with offence and shock given to many, and the disputants leave off with but a mean opinion of each another. Yet it never occurred to either party that the dispute was strictly preposterous,[82] that is, began at the wrong end, and that each should have first ascertained what the other understood by the word *Poetry*. If the veracious Lemuel Gulliver on his return from his celebrated Travels, and previous to his publication, had mentioned to us the names of two public characters in the country which an unfortunate alien act had compelled him to leave, and then asked–which of the two we thought the *nobler* Houyhnhnm, we should most certainly, if only we could neigh out the word, answer him by asking him–what *is* a Houyhnhnm? What do you mean by the word?[83] The endless disputes where no real difference existed in the disputants, which I have witnessed and often, and I doubt not taken a warm part in, and those in morals, politics and religion, as well as in literature, convince me I have no less reason to commence by explaining the various sense of the word *Poetry* before I can address you on the comparative merits of certain Poets, and assign that one sense to which I shall confine my use of the Term and my reasons for so confining it.

Words are used in two ways:–

1. In a sense that comprizes every thing called by that name. For instance, the words 'poetry' and 'sense' are employed in this manner, when we say that such a line is *bad poetry* or *bad sense*,

---

[82] The Latin *praeposterus* (*prae*, 'before' + *posterus* 'coming after') means 'with the hinder part before, reversed, inverted'.

[83] The Houyhnhnms are the intelligent equine race Gulliver encounters upon the fourth and last voyage he narrates in Swift's *Gulliver's Travels* (1725). The 'Alien Act' of 1704 decreed that Scots living in England were to be treated as foreign nationals, in some cases having their property seized and themselves repatriated (it was repealed in 1707). In fact, in Swift's book the Houyhnhnms do not expel Gulliver; he is rescued (against his will) by a Portuguese ship. The whole first portion of this paragraph, to this point, follows S. T. C.'s own notes rather than Collier's speculative transcription, which reads 'Poetry is not merely invention: if it were, *Gulliver's Travels* would be poetry.' Collier's own shorthand notes at this point in fact say: 'he illustrated this sentiment further by an allusion to Gulliver's Travels, which I did not exactly comprehend' (CC 5:1, 204). R. A. Foakes observes: 'C's point, that one cannot judge between Houyhnhnms without knowing what they are, was lost on Collier.'

when in truth it is neither poetry nor sense. The same remark may be applied to 'metre': bad metre is not metre.

2. In a Philosophic sense, which must include a definition of what is essential to the thing. No one means in reality merely *metre* by poetry; so, mere rhyme is not poetry. Something more is required, and what is that something? It is not wit, because we may have wit where we never dream of Poetry. Is it the just observation of human life? Is it a peculiar selection of words? This, indeed, would come nearer to the taste of the present age, when sound is preferred to sense; but I am happy to think that this taste is fast waning. The Greeks and Romans, in the latter period of their literature, were entirely ignorant of any such taste. In the Attis of Catullus it is impossible that more simple language could be used; there is scarcely a word or a line, which a lamenting mother in a cottage might not have employed.[84]

liquidaque mente uidit sine quis ubique foret,
animo aestuante rusum reditum ad uada tetulit.
ibi maria uasta uisens lacrimantibus oculis,
patriam allocuta maestast ita uoce miseriter.

I will venture to give the following definition of Poetry.

It is an art (or whatever better term our language may afford) of representing, in words, external nature and human thoughts and affections, both relatively to human affections, by the production of as much immediate pleasure in parts, as is compatible with the largest sum of pleasure in the whole.

Or, to vary the words, in order to make the abstract idea more intelligible:–

It is the art of communicating whatever we wish to communicate, so as both to express and produce excitement, but for the purpose of immediate pleasure; and each part is fitted to afford as much pleasure, as is compatible with the largest sum in the whole.

You will naturally ask my reasons for this definition of poetry, and they are these:–

'*It is a representation of nature;*' but that is not enough: the anatomist and the topographer give equally representations of nature; therefore I add:

---

[84] Collier's shorthand notes read 'In the Agis of Catullus', presumably a mishearing for the lament of Attis (Catullus 63). The Latin is not recorded by Collier and the particular passage quoted here is an editorial speculation. It means: 'And she saw with a clear mind all that she had lost. She turned back to the sea, viewing it with streaming eyes and spoke with tearful voice' (Catullus 63: 46–9).

'*And of the human thoughts and affections.*' Here the metaphysician interferes: here our best novelists interfere likewise,–excepting that the latter describe with more minuteness, accuracy, and truth, than is consistent with Poetry. Consequently I subjoin:

'*It must be relative to the human affections.*' Here my chief point of difference is the novel-writer, the Historian, and all those who describe not only nature, and the human affections, but relatively to the human affections: therefore I must add:

'*And it must be done for the purpose of immediate pleasure.*' In Poetry the general good is to be given through the Pleasure, and if the Poet do not do that he ceases to be a Poet to him to whom he gives it not. Still, it is not enough, because we may point out many prose writers to whom the whole of the definition hitherto furnished would apply. I add, then, that it is not only for the purpose of immediate pleasure, but–

'*The work must be so constructed as to produce in each part that highest quantity of pleasure, or a high quantity of pleasure.*' There Metre introduces its claim, where the feeling calls for it. Our language gives it a certain measure, and will in a strong state of passion admit of scansion from the very mouth. The very assumption that we are reading the work of a Poet supposes that he is in a continuous state of excitement, and thereby arises a language in prose unnatural, but in poetry natural.

There is one error which ought to be peculiarly guarded against, which young Poets are apt to fall into, and which old Poets commit, from being no Poets, and who are desirous of the end which true Poets seek to attain. No: I revoke the words; they are not anxious of that of which their little minds can have no conception. They have no desire of fame–that glorious immortality of true greatness–but they seek for *reputation*, that echo of an echo, in whose very etymon its signification is contained.[85] It is into this error that the author of *The Botanic Garden*[86] has fallen, through the whole of which work there are not to be found twenty images which are described as they would be described by a man in a state of excitement. The poem is written with all the industry of a milliner or tradesman, who is anxious to dress up his ideas in silks and satins by collecting all the sonorous and handsome-looking words. This is not poetry, and I subjoin to my definition–

85 An etymon is the etymological source word for any given term; in this case the Latin *reputatio*, which originally meant a reckoning, computation, or thinking over.
86 Erasmus Darwin, *The Botanic Garden: a Poem in Two Parts* (London: J. Johnson 1791), a set of two poems (*The Economy of Vegetation* and *The Loves of the Plants*) by British poet and naturalist Erasmus Darwin (1731–1802).

'*As much pleasure in each part as is compatible with the greatest sum of pleas-ure in the whole.*' In reading the works of Milton, scarcely a line will be found which in itself could be called good. Milton would not have attempted to produce what is called a good line: he sought to produce glorious paragraphs and systems of harmony, or, as he expresses it,

> With many a bout
> Of linked sweetness long drawn out.[87]

Such as I have now defined it, I shall in future lectures consider the sense of the word 'Poetry': pleasurable excitement is its origin and object; pleasure is the magic circle out of which the poet must not dare to tread. Part of my definition, you will be aware, would apply equally to the arts of Painting and Music, as to Poetry; but to the last must be added *words* and *metre*, so that my definition is strictly and log-ically applicable to Poetry, which produces that delight which is the parent of many virtues. When I was in Italy, a friend of mine,[88] who pursued painting with the highest enthusiasm, believing it superior to every other art, heard the definition I have given, acknowledged its correctness, and confessed the superiority of Poetry.

I never shall forget the acute sensation of pain I experienced on beholding the Cartoons of Raphael and 'The Florentine'[89] at Rome, and on reflecting that their being painted in *Fresco* was the only reason why they yet remained and had not like others becomes victims of insatiate avarice or wanton barbarity. How grateful ought mankind to be, that the works of Euclid, and Plato still remain to us,–and that we were yet possessed of Newton, of Milton, and of Shakespeare, the greatest *living dead* men of our own island, and that they would not now be in danger of a second irruption of the Goths and Vandals. They will never cease to be admired till man shall cease to exist and at the present moment the greatest name our isle can boast has but received the first fruits of his glory, which glory must forever increase wherever our language is spoken. Some prejudices have been attached to the name of our illustrious countryman which it will be necessary for me first to attempt to obviate. On the Continent the works of Shakespeare are honoured in a double way; by the admiration of Italy and Germany and by the contempt of the French.

Mr Pope, in his edition of Shakespeare, elaborates the nature of

---

[87] *L'Allegro* (1645), 139–40. Milton actually wrote '. . . many a winding bout'.
[88] John Miers (1756–1821), celebrated in his day for his silhouette portraits. S. T. C. was in Italy in 1805.
[89] Michelangelo.

Shakespeare's mind almost as a gloss upon his verse that a man might grow immortal in his own despight.[90]

> By a talent very peculiar, something between penetration and felicity, he hits upon that particular point on which the bent of each argument turns, or the force of each motive depends. This is perfectly amazing, from a man of no education or experience in those great and public scenes of life which are usually the subject of his thoughts: so that he seems to have known the world by intuition, to have look'd through human nature at one glance, and to be the only author that gives ground for a very new opinion, that the philosopher, and even the man of the world, may be born, as well as the poet. It must be own'd, that with all these great excellencies, he has almost as great defects; and that as he has certainly written better, so he has, perhaps, written worse, than any other. But I think, I can in some measure account for these defects, from several causes and accidents; without which it is hard to imagine that so large and so enlighten'd a mind could ever have been susceptible of them. That all these contingencies should unite to his disadvantage seems to me almost as singularly unlucky, as that so many various (nay contrary) talents should meet in one man, was happy and extraordinary.[91]

Such was the language employed by those who thought Sophocles the most perfect model for tragedy, and Aristotle its great censor; and finding that *Hamlet, King Lear, Macbeth,* and other of Shakespeare's Tragedies not framed in the same mould, and not having courage to deny the justness of that model or the propriety of those rules have asserted that Shakespeare was a sort of irregular writer–that he was tasteful but incorrect; and, in short, that he was a mere child of nature.

It is an old, and I have hitherto esteemed it a just, Latin maxim, *Oportet discentem credere, edoctum judicare*; but modern practice has so perverted the sense that it ought rather now to stand, *Oportet discentem*

---

90   Alexander Pope, *Poems Imitations of Horace* (London: Dodsley, 1738), 2:72.
91   This whole paragraph, from 'Mr Pope, in his edition. . .' to the end of this quotation (it is from Pope's 'Preface' to his own edition of Shakespeare (1725)), is an editorial hypothesis. Collier's *Seven Lectures* has nothing here, although his shorthand notes are as follows: 'Coleridge here read a Passage from I think Theobald on the nature of Shakespeare's mind in which it was said that he seemed a great man in his own despite and that where he was not much above all other writers he was equally below them: that he was a man of an irregular mind' (CC 5:1, 208). There is nothing like this in Theobald, and the present editor concurs with Foakes that the line from Pope's *Imitations of Horace*, and the sentiment from the Preface, strongly suggest that S. T. C. here read from Pope's Preface.

judicare, edoctum credere.[92] And for this mistake, or rather infatuation, there is but one remedy, namely the acquirement of knowledge. I have often applied to the ignorant, who assumed the province of judges, a ludicrous but not inapt simile: they remind me of frogs croaking in a ditch or bog, involved in darkness, until the moment a lantern is brought near the scene of their disputating society, when they cease their discordant harangues. At other times they remind me of the night fly, which flutters round the glimmering of every feeble taper, but are overpowered by the dazzling glory of the noon. Nor will it be otherwise, until the idea be exploded, that knowledge is easily taught, and until we learn the first great truth, that to conquer ourselves is the only true knowledge.

Plato called the mathematical Sciences τοῦ γὰρ ἀεὶ ὄντος γνῶσις.[93] Now, some persons have contended that mathematics ought to be taught by making the illustrations obvious to the senses. Nothing can be more absurd or injurious: it ought to be our never-ceasing effort to make people *think*, not *feel*; and it is owing to this deficiency that Shakespeare has been found too difficult for the comprehension of such persons.

If it were possible to say which of the great man's extraordinary powers is more admirable than his other powers, it appears to me that his judgment is the most wonderful. This opinion I have formed after a careful comparison of Shakespeare's works with the best and greatest of his contemporaries.

If the *Lear* were to be tried by those rules on which Sophocles constructed his *Oedipus*, it must be admitted that it was a very irregular piece. If it be allowed that Aristotle's rules were founded on man and nature, Shakespeare must be condemned for arraying his works in charms with which according to those rules they ought never to have been decorated. I have no fear, however, that I shall be able to show

---

92　The maxim is Francis Bacon's: 'although the position be good, *Oportet discentem crederes* ['we must believe, in order to be able to learn'] yet it must be coupled with this, *Oportet edoctum judicare* ['we must learn, in order that we are able to judge']: for disciples do owe unto masters only a temporary belief, and a suspension of their own judgment till they be fully instructed, and not an absolute resignation, or perpetual captivity' (Bacon, *On the Advancement of Learning* (1605) 1, §12). Coleridge's two Latin phrases mean, respectively: 'we must believe in order to learn, and the learned should judge' and 'we must judge in order to learn, and the learned should believe'.

93　Plato's *Republic* 527B: 'τοῦ γὰρ ἀεὶ ὄντος ἡ γεωμετρικὴ γνῶσις ἐστιν' 'for Geometry is the knowledge of that which is eternally existent'. *Seven Lectures* omits this sentence, and Collier's notes have 'Plato had called the mathematical Science the', breaking off (as Foakes suggests) presumably because he was unable to follow as Coleridge quoted in Greek.

that the great men of Greece and the great man of England proceeded in the same process.

Respecting the origin of tragedy among the Greeks, it grew particularly from the celebration of feasts of Bacchus. This story is given in very clear and excellent manner in Goldsmith's 'Essay on the Origin of Poetry'; the same author gives the rise and progress of Comedy.[94] The Unities originated in the size and origin of the ancient theatres and were made to include within a short space of time events which it was impossible could have occurred in that short space of time, and they could not be fit and true unless it were possible to imagine all theatrical representations *ideal*. If mere pain for the moment were wanted, can we not go to our hospitals? if we require mere pleasure, can we not be present at our public fêtes? This is not what is required from dramatic exhibition: we want a continual representation of it before our eyes. The real pleasure we derive is from knowing that the scene represented is unreal and merely an imitation.

Performances in a large theatre made it necessary that the human voice should be unnaturally and unmusically stretched; and hence the introduction of Recitative, for the purpose of making pleasantly artificial the distortion of the voice occasioned by the magnitude of the building.

The origin of the English Theatre is less boastful than that of the Greeks; like the Constitution by which we are governed, which though more barbarous in its derivation, gives more genuine and more diffused liberty, than Athens in the height of her political glory ever possessed. Our Ancient religious mysteries were, we may notice, filled with blasphemies that the most hardened to vice in the present day would not dare to utter. In these performances Vice and the Devil were personified; and from thence arose the introduction of our Fool and Clown.

Shakespeare at the same time that he accommodated himself to the taste of the times employed these characters to a most terrible effect, in heightening the misery of his most distressing scenes. Permit me to

---

[94] This essay first appeared anonymously in the *British Magazine* (1761) as 'On Taste'. It was included as 'Essay XV' in Anon (ed.), *Essays and Criticisms, by Dr. Goldsmith; With an Account of the Author* (3 vols, London: Johnson, 1798), 2:163–80; and was often reprinted as 'Origin of Poetry'. In point of fact, modern critics have challenged the idea that this essay *was* written by Goldsmith, although without coming to any consensus on the actual author. The essay describes the origins of drama 'at the orgies of Bacchus': 'tragedy herself, which afterwards attained to such dignity as to rival the epic muse, was at first no other than a trial of crambo, or iambics, between two peasants, and a goat was the prize. Hence the name τραγῳδια, signifying the goat-song, from τράγος' ('goat').

conclude by quoting a passage from a paper written by a friend:[95] 'we
may observe upon the high colouring given by *contrast* to the scene
where Lear in the very pitch of his agony, complains to the warring
elements of the ingratitude of his daughters:–

>   Spit, fire! spout, rain!
> Nor rain, wind, thunder, fire are my daughters:
> I tax not you, you elements, with unkindness,
> I never gave you kingdom, call'd you children;
> You owe me no subscription: then, let fall
> Your horrible pleasure; here I stand, your slave,
> A poor, infirm, weak and despis'd old man.[96]

–and is mocked by the mimicry of the fool, his only attendant in his
calamities:

> The cod-piece that will house
> Before the head has any,
> The head and he shall louse;
> So beggars marry many.
> The man that makes his toe
> What he his heart should make
> Shall of a corn cry woe,
> And turn his sleep to wake.'

---

[95] Collier's notes record that at this point in the lecture S. T. C. 'quoted a passage from a
      Paper written by a friend, which observed upon the high colouring given by the con-
      trast to the Scene where Lear, in a very pitch of agony, complaining to the Elements
      & accusing them of ingratitude, is mocked by the mimicry of the fool' (CC 5:1, 212).
      Foakes thinks it likely this 'friend' is a rhetorical device, the paper non-existent, and
      these thoughts S. T. C.'s own.
[96] *King Lear*, III, ii, 14–20. The fool's reply, quoted next, is lines 27–34.

LECTURE 3

Understanding that the definition, or rather description, I gave of poetry in the previous lecture has left no definite idea in the minds of my auditors; and given that the whole of the Fabric I should raise in a manner rested of upon[97] laying the foundation firmly and distinctly, I consider it necessary to add something to what I said before. It is easy to define Gold so as to distinguish it from any of the Earths, or to show the difference between a circle and a square; but with poetry it is as if I were verbally to give to an American a distinction between the English Sycamore and the American Maple—the points of similarity are so numerous that it would require much explanation and attention to show the points of distinction. The intelligibility of almost everything I have to say on the subject of poetry will depend upon me being perspicacious in my definition, because, as I have said before, it often happens that differences between men of good sense arise solely from having attached different ideas to the same words. I have been supposed by some persons to have spoken disrespectfully of that great and admirable writer, Pope—I have not perhaps determined whether or not he deserves the name of *poet*, but in many cases I think that if the words 'excellent and delightful writer' were substituted, persons disputing the merits of individual authors would agree in confessing the instance of Pope that they never looked into his writings without pleasure or laid them down without instruction.

I hope I may first be permitted to express my view that poetry is no proper antithesis to prose—in the correct opposite of poetry is science, and the correct antithesis of prose is metre. The immediate object of science is the communication and acquirement of truth; the immediate object of poetry is the communication of pleasure. Yet it would be acknowledged by all that when we read Newton's *Principia* or Locke's works, the immediate object is not pleasure but to obtain truth which might hereafter enlighten and the pursuit of pleasure, or of something nobler, for which we have not a name, but distinct

---

[97] Tomalin, transcribing this lecture, marked the phrase 'rested of' with '(sic)'. This is an unusual, but not unprecedented, locution in nineteenth-century discourse, and can be followed by various modifiers, including 'upon'.

altogether from what in the ordinary language of common sense can be brought under the name of pleasure—but which *was* expressed in the sacred writings as a peace that passeth all understanding,[98] the delight of which could never be known but by experience, which, consisting of no difference in parts, but being in itself entire must be altogether unknown, or *fully* known.

So on the other hand, with regard to Poetry, I doubt not but that the most important moral truths might be impressed by poetry—but such is not the immediate object of the poet. Its immediate object is pleasure, and it is that which constitutes a poet, to what purpose he employs his means, and it is that which constitutes him a bad or good man. I therefore define poetry as: *the communication of immediate pleasure.*

This definition will be useful, inasmuch as it distinguishes poetry from science, but it will be inadequate, inasmuch as it includes novels, romances, and other works of fiction, not called poems. Therefore there must be some additional characters to poetry distinguishing it from those modes of composition which though similar are different.

How is this to be effected? In animated prose, the beauties of nature, and the passions and accidents of human life, including all that is comprized under the names of the heart and the head, are often expressed in the natural language which may be dictated by the incidents—yet still neither the reader nor the writer called the work a poem, though no work could deserve the title of poem which did not include those circumstances—but *together with something else.*

One amiable female writer of the present day,[99] speaking of Richardson, wonders why we should hesitate to call him a *great poet* and place him in the same class with Shakespeare and Milton. The first answer would be that Mankind had not so placed him and there must be some reason for it. This we all feel, though it requires great thought and a patient investigation to discover causes—for nature has gifted us with a large portion of knowledge which might be called the rude stock, which we are to work upon; and our intellectual life is

---

[98] Philippians 4: 7.

[99] Anna Letitia Barbauld (1743–1825), editor of *The Correspondence of Samuel Richardson* (London: Richard Phillips, 1804). This claim is from the Preface: 'is not easy therefore to say, why the poet should have so high a place allotted him in the temple of Fame, and the romance-writer so low a one . . . the invention of a story, the choice of proper incidents, the ordonnance of the plan, the exhibition of the character, the gradual development of a plot, occasional beauties of description, and, above all, the power exercised over the reader's heart, by filling it with the successive emotions of love, pity, joy, anguish, transport, or indignation, together with the grave impressive moral resulting from the whole, imply talents of the highest order, and ought to command our warmest praise' (p. ix).

passed not so much in acquiring new facts as in acquiring a distinct *consciousness,*–in making a mere gift of nature, as it were, *our own,* so that it is not longer a something which we now have and now is lost, but continuing with our thoughts, a regular series of cause and effect, it becomes in the truest sense our own–the possession of the present, and the dowry of our future nature.

What then is this something? With much diffidence, I would answer that *it is that pleasurable Emotion, that peculiar state and degree of excitement that arises in the poet himself in the act of composition.*

And in order to understand this we must combine under the notion of true poet more than ordinary *sensibility*, occasioning a more than ordinary *sympathy* with the objects of nature or the incidents of human life. This, again, united with a more than ordinary *activity* of mind in general, but more particularly of those faculties of the mind we class under the names of fancy and imagination–faculties (I know not how I shall make myself intelligible) that are rather spontaneous than voluntary–they excite great activity, but such as is greatly beyond all proportion to the effects occasioned by them.

All persons are aware of the difference between our moral feelings, faculties and so on being called forth and gratified when a soft piece of music by Cimarosa or Handel,[100] or a fine picture by Raphael or Michael Angelo, are contemplated. In both instances the faculties are called forth, but, in one also, a painful effort, unless the prospect of what we are to gain interferes and still urges us on. That which excites us to all the activity of which our nature is capable and yet demands *no* painful effort, and occasions no sense of effort–This is the state of mind (for I wish to impress particularly that it is the pleasure derived from the spontaneous activity, and our best faculties *not* accompanied by painful effort) which admits the production of a highly favourable whole but of which each part shall communicate a distinct and common pleasure–Hence arises the definition that *Poetry is a species of composition opposed to science as having intellectual pleasure for its object and not truth–and attaining that end by the language natural to all persons in a state of excitement.*

So far it is opposed to Science, but distinguished from other species of *composition* not excluded by this criticism, but admitting pleasure from the whole, consistent with a consciousness of pleasurable excitement from the component parts, and the perfection of which is the

---

[100] Domenico Cimarosa (1749–1801), Italian composer of over eighty operas, including his most famous *Il matrimonio segreto* (1792); George Frideric Handel (1685–1759), the most celebrated composer of his generation.

acquirement from each part of the greatest immediate pleasure compatible with the largest sum of pleasure in the whole.

This will vary with the different modes of poetry in all that which distinguishes poetry from all other classes of composition–is in truth the poet himself.[101] We expect from him all the faculties we are possessed of: accurate observation and meditation, in what he has observed; sympathy in the sufferings and joys he either witnesses or imagines; and besides, we look for an activity of those faculties which justify at each moment his writing in metre.

Physicians assert that each passion has its proper pulse. So it is with metre when rightly used. A state of excitement produced is, in truth, an *analogy* of the language of strong passion–not that strong passion always speaks in metre, but it has a language more measured than is employed in common speaking.

In reading a poem, we look not only for a just description of material objects, or human affections, but we expect to find them represented in such constant activity of mind, arising from the poet himself, as shall give a greater pleasure to that which is already pleasurable, and shall bring within the bounds of pleasure that which would otherwise be painful. I would even venture to give the definition of poetry as being *That which, from the always present, though always conscious Idea that it is poetry in the mind of the reader, allows a greater attention to each particular part of a composition the greater power of giving pleasure and attracting attention from each part than would be permitted in ordinary writing though writing a fiction*–and the great rule by which a poet is to be judged is *the balance between them*. Is there more pleasure in the particular lines than is consistent with the whole? Is the sense of totality injured or not injured by the splendour of particular passages?–for the great object of a poet must be to produce the great total effect.

So closely connected is metre with passion that many of the finest passages we read in prose are in themselves, in point of metre, poetry– only they are forms of metre which we have not been familiarized to and not brought forward to us and other English readers in the shape of metre. I have myself paid particular attention to language of the Bible and have found that all persons have been affected with a sense of their high poetic character, not merely from the thought conveyed in them, but from the language enclosing those thoughts–from the stately march of the words, which affect them in a degree and kind altogether different from that of common writing, and different again from the narrative and perceptive parts of the same books. It has been

[101] Marked '(sic)' in the original transcript.

my business to discover the cause, and I have found that in almost every passage brought before me, as having produced a *particular* effect, there is metre and very often poetry: not indeed, regular–not such as could be scanned on the fingers–but in some cases fragments of hexameter verses, not unlike the line of Pope

Awake, my St John, leave all meaner things[102]

where the line consists nearly entirely of Iambics, but regularly of dactyls and spondees, forming sometimes a complete Hexameter verse, as in

Gōd wēnt/ ūp wĭth ă/ shōut, ōur /
Lōrd wĭth thĕ/ sōund ŏf thĕ/ trūmpēt[103]

forming a line exactly similar with the first of Homer and Virgil. In another it is equally evident

There is a river the flowing whereof &c[104]

This taking the first chapter of Isaiah, without more than four or five transpositions and no alteration of words, I have reduced it to complete Hexameters–so true it is that wherever passion is, the language becomes a sort of metre.

It is necessary for me, in the first place, to enquire whether poetry ought to be a copy, or only an *imitation* of what is true nature? According to every effect I have been able to trace, I am of opinion that the pleasure we receive arises, not from its being a copy, but from its being an imitation, and the word imitation itself means always a combination of a certain degree of dissimilitude with a certain degree of similitude. If it were merely the same as looking at a glass reflection, we should receive no pleasure. A waxen image after once it has been seen pleases no longer, or very little, but when the resemblance of a thing is given upon canvas or flat surface, then we are delighted.

In poetry it is still more so; the difference there is of a higher character. We take the purest parts and combine it with our own minds, with our own hopes, with our own inward yearnings after perfection, and being frail and imperfect, we wish to have a shadow, a sort of

---

[102] This is the first line of Pope's *An Essay on Man* (1734).

[103] Psalm 47: 5. The King James Version actually reads 'God is gone up with a shout, the Lord with the sound of a trumpet.' This, though, is prosodically equivalent to the version S. T. C. cites.

[104] Psalm 46: 4, which in the King James Version reads 'There is a river, the streams whereof shall make glad the city of God, the holy place of the tabernacles of the most High.'

prophetic existence present to us, which tells us what we are not, but yet, blending in us, much that we are, promises of great things of what we may be. It is the Truth, and poetry results from that instinct the effort of perfecting ourselves—the conceiving that which is imperfect to be perfect and blending the nobler mind with the meaner object.

Thus, in Shakespeare, I have often heard it said that he was a close copier of nature—that, indeed, he was a child of nature—like a Dutch painter copying exactly the object before him. He *was* a child of nature, but it was of *human* nature and of the most important part of human nature. In the meanest characters it is still Shakespeare: it is not the mere Nurse in *Romeo and Juliet*; or the Dogberry in *Much Ado about Nothing*, or the blundering Constable in *Measure for Measure* but it is this great and mighty being changing himself into the Nurse or the blundering Constable that gives delight. We know that no Nurse talked exactly in that way, though particular sentences might be to that purpose. One might compare it to Proteus, who now flowed a river; now raged a fire; now roared a lion—he assumes all changes, but still in the stream, in the fire, in the beast, it is not only resemblance, but it is the Divinity that appears in it, and assumes the character.

I include Music and Painting under the great Genus of Poetry, and we cannot understand those, unless we first impress upon the mind that they are ideal: not the mere copy of things, but the contemplation of mind *upon* things. When you look upon a portrait, you must not compare it with the face when present, but with the recollection of the face. It refers not so much to the senses, as to the ideal sense of the friend not present.

Hitherto I have judged of Shakespeare by the Ancients. In my last lecture, I endeavoured to detect the error of this mode of judging. When I said the Grecian Theatre, I alluded to the great works of Euripides, and Aeschylus and Sophocles, which have been held out as models: not of what is essential to the Drama in all possible states; but as ideal of the *construction* of the drama. I have tried to show that the construction of the Greek Drama was owing to pure accident and that of those accidents they made the best possible use. The origin of it was the Song of the Goat and at first the principal part was the Chorus; then Dialogue was introduced; and then they sought to make the two consistent with each other. The size of the Theatre rendered it impossible to make the human voice intelligible without artificial means, and being resolved that it should be delightful, artificially they introduced music. But as in a good picture, it is necessary that all things should be in keeping, and as the Chorus is always present it enforces the preservation of the Unities, for it would have been too great an extravagation from nature to have had the same men and characters on the stage when the scene was totally different. As the Chorus was always on the stage, there was no dropping of curtains; the same men could not be at the same time at Thebes and at Rome.[105] It therefore became necessary that the same scene should be presented to the eye, constituting the *Unity of place*; and that the piece should be acted nearly within the time that the events could have occurred in; and, lastly, they had, what is common to all dramas, a *unity of interest* and *action*.

The two first I have shown to be mere effect of accident in the Grecian drama, and I would venture to add, that they were most unfortunate effects—because in the very best of their plays, it involved the authors in absurdities. It frequently happened that seventy or eighty plays were written on the same subject and with the same characters, so few were the subjects which could be represented con-sistently with the preservation of the unities. In our earliest youth there were none who had not listened to the 'tale divine of Troy',[106] and Pope's popular translation was in the hand, nay, in the mouth of every person[107]—while the translations of Sophocles, of Aeschylus or Euripides were found only in the libraries of those who did not want them, scarcely making any impression on the community at large.

I have thus attempted to show that the Unities of time and place are not essential to the drama, and that to suppose them necessary is to suppose as evident a falsehood as that the Drama impresses with pleasure only, as it is supposed to be reality. The truth is, it is never believed to *be real*. In a farce written to ridicule ancient plays the chorus is represented as lamenting for some crime which a man who had just escaped had committed, when one of the characters comes in and exclaims—'Why don't you run for a constable, why do you remain there and do nothing?'[108] The height of delusion, the utmost point to which it can arrive is that we do not think about its being

---

[105] A reference to Horace's *Epistles* 2.1.213, 'Ut magnus; et modo me Thebis, modo ponit Athenis'. That, rather like a magician, the dramatist will 'snatch me, o'er the earth, or through the air,/To Thebes, to Athens, when he will, and where' (Pope, *Imitations of Horace* (1733) 1:346–7).

[106] 'Sometime let gorgeous tragedy/In sceptred pall come sweeping by,/Presenting Thebes, or Pelops' line,/Or the tale of Troy divine'; Milton, *Il Penseroso* (1645), 96–100.

[107] Pope's translation of the *Iliad* appeared 1715–20, and of the *Odyssey* 1726.

[108] Henry Carey's comic *The Contrivances* (1715) mocks, as its title implies, the conventions of Classical drama. In Scene 5 Argus is robbed and his wife Arethusa kidnapped. A mob finds him: 'All: What's the matter? what's the matter? [*They ungag him*]. Argus: Oh! neighbours, I'm robbed and murdered, ruined, and undone for ever. 1st Half of Mob: Why, what's the matter, master? Argus: There's a whole legion of thieves in the house; they gagged and blindfolded me, and offered forty naked swords at my breast . . . 2nd Half of Mob: Then if you please, I'll run and call a constable. All: Ay, ay; call

real or false, but are affected only by the vividness of the impression, independent of the thought of reality. This difference between a sense of reality and falsehood admits of various degrees, from the domestic tragedy, which is too real to be compatible with pleasure, to Shakespeare, who seems to have taken the due medium and to gratify our senses from the imitation of reality, and down to the mere dance at an Opera, which is yet capable of giving us the highest pleasure, and which, with music and harmonious motions of the body, can, by thus explaining some tale, deeply affect and delight an audience.

I do not blame the authors of the French Drama that they had less reality—but that many of their thoughts are painfully false in logic, and never could have occurred to minds of men placed in the same situation. I never dreamed that Lear could think what he said according to Shakespeare—but it *was* the language of nature, and such language, that while we weep it mingles wisdom with our tears. It might give pain, but not such pain as is inconsistent with pleasure.

Shakespeare had advantages as well as disadvantages in forming the class of writing which he took, and it has been truly said, that it was a magic circle in which he himself could only tread.[109] This remark had been applied to his tragic characters only, and it can be added that in this alone Shakespeare succeeded, but it would be found equally true that in the whole scheme of his Drama, he invented a work which was peculiar to himself, and not to be compared with the productions of any writer of any nation, in which he had neither follower nor second.

How was he able to effect his? He lived in an age in which, from the religious controversies, carried on in a way of which we have no conception, there was a general energy of thinking, a pleasure in hard thinking and an expectation of it from those who came forward to solicit public praise of which, in this day, we are equally ignorant. Consequently the judges were real amateurs. The author had to deal with a learned public, and he had no idea of a mixed public—it was divided, in truth, between those who had no taste at all and who went merely to amuse themselves, and those who were deeply versed in the literature to which they gave encouragement.

Although the piety of the times, narrowed the numbers of those who attended the Theatre, it made those who did visit it especially

---

a constable, call a constable' (*Dramatick Works of Henry Carey* (London: S. Gilbert, 1743), 207–8).

[109] 'But Shakespeare's magic could not copied be,/Within that circle none durst walk but he', John Dryden, 'Preface', in John Dryden and William Davenport, *The Tempest, or the Enchanted Island* (London: J. Debrett, 1699), 19–20.

conversant with what they ought to expect. The Theatre itself had no artificial, extraneous inducements—few scenes, little music, and all that was to excite the senses in a high degree was wanting. Shakespeare himself said, 'We appeal to your imaginations; by your imagination you can conceive this round O to be a mighty field of monarchs, and if you do not, all must seem absurd.'[110] The circumstances of acting were altogether different from ours: it was much more of recitation, or rather, a medium between recitation and what we now *call* recitation. The idea of the poet was always present, not of the actors, not of the thing to be represented. It was at that time more a delight and employment for the intellect, than amusement for the senses.

It was natural that Shakespeare should avail himself of all that imagination afforded. If he had lived in the present day and had seen one of his plays represented, he would the first moment have felt the shifting of the scenes. Now, there is so much to please the senses in the performance and so much to offend them in the play, that he would have constructed them no doubt on a different model. We are grateful that he did not,—since there can be no comparative pleasure between having a great man in our closet and on the stage. All may be delighted that Shakespeare did not anticipate and write his plays with any conception of that strong excitement of the senses, that inward endeavour to make everything appear *reality* which is deemed excellent as to the effort of the present day. Surely, we may be grateful that we may take Shakespeare out of the rank of mere stage-writers to place him among the Miltons, the Homers, the Dantes, the Ariostos and the great men of all nations and of all ages.

I may add that what gives delight to the present is a very bad criterion indeed of what had pleased a former age. I may confirm this opinion by reading a quotation from Dryden in response to Rymer's structures upon English tragedy:

He who undertakes to answer this excellent critique of Mr. Rymer, in behalf of our English poets against the Greek, ought to do it in this manner: either by yielding to him the greatest part of what he contends for, which consists in this, that the design and conduct of it, is more conducing in the Greeks to those ends of tragedy, which Aristotle and he propose, namely, to cause

---

[110] A confection of phrases from the opening prologue to *Henry V*: 'A Kingdom for a Stage, Princes to Act,/And Monarchs to behold the swelling Scene ... Can this Cock-Pit hold/The vastie fields of France? Or may we cram/Within this Wooden O, the very caskes/That did affright the air at Agincourt? ... within the Girdle of these Walls/Are now confin'd two mighty Monarchies' (4–20).

terror and *pity*; yet the granting this does not set the Greeks above the English poets. The English, which have both underplot and a turned design, which keeps the audience in expectation of the catastrophe; whereas in the Greek poets we see through the whole design at first. For the characters, they are neither so many nor so various in Sophocles and Euripides, as in Shakespeare and Fletcher. The thoughts and words are certainly more noble and more poetical in the English than in the Greek. And if we should grant that the Greeks performed this pity and terror better, perhaps it may admit of dispute, whether pity and terror are either the prime, or at least the only ends of tragedy. Tis not enough that Aristotle has said so; for Aristotle drew his models of tragedy from Sophocles and Euripides; and if he had seen ours, might have changed his mind.[111]

Hence the excellence of the English Drama is that it possesses that which delights both classes, but in different ways. One man would carry away nothing but the jokes and what was externally ludicrous, while the other would be pleased that his fellow-citizens had received an innocent enjoyment, which had been to him a profitable employment. He saw that which gave him a deeper knowledge of his own heart, and of the actions of his fellow-creatures, and he wonders that this great man could at the same time excite the admiration of the most profound metaphysician and draw tears or awake laughter from the most ignorant.

There was, in truth, an energy in the age, an energy of thinking, which gave writers of the reigns of Elizabeth and James, the same energy. At the present, the chief object of an author is to be intelligible at the first view; then, it was to make the reader think— not to make him understand at once, but to show him rather that he did *not* understand, or to make him to review, and re-meditate till he had placed himself on a par with the writer.

---

[111] Tomalin's notes include the following quotation, which is attributed to 'Webster': 'In other words the learned would have English Tragedians to be mere reflections of the Greek, or of the oratorical declamation in dialogue under the name of Seneca.' This has not been traced, neither in any work by Webster, nor anywhere else. The quoted text above is an editorial hypothesis, taken from Walter Scott (ed.), *The Works of John Dryden Now First Collected* (18 vols, London: William Miller, 1800–8), 15:387–8, based on the theory that Coleridge here quoted Dryden's response to English critic Thomas Rymer (1643–1713)'s *A Short View of Tragedy* (1693), which in turn argued that the Greek and Roman tragedians must stand as models to English writers. Dryden responded to this at length, asserting that English writers ought not to be mere reflections of the Greeks. The precise terms of the quotation transcribed by Tomalin do not occur in Dryden, but the sentiments are close.

With regard to his education, it was little more than might be expected from his character. Conceive a profound metaphysician and a great poet, intensely occupied in thinking on all subjects, on the least as well as the greatest—on all the operations of nature and of man, and feeling the importance of all the subjects presented to him—conceive this philosophical part of his character combined with the poetic— the twofold energy constantly acting; the Poet, and the Philosopher embracing, but, as it were, in a war embrace, when if both had not been equal one or the other must have been strangled.

With this rule the reader might go through what was really Shakespeare's, and distinguish him from every man that ever lived. His education was the combination of the Poet and the Philosopher,—a rapid mind, impatient that the means of communication were so few and defective compared with what he possessed to be communicated. From this cause his images followed upon each other and if his genius had not guided him to the stage Shakespeare would by them have been rendered a writer rather to be wondered at than admired.

Therefore it is, that in all the great characters, it is still Shakespeare,— now imitating this, now imitating that,—now displaying the operations of a mind under the influence of strong intellect,— sometimes without, and sometimes against the moral feeling.

LECTURE 4

Various attempts have been made to arrange the plays of Shakespeare, each according to its priority in time, by proofs derived from external documents. How unsuccessful these attempts have been might easily be shown, both from the widely different results of men, all deeply versed in the black-letter Books, Old Plays, Pamphlets, and Manuscript Records and Catalogues of that age, as also from the fallacious and unsatisfactory Nature of the Facts and Data on which the Evidence rests. In that age, when the Press was chiefly occupied with controversial and practical Divinity; when the Law, the Church and the State engrossed all honour and respectability; when a degree of Disgrace, *quaedam levior infamiae maculae*,[112] was attached to the publication of Poetry, and even to have sported with the Muse, as a private relaxation, was supposed to be a venial fault, indeed, but yet something beneath the gravity of a wise Man.

This fact might be proved from a letter of Dr Donne, wherein he expressed his mortification that any of his poems should have been published, and he thereby have incurred the disgrace of being a poet:

> of my Anniversaries, the fault that I acknowledge in myself is to have descended to print any thing in verse, which, though it has excuse even in our own times by men who profess and practise much gravity, yet I confess I wonder how I declin'd to it, and do not pardon myself.[113]

---

[112] A legal phrase meaning 'a certain faint taint of infamy'. It originates with the Pomeranian jurist David Mevius (1609–70), who laid down the principle that a defendant who pays reparations thereby in effect confesses and so lessens the stain of disgrace attaching to his delinquency ('in reo est datio alicuius pecuniae injuriae confessio, inde infamiae macula non levior'; David Mevius, *Decisiones super causis praecipuis ad summum tribunal regium Vismariense delatis* (Frankfurt: Johannus Jungius, 1698), 178).

[113] Donne to George Gerrard, 14 April 1612. This letter was reproduced in John Donne's *Poems* (London: H. Herringman, 1669), a copy of which S. T. C. read and annotated. His marginalium upon this comment reads, in part: 'The idea of degradation & frivolity which Donne himself attached to the character of a professed Poet, & which was only not universal in the reigns of Elizabeth & James, which yet exhibited the brightest Constellation of Poets ever known, gives a *settling* answer to the fashionable outcry about Patronage' (CC 12:2, 234–5).

Another cause of the obscurity hanging over the works of Shakespeare is the poverty of the professed Poets, so poor they that the very expenses of the press demanded the liberality of some wealthy Individual, so that two thirds of Spencer's poetic works, and those most highly praised by his learned admirers and friends, remained for many years in Manuscript, and in Manuscript perished. Half his Fairy Queen, his Comedies, his Hymn and a number of his Epistles were thus lost to the world.

The religious zeal of the age rendered besides the Amateurs[114] of the stage comparatively few, and therefore for the greater part more or less known to each other. And lastly, we know that the Plays of Shakespeare, both during and after his life, were the *property* of the Stage, and published by the Players, doubtless according to their notions of acceptability with the visitants of the Theatre—neither can an allusion or reference to any Drama or Poem in the publication of a contemporary be received as evidence, that such Poem or Drama had at that time been published. Nor can the priority of publication itself prove any thing in favour of actually prior composition. Accordingly I shall proceed by the few certain dates that are known of an external kind which tend to corroborate the internal testimony.

We are certain, indeed, that the *Venus and Adonis,* and the *Rape of Lucrece,* were his two earliest poems, and though not printed until 1593, in the twenty-ninth year of his age, yet there can be little doubt that they had remained by him in manuscript many years. For Mr. Malone has made it highly probable that he had commenced as a writer for the stage in 1591, when he was twenty-seven years old,[115] and Shakespeare himself assures us that the *Venus and Adonis* was the first heir of his invention.[116]

Baffled, then, in the attempt to derive any satisfaction from outward documents, we may easily stand excused if we turn our researches towards the internal evidences furnished by the writings themselves, with no other positive data than the known facts that the *Venus and Adonis* was printed in 1593, the *Rape of Lucrece* in 1594, and that the *Romeo and Juliet* had appeared in 1595,[117]—and with no other presumptions than that the poems, his very first productions, were written many years earlier—(for who can believe that Shakespeare could have

---

[114] In the sense of 'lovers'.
[115] Edmond Malone makes this claim in his *An Attempt to Ascertain the Order in Which the Plays Attributed to Shakspeare Were Written* (London: C. Bathurst, 1778).
[116] Shakespeare dedicated the poem to the Earl of Southampton, adding 'But if the first heir of my invention prove deformed, I shall be sorry it had so noble a godfather'.
[117] In fact the first quarto publication of *Romeo and Juliet* was 1597.

remained to his thirtieth year without attempting poetic composition of any kind?),–and that between these and *Romeo and Juliet* there had intervened one or two other dramas, or the chief materials, at least of them, although they may very possibly have appeared after the success of the *Romeo and Juliet*, and some other circumstances, had given the poet an authority with the proprietors, and created a prepossession in his favour with the theatrical audiences.

I pay little attention to the anecdotes, or rather, hearsay stories, regarding Shakespeare's having held horses,[118] snuffed candles at the theatre, etc.;–the facts of his history confute them. Those offices were wholly unworthy of his birth and inconsistent with the circumstances of his having so soon purchased himself a share in the Theatre, and retired at so early an age with an independent fortune. I rather think that Shakespeare early felt an impulse for a species of poetry different from that he first attempted;–the very imperfections of which seemed to imply a dormancy and yet at the same time a powerful prompting of his powers to the Drama.

We shall be better able to judge of the facts after contemplating the characteristics of Shakespeare's first poem: the *Venus and Adonis*.

The subject is one which few with Shakespeare's mind would have chosen, and which none but a mind like Shakespeare's could have treated as he did. It appeals not to the senses–it places it out of the ordinary feelings, and on reading it the loves of Venus and Adonis, as far as our passions are concerned, as little affect us as the amours of the Faery Queen with Nick Bottom.[119] My object in making these remarks is not so much to illustrate the character of Shakespeare as to illustrate the principles of Poetry. We should then see what principles in this work had led us to more intimate knowledge of our great poet, and to form a foundation of a rational system concerning poetry in general.

The first thing which strikes us on reading the *Venus and Adonis* is the perfect sweetness of the versification, so well adapted to the subject without possessing more majestic rhythm than the subject requires, and the propriety of preserving the melody. There is a

---

[118] 'When Shakspeare fled to London from the terror of a criminal prosecution, his first expedient was to wait at the door of the playhouse, and hold the horses of those that had no servants, that they might be ready again after the performance. In this office he became so conspicuous for his care and readiness, that in a short time every man as he alighted called for Will. Shakspeare, and scarcely any other waiter was trusted with a horse while Will. Shakspeare could be had' (Isaac Reed (ed.), *The Plays of William Shakspeare* (21 vols, London: George Bell, 1803) 1:120).

[119] A reference to *A Midsummer Night's Dream*, of course; not to Spenser.

delightful sweetness of sound,—even to faulty excess. At the same time it is completely distinguishable from that mechanic metre where, in truth, there is no richness or sweetness,—but by being scanned by the fingers, could such scansion be learnt. If we put this sort of poetry out of our minds in reading the *Venus and Adonis*, we shall find it possesses that delight, that richness and sweetness which could not but be regarded as a highly favourable promise of future excellence.

I am not certain that the 'man who hath not music in his soul'[120] will be liable to all that Shakespeare has charged him with, but I am well assured that such a being could never be a poet. Images might be copied from works of voyages and travels, or of Natural History and even from Nature herself. In like manner affecting incidents might be obtained from observation, or from reading—and curiosity might be kept up in the detail. Domestic feelings themselves of the best and tenderest kind might be borrowed not only from books, but even from the heart, and all might be so happily combined by wit as to make a pleasing work;—and yet the man not be a *poet*. He might have talent, and a good education and yet have mistaken (perhaps, for his own interest, wisely) an intense *desire* for poetic reputation for a natural genius and poetic powers. He might mistake, as we all too often do, the strong thirst for the end, for a natural capability of the means.

That gift of true Imagination, that capability of reducing a multitude into unity of effect, or by strong passion to modify series of thoughts into one predominant thought or feeling;—these are faculties which might be cultivated and improved, but cannot be acquired. Only such a man as possesses them deserved the title of *Poeta* who *nascitur non fit*[121]—he is that Child of Nature, and not the creature of his own efforts.

The second sure promise of Genius, is the choice of the subject remote from the private interests, circumstances and feelings of the poet himself. I myself have been more than once deluded and led into a false expectation of Genius from the perusal of very affecting poems in which the poet had described those incidents and passions which misfortune, disease, or any other cause had made the poet himself possess. Grant to such a man knowledge of language, and what would follow?—a lively description,—yet he is not a Poet. He will not be the man, who, though happy in his domestic and conjugal relations, can yet paint a noble and generous mind under the pangs of jealousy,

[120] 'The man that hath no music in himself'; *Merchant of Venice*, 5.1.83.
[121] The origin of this proverbial phrase ('a poet is born, not made') has never been traced. See William Ringler, 'Poeta Nascitur Non Fit: Some Notes on the History of an Aphorism', *Journal of the History of Ideas*, 2:4 (1941), 497–504.

loving to desperation a being whom he believes unworthy of that love. He never can be the man who from a handkerchief can weave a dreadful tissue of human calamity. He never can be the being who could paint a Lear or Othello.

If it were not that it fell too much below the subject, I could relate a tale told by one of the ancients more illustrative of the truth of his position, than consistent with the feelings of his auditory. There is said to be a statuary[122] in ancient Greece whose figures were awkward and unideal in every respect but one—he had gained much praise from the beautiful feet and ancles of Venus. His name was introduced in a company of which his wife formed a part, and with as much delicacy as possible the merits of the husband were discussed. One person dwelt with much warmth of praise on the symmetry and grace of the feet and ancles of the Venus he had just completed. The wife was so transported at the compliment that she interrupted the eulogist by observing that her husband always took her for his model and she was always reckoned to have a most beautiful foot and ancle. As little could a poet by profession become a poet by nature, because he had happily succeeded in painting those circumstances and scenes which were not created by him, but by which he was possessed and employed no creative faculty.

This excellence is perhaps carried too far in the *Venus and Adonis*, but not too far if we regarded it as a fragment in the history of the mind of Shakespeare. It appears to me as if Shakespeare in this instance had been a mere passive being, not actuated by the passions and feelings he displayed under the agency of some superior spirit;—had represented every look and action and feeling, without himself participating. I think or should have conjectured from this poem, and *Lucrece*, that, even then, the impulse to the Drama was secretly working in him. The scenes of unbroken images, unbroken and therefore minute and as picturesque as language is capable of, and of a far higher order than any other poet had produced, seem to fit him admirably for the line of composition he afterwards pursued. His *Venus and Adonis* seems at once the characters themselves, but, more, the representations of those characters by the most consummate actors. Throughout, you seem to be *told* nothing and to *hear and see* everything.

The poem is certainly unfit for public recitation, but never was any work written that was less dangerous in a moral point of view. Instead of doing as Ariosto, or in a still more offensive way, Wieland, has done—degrading the struggles of passion into a low animal

---

[122]   That is, sculptor. The source for this story has not been identified.

feeling—Shakespeare has dissipated the reader's attention by a thousand outward images which form the drapery and scenery of his tale, or diverted us by sallies of wit and bursts of profound reflection which the active mind of the poet diffuses through and blends with the images and incidents.[123] The reader's thoughts are forced into too much action to sympathise with what is merely passion in our nature. As little could the noisome mist hang over our northern Windermere, when a strong and invigorating gale was driving the lake in foam and billows before it!

I have said before that images taken from Nature and most accurately described do yet not characterise *the Poet*. They must be blended or merged with other images, the offspring of imagination and blended, besides, with the passions or other pleasurable emotions which contemplation has awakened in the poet himself. Many have witnessed the rising of the sun without any poetic sensations, but who would not feel the beauty of this passage?—

> Full many a glorious morning have I seen
> *Flatter* the mountain-tops with sovereign eye.[124]

Here is a union of thoughts, a bringing all into one. You see not only the sun rising over the mountains, but you have also the moral feeling with which the rapidity of the poet's mind has connected it. You behold the sun the sovereign of the world, the elation of the high mountain flattered by a glance of his beams, and the activity of the poet's mind, which, in one image, has merged so many associations. You feel him to be a poet inasmuch as, for a time, he has made you one—an active creative being. I introduce another instance of the same kind:

> Since I left you, mine eye is in my mind;
> And that which governs me to go about
> Doth part his function and is partly blind,
> Seems seeing, but effectually is out;

---

[123] Coleridge reused this passage in the *Biographia Literaria*, Chapter 15. The two poets named are Italian Ludovico Ariosto (1474–1533) and German Christoph Wieland (1733–1813). Coleridge broadly admired the latter's epic *Oberon* (1780), although it also offended his pudeur. In the 'Satyrane's Letter' chapter of the *Biographia* he records Wordsworth's criticism that its 'interest . . . turn[s] entirely upon animal gratification'. It was translated, and bowdlerised, by Coleridge's friend William Sotheby in 1798, an edition of which one reviewer said: 'much of the voluptuous scenery, which abounds, is concealed by the decorum of the translator behind a thicker veil than Wieland had provided' (Anon., 'Sotheby's Oberon', *The Annual Review and History of Literature* 5 (1807), 501).

[124] Shakespeare's 'Sonnet 33', lines 1–2.

For it no form delivers to the heart
Of bird, of flower, or shape which it doth latch:
Of his quick objects hath the mind no part,
Nor his own vision holds what it doth catch;
For if it see the rud'st or gentlest sight,
The most sweet favour or deformed'st creature,
The mountain or the sea, the day or night:
The crow, or dove, it shapes them to your feature.
Incapable of more, replete with you,
My most true mind thus maketh mine untrue.[125]

That blending of thoughts into each, or, rather, into one passion at the time it contemplates, is one of the greatest criterions of a true poet, because it is impossible *excepting* to a true poet,—which implies three constituent parts, namely, *sensibility, imagination* and the powers of *association*. We shall hereafter have so many occasions to point out such blending in his *Lear* and other plays.

Lastly, the metaphor must be combined with the poetic feeling itself, so that the pleasure of the reader, as well as the vividness of the description is in part derived from the force and fervour of the describer. The latter excellence is, I admit, though the least of a great poet, still an excellence characteristic and indispensable. In the instances I shall now give from Shakespeare I would ask my auditors to recollect that they must consider him as a young poet presented to their promise just rising into notice at the age of twenty-three or twenty-four years. Here is the description of the horse of Adonis:

Imperiously he leaps, he neighs, he bounds,
And now his woven girths he breaks asunder;
The bearing earth with his hard hoof he wounds,
Whose hollow womb resounds like heaven's thunder;
The iron bit he crusheth 'tween his teeth,
Controlling what he was controlled with.

His ears up-prick'd; his braided hanging mane
Upon his compass'd crest now stand on end;
His nostrils drink the air, and forth again,
As from a furnace, vapours doth he send:
His eye, which scornfully glisters like fire,
Shows his hot courage and his high desire.

---

[125] Shakespeare, Sonnet 113.

Sometime he trots, as if he told the steps,
With gentle majesty and modest pride;
Anon he rears upright, curvets and leaps,
As who should say, Lo! thus my strength is tried;
And this I do to captivate the eye
Of the fair breeder that is standing by.

What recketh he his rider's angry stir,
His flattering 'Holla', or his 'Stand, I say'?
What cares he now for curb or pricking spur?
For rich caparisons or trapping gay?
He sees his love, and nothing else he sees,
Nor nothing else with his proud sight agrees.

Look, when a painter would surpass the life,
In limning out a well-proportion'd steed,
His art with nature's workmanship at strife,
As if the dead the living should exceed;
So did this horse excel a common one,
In shape, in courage, colour, pace and bone.

Round-hoof'd, short-jointed, fetlocks shag and long,
Broad breast, full eye, small head, and nostril wide,
High crest, short ears, straight legs and passing strong,
Thin mane, thick tail, broad buttock, tender hide:
Look, what a horse should have he did not lack,
Save a proud rider on so proud a back.

Sometimes he scuds far off, and there he stares;
Anon he starts at stirring of a feather;
To bid the wind a base he now prepares,
And where he run or fly they know not whether;
For through his mane and tail the high wind sings,
Fanning the hairs, who wave like feather'd wings.[126]

And here the description of the Hare.

And when thou hast on foot the purblind hare,
Mark the poor wretch, to overshoot his troubles
How he outruns the winds, and with what care
He cranks and crosses with a thousand doubles:
The many musits through the which he goes
Are like a labyrinth to amaze his foes.

[126] Shakespeare, *Venus and Adonis*, 265–306.

Sometime he runs among a flock of sheep,
To make the cunning hounds mistake their smell,
And sometime where earth-delving conies keep,
To stop the loud pursuers in their yell,
And sometime sorteth with a herd of deer;
Danger deviseth shifts, wit waits on fear:

For there his smell with others being mingled,
The hot scent-snuffing hounds are driven to doubt,
Ceasing their clamorous cry till they have singled
With much ado the cold fault cleanly out;
Then do they spend their mouths: Echo replies,
As if another chase were in the skies.

By this, poor Wat, far off upon a hill,
Stands on his hinder legs with listening ear,
To hearken if his foes pursue him still:
Anon their loud alarums he doth hear;
And now his grief may be compared well
To one sore sick that hears the passing bell.[127]

In these quotations the auditors will perceive that there is accuracy of description blended with the fervour of the poet's mind, thereby communicating pleasure to the reader. In the description where Adonis flies from Venus prior to the hunt in which he lost his life, there seems to be all that could be expected from the imagination. It is a complete picture informed with all the passions of the person viewing it.

With this he breaketh from the sweet embrace
Of those fair arms which bound him to her breast,
And homeward through the dark laund runs apace;
Leaves Love upon her back deeply distress'd.
Look, how a bright star shooteth from the sky
So glides he in the night from Venus' eye;[128]

How many images and feelings are here brought together without effort and without discord, in the beauty of Adonis, the rapidity of his flight, the yearning, yet hopelessness, of the enamoured gazer, while a shadowy ideal character is thrown over the whole! The suddenness, beauty, and fancifulness of the image, all joined with the characters, exemplifies what I am advancing better than any other passage I remember.

[127] Shakespeare, *Venus and Adonis*, 679–702.
[128] *Venus and Adonis*, 811–16.

The *Venus and Adonis* does not allow the lofty and moral mind to display its deeper and nobler qualities. I therefore take the well-known story *Lucrece*, although I do confess there is nothing in the poem *highly* pathetic or dramatic. The same minuteness of imagery with a more profound display of reflection, with dominion—sometimes even a domination—over the whole world of language is to be found in it.

What then shall we say of Shakespeare? That he was a mere child of nature, Automaton of Genius, and that he was possessed of a feeling that he had no power to control? No! But that like a great man, he first studied deeply, read and thoroughly understood every part of human nature, which he joined with his poetical feeling, till at length it gave him that wonderful power in which he had no equal—not even a second in his own class.

It is this which entitles him to occupy one of the two Golden Thrones of the English Parnassus—*Milton* on the one and *Shakespeare* on the first. He, darting himself forth, and passing himself into all the forms of human character and human passion. The other attracting all forms and all things to himself into the unity of his own grand ideal. Shakespeare became all things well into which he infused himself, while all forms, all things became Milton—the poet ever present to our minds and more than gratifying us for the loss of the distinct individuality of what he represents.

In speaking of the Dramas of Shakespeare, I shall be inclined to pursue a *psychological*, rather than a historical, mode of reasoning. I shall take them as they seem naturally to flow from the progress and order of his mind. As the first of his poems, or, rather, amongst the first, I shall place *Love's Labour's Lost*, together with the *All's Well that Ends Well*, *Romeo and Juliet*, *Midsummer Night's Dream*, *As You Like It*, *The Tempest*, *Winter's Tale*, *Twelfth Night*—all, in short, in which the Poet still blends with the Dramatist, but in which the Dramatist still seems to press forward and never loses his own being in the character he represents to us.

In the next class I shall present him as on his journey to the last and most complete forms of his genius; when he was growing towards it with some of the awkwardness of growth. I would then take *Troilus and Cressida*, *Cymbeline*, *Merchant of Venice*, *Much Ado about Nothing*.

Finally, I shall comment upon the Plays which might be considered as the greatest works of our immortal poet viz: *Macbeth*, *King Lear*, *Hamlet*.

I shall afterwards, and in conclusion, consider Shakespeare's Historical Dramas, as a distinct class, in order to state my reasons not only for rejecting whole plays hitherto considered as Shakespeare's, but also many scenes in his other works—likewise to point out this as one species of composition in which Shakespeare alone succeeded, and which he would fain prove, was his, and his only—neither imitated with success by his followers nor anticipated by his predecessors.

Having proceeded thus far I must revert to what I had alluded to in my second Lecture;—that is, that it was the accidents of the Greek stage which gave rise to the ancient Unities, and the accidents of the English Stage which gave rise to Shakespeare's Dramas. These latter accidents left Shakespeare to rely on his own imagination, and to speak not to the senses as is now done, but to the mind. He found the stage as near as possible a closet, and in the closet only could it be fully and completely enjoyed. Those who go to the Theatre in our own day, when any of our poet's works are represented, go to see Mr Kemble *in* Macbeth, or Mrs Siddons *as* Isabel,—to hear speeches usurped by fellows who owed their very elevation to dexterity in snuffing candles, since all the inferior characters, through which our poet shines no less conspicuously and brightly are given them to deliver.

Then I must, in the warmest language, censure those who have attempted to alter the works of Shakespeare, in order to accommodate him to modern ears. It will scarcely be believed that a man like Dryden[129] had transformed the purity of Milton's Adam and Eve into such a shape as imagination, even memory, turns aside from in loathing.

I now must correct the definition I gave of poetry in earlier lectures, and substitute the following:—*It is that species of composition which being together with some others opposed to Science, as having for its immediate object the communication of pleasure, not of Truth is yet distinguished from all others by proposing to itself such a delight from the whole as is compatible with the distinct gratification from each component part, and thence enables us to place the perfection of a poem in the power of communicating the greater degree of pleasurable excitement from each part as is consistent with the largest possible portion of pleasurable excitement from the whole.* Pleasure alone is not sufficient. I have always drawn delight from a passage in Burns alluding to the transitoriness of Pleasure:

---

[129] Tomalin leaves a blank for this name, but Foakes is surely correct in identifying John Dryden (1631–1700) as the reference here. Dryden's libretto *The State of Innocence and Fall of Man* (1677) adapted the story of *Paradise Lost* into a stage musical concentrating on the relationship between Adam and Eve. Coleridge elsewhere expressed his belief that Dryden sacrificed the dignity of Milton's poem to mere entertainment.

Like snow that falls upon a river
A moment white, then gone for ever.[130]

What is a poet? He is a person who balances sameness with difference; and triteness with novelty;—who reconciles judgment with enthusiasm and vehemence with feeling. He mixes Art with Nature; the manner with the matter, and our admiration of the poem with the sympathy with the characters and incidents *of* the poem. The importance of this observation can be seen in comparing the works of our dramatist with French Plays, and with those of the Greeks from which the French are little better than translations.

I can no better conclude than by quoting the following passage from Sir John Davies, where he speaks of the mind which is equally applicable to the mind in its highest state of perfection in a great poet:—

Doubtless this could not be, but that she turns
Bodies to Spirit, by sublimation strange;
As fire converts to Fire the things it burns,
As we our food into our Nature change.

From their gross matter she abstracts the forms,
And draws a kind of Quintessence from Things
Which to her proper Nature she transforms
To bear their light on her celestial Wings.

Thus doth she when from *individual States*
She doth abstract the universal kinds
Which there recloath'd in diverse names and fates
Steal access thro our Senses to our minds.[131]

The words and lines in the last stanza, emphasized here, I have added the better to apply Sir John's verses to the *Poetic* Genius.

---

[130] Burns 'Tam o'Shanter' (1791), 61–2. The lines as Burns actually wrote them are: 'Or like the snow falls in the river,/A moment white—then melts for ever'.

[131] Sir John Davies, *Nocse Teipsum: The Soul of Man and the Immortalitie Thereof* (1599). The passage S. T. C. quotes is from section 4 of this work, 'That the Soul is a Spirit'. In Davies' original the final stanza is as follows: 'This doth she, When from things particular/She doth abstract the universal kinds,/Which bodiless and immaterial are,/And can be only lodg'd within our minds.'

LECTURE 5

Among the strange differences between our ancestors and their descendants of latter days is the wide difference between the feelings and language of commentators on great classical works. At the restoration of letters, when men discovered the manuscripts of the great Ancients, as some long hidden treasure, the editors of even the most trivial work were exuberant in phrases of panegyric, and superlatives of praise seemed to be almost their only terms. In the editing of modern writers, on the contrary, we find the commentator everywhere assuming a sort of critical superiority over the author he edits. Which of the two is to be blamed? I must confess that the former (even admitting him more deficient in judgment, which I am by no means prepared to allow) is more congenial with the *moral* feelings, and better suited to all purposes of instruction, for though too much love for an author is like a mist which magnifies unduly, it brings forward objects that would otherwise have passed unnoticed. Never will I cease to deprecate that haughty insolence of the modern critic[132] whose name would pass unknown were it not for the great and awful being on whom he exercises his art—like a monkey who has seated himself on the top of a rock, it is the rock which enables him to reach the eminence where he is making his grimaces. In the course of the Lectures it will be necessary to point out many instances of this kind.

It might be proper here to examine what have been the causes of this remarkable change—and to understand the matter it will be necessary to look back into history. There, perhaps, never was a time in civilized and christianized Europe which would be called an age of universal and complete darkness. When we speak of the dark ages, we ought often rather to say the ages in which *we* were in the dark—for

---

[132] It is unclear whether Coleridge invokes a generic modern critic, or has a specific person in mind. If the latter it might be Voltaire (Foakes's suggestion), or Francis Jeffrey, or some other figure. Alternatively Coleridge may have had in mind, and conceivably even quoted at this point in the lecture, George Chalmers's rebuke to the critic T. J. Mathias: 'You came out monkey-like, to reform literature, at whatever hazard of mischief, or certainty of wrong: And, like a true monkey-critic, you censured a book, which you had never read' (George Chalmers, *A Supplemental Apology for the Believers in the Shakspeare-papers* (London: Thomas Egerton, 1799), 495).

there was always a chain along which this bright electric spark was conveyed, from the periods of its pristine brightness, even to our own day.

During the reign of Henry VI and within a short time afterwards when the art of printing was discovered the ancient manuscripts were chiefly found. In Russia we have seen monarch after monarch encouraging men of learning and placing them at the head of literary societies,[133] and endeavouring to bring man in from his state of first being, neither angel nor animal, but which according to circumstances is capable of rising to the one or sinking to the other. What has been the consequence? Travellers tell us that men of talents and fine understandings in Russia, are like the plants of tropical climates thither. They can only flourish under *glasses* with the utmost care and attention. They are wells from which water can be drawn by those who could discover the well, but the people at large, from the nobleman down to the peasant, are without interest or enthusiasm. If any desire of improvement is shown, it is that of the ape–a mere imitation of those around them. They copied the wit, the genius and the philosophy of the *French*, who, in truth, are ignorant of Philosophy, incapable of Poetry, and have never soared as high as Religion. It is an undoubted fact, that since the days of Descartes and Malebranche[134] they have not had a Philosopher among them.

Contrast the progress of the sciences in Russia with its advance in other parts of Europe at the first restoration of letters, when learning sounded throughout Christendom like a trumpet;–when all classes, headed even by Kings, hurried forward as if it were the moment of their Redemption; when 50,000 from different parts of Europe were collected to attend a single teacher; when an Erasmus or a Melancthon, the children of boors,[135] hastened to drink at the fountain

---

[133] Catherine I had founded an Academy of Sciences in 1725, and Catherine the Great had established an Academy of Fine Arts in 1783. Specifically literary societies were a more recent development. One in particular might have been in S. T. C.'s mind at the time of delivering this lecture: 'The Society of friends to Russian Literature, opened its sittings on the 26th of March. The principal object of this institution is to accelerate the progress of Russian literature; to oppose and correct bad taste, even though favoured by distinguished talents; to purify the language, [and] to banish foreign expressions and idioms' (*The Literary Panorama* 11 (1811), 127).

[134] René Descartes (1596–1650) and Nicolas Malebranche (1638–1715).

[135] That is, farmers. Catholic humanist and theologian Erasmus (1466–1536) was actually the son of a churchman and Protestant scholar Melancthon (1497–1560) the son of an armourer; both were therefore from more well-to-do families than Coleridge here implies. The story about reading by moonlight for want of a candle is derived from a religious tract by the Reverend John Jortin: '[in] the first protestant schools and universities of Germany, most of the students were very poor: they supported themselves by

of knowledge; when they could starve for the sake of learning and read their folios by moonlight because they could not afford tapers; when they pursued the carriages of the great exclaiming *Date obolum pauperio discipulo.*[136]

The result of this eagerness was afterwards an abasement of mind under authority. Authority was substituted for reason and the *ipse dixit*[137] of a philosopher for a due appreciation of those grounds which justified the philosopher in the formation of his judgment. Thence arose another race of men; and, how could it be otherwise? For if ignorance is to begin to judge of the highest points to which knowledge has been carried, that knowledge must appear absurd to necessity—because the ignorant cannot understand all the prior knowledge, all the previous process in which the most perfect exemplification of the human mind is built.

They then began, as a new discovery, with the last point of the human mind, that is, the simple observation of facts;—facts, taken as the senses recorded them without even a psychological connection; and finding that the more learned talked without applying them in the spirit, they understood and used those words as incapable of conveying any thing else, and therefore, where they could not find a distinct image which could be touched as well as seen they rejected it. With such persons a shoemaker might have been the admiration of mankind while the name of Shakespeare was consigned to oblivion, not knowing that our passions, the mere passivity of our nature must diminish in proportion as our intellectual faculties become active.

Hence naturally arose a general contempt for the ancients. But when a great man arose among them, it was a new source of delusion, and this was of the utmost importance to be explained, in order to reach the true understanding of the merits of Shakespeare.

All things that have been highly admired by mankind at any time,

---

begging and singing psalms from door to door: they studied by moonlight, for want of candles; they were almost starved for want of fire; and often went to bed with an empty stomach: Yet the earnest desire of erudition conquered all these difficulties, and they became private tutors, schoolmasters, preachers, and professors. Our young folks how have not the tenth part of these hardships to endure, nor a tenth part of their industry and learning' (John Jortin, 'Cursory Observations', in *Tracts, Philological, Critical, and Miscellaneous* (2 vols, London: T. Bensley, 1790) 1: 432–3). Coleridge passed this story to Wordsworth who used it in *The Prelude* (1850) 3:475–91.

136   'Give a penny to the poor scholar'. The phrase 'Date obolum Belisario' ('give a penny to Belisarius') was well known: the celebrated Roman general (505–65) ended a life of remarkable military glory by being reduced to penury, and having to beg in the streets of Constantinople.

137   'he himself said it': a way of citing an authority in a learned text.

or which have gone into excess must have been *originally* applicable to some part or other of our nature. They have become ridiculous only in the excess; but great geniuses having used them with the truth of nature and the force of passion, have extorted from all mankind praise, or rather won it by their instinctive sympathy. Men afterwards, most desirous of the end, and mistaking the desire of the end for a capacity of the means, have mechanically, and devoid of that spirit of Life, employed the terms. They enquired *what pleased or struck us?* It was this or that—and they imitated it without knowing what it was that made them excellent; or, that, excellent as they were, they would be ridiculous in another form. Such was the nature of *metaphors, apostrophes* and what were called *conceits.* I would venture to add, though it may excite a smile—*punning.* There are states in all our passions when even punning is no longer ridiculous, but is strictly, in a philosophical sense, a *natural* expression of *natural* emotion.

It is known that all deviations from ordinary language (by which I mean, such language as is used, by a man speaking without emotion, to express any thing simply; not that I am quite correct in using the last phrase, because all language arises out of passion);–the only difference is in the *figure* that is employed, old or new;– thus, we say, the tops of trees, or the heads of mountains, which expressions, with innumerable others in common use, are figurative, and originally used in a state of emotion; but they are now worn out. Passion is the true parent of every word in existence in every language.

But in the present state of language, in expressing an abstract Idea, such as *Virtue* or a particular Thing, such as a *Table*, all deviations from ordinary language must be justified by some passion which renders it natural. How ridiculous would it seem in a stage of comparative insensibility to employ a figure used only by a person, only under the highest emotion—Such as the impersonation of an abstract being, and an apostrophe to it as if it were not only in existence, but actually present. What if this be used as a vulgar artifice of poetic connection, just as I have heard in a Methodist meeting the minister in his prayer, at a loss for an idea, and when there seemed to be no natural connection, he would unite his thoughts by a new string of epithets applied to the Supreme Being, thus degrading the highest exertion of the human faculties to a mere art to give a pretence of connection where none exists.

In the poems produced in modern days I have observed the same thing. I have seen works which have acquired great fame, or at least what is called fame, such as *The Pleasures of Tea Drinking; The Pleasures of Wine-drinking; The Pleasures of Hope; The Pleasures of Fear*, and so on[138]–which are mere abstract ideas, and which poems are made up by heaping together a certain number of images and a certain number of thoughts, and then merely tying them together with a string as has been bought at a penny the yard. What is the consequence? When the artist has come to the end of one thought, another must arise between which there is not the least connection of mind, or even of logic (which is the *least* connection of a poet) or of passions frequently acting by contrast, but always justifying themselves–no, there is no such connection, but a full pause ensues and the reader must begin again.

Oh there, prophetic Hope! thy smile bestow,
And chase the pangs that worth should never know &c.[139]

The conceits which have been so rudely treated arise, one and all, from this circumstance that language is not, was not, and never will be the mere vehicle of representing external objects or simple information.

Horne Tooke called his book Ἔπεα πτερόεντα, 'winged words'.[140] In my judgment it might have been much more fitly called *Verba Viventia*, or 'living words'[141] for words are the living products of the living mind and could not be a due medium between the thing and the mind unless they partook of both. The word is not to convey merely what a certain thing *is*, but the very passion and all the circumstances which are conceived as constituting the perception of the thing by the person who used the word.

Hence the gradual progression of language: for could it be supposed that words should be no object of the human mind? If so, why is style cultivated in order to make the movement of words correspond with the thoughts and emotions they are to convey, so that the words themselves are part of the emotion? And in my opinion it would be no ill compliment to call another, 'a man of

---

[138] Several dozen eighteenth- and nineteenth-century long poems followed this naming convention, including Mark Akenside's *The Pleasures of Imagination* (1744), Thomas Warton's *The Pleasures of Melancholy* (1747), Samuel Rogers' popular *The Pleasures of Memory* (1792) – Foakes notes that Rogers was actually present in the audience during this lecture – and Thomas Campbell's very successful *The Pleasures of Hope* (1799). Apart from the reference to this latter title, the names listed here are all satirical inventions of Coleridge's, although the second may make glancing reference to John Philips' *Cider: a Poem in Two Books* (1791).

[139] Campbell, *The Pleasures of Hope*, 1:207–8.

[140] Horne Tooke's Ἔπεα πτερόεντα or the *Diversions of Purley* (London: Thomas Tegg, 1786) is a series of prose dialogues concerning the history and nature of language.

[141] 'Verba viventia' ('living words') is the Latin phrase in the Vulgate for what the angel in Mount Sina speaks in Acts 7: 38. The King James Version translates the phrase as 'lively oracles'.

words' if the term were used in all the force and sublimity they naturally contain.

The general desire of knowledge, and its diffusion, which in the first instance must produce shallowness, had rendered necessary a set of men called *Reviewers*. With them Plato and Bacon talked nonsense, and Locke was the only man who understood any thing. The others were fellows who talked of Ideas as distinguished from Images— true knowledge only began with Mr John Locke.[142] These reviewers might be compared with the Roman *Praegustatores* whose business it was to tell you what was fit to be eaten, and like the Praegustatores the Reviewers give their opinions, but carefully conceal all the reasons for such judgments. They are incapable, in the first place of writing themselves and therefore have more time to criticize others. Besides, according to them, all the noblest faculties of the human mind are incompatible with each other. Had a man Imagination, Fancy, or a power of exciting emotion, he must necessarily be devoid of Judgment; but if they see a man stripped of all those faculties–as in point of charity, they are bound to cloathe the naked–they decree him to be *Judicious*. If they review one man who has neither Heart, Fancy, nor Sympathy, derived from the relations of Life, or from the instincts and yearnings of our nature, he is declared to be *profound*, for he is *quite below* all others–he is said to be beyond all sight, simply because there is nothing to be seen.

I own that I bear Reviewers no good will, although for one scratch they had given me, they have bestowed twenty plasters of Basilycon flattery,[143] but I deem the business degrading from the beginning, and am convinced that to be connected with a review is below a gentleman and a man of honour.

The Reviewers have produced more superficiality, more bad feelings, and have put a more complete stop to the progress of knowledge than any other causes. Let it be granted they have written books: they are generally bad ones; and they are therefore more acquainted with the means of manufacturing such things. It is a hint I have taken from a German writer, that anciently when a certain Saint Nepomuc was thrown over a Bridge, he was constituted immediately Guardian of all Bridges.[144] This is very applicable to Reviewers: they attempted

---

[142] Coleridge expands upon the reasons for his hostility to reviewers, and Locke, in the *Biographia Literaria*, Chapters 3 and 5.

[143] 'BASILICON: in *Pharmacy*, denotes an officinal ointment, composed of wax, rosin, pitch, and oil of olives' (John Marchant and Daniel Gordon, *A New Complete English Dictionary* (London: J Fuller 1760).

[144] John of Nepumuk (c.1345–93) was martyred for his Christian faith by being drowned

to pass the Bridge of Literary Reputation, they were thrown into the stream of Oblivion, which in its buffeting against piers produced a coarse imitation of laughter; then, they were dragged by some reanimated power, restored to their senses (not to their wits), and were appointed a sort of literary toll-gatherers from all who afterwards attempted to pass. In the opinion of such persons, Shakespeare was an ignorant man, a child or nature, a wild genius, a strange medley–at least as the most admired of critics, such as Dr Johnson, thought.[145]

He is indeed such a mixture of contraries, that I can only compare him to a Chessboard, with here a white square, there a black square. Here Shakespeare is below contempt–there he rises above all praise–Here he displays an utter ignorance of human nature, there a most profound acquaintance with it: so proceeding with one sentence giving the lie to the anterior–that I trust in the next Lecture I shall be able to produce a Table of their opinions which if read across would contradict itself in every line. They, in short, had made him here white and there black, and the only wonder was that after so much trampling they had not made him black and blue.

Logic is sometimes cloathed in Rhetoric as in former cases, but that two-fold being of Shakespeare, the Poet and the Philosopher, availing himself of it to convey profound truths in the most lively Images, and yet the whole faithful to the character supposed to utter the lines and a further development of that character:

Other slow arts entirely keep the brain;
And therefore, finding barren practisers,
Scarce show a harvest of their heavy toil:
But love, first learned in a lady's eyes,
Lives not alone immured in the brain;

in the Vltava River. The irony of his subsequent position as the patron saint of bridges was widely remarked in eighteenth-century writing. Coleridge reused this example, with respect to reviewers, in *Biographia Literaria*, Chapter 3. The 'German writer' mentioned here is Jean Paul Richter, in whose *Geist oder Chrestomathie* (Graz: Tanzer, 1801) Coleridge found the story.

145 In his *Mr Johnson's Preface to His Edition of Shakespear's Play* (London: J. and R. Tonson, 1765), Samuel Johnson wrote: 'The work of a correct and regular writer is a garden accurately formed and diligently planted, varied with shades, and scented with flowers; the composition of Shakspeare is a forest, in which oaks extend their branches, and pines tower in the air, interspersed sometimes with weeds and brambles, and sometimes giving shelter to myrtles and to roses; filling the eye with awful pomp, and gratifying the mind with endless diversity. Other poets display cabinets of precious rarities, minutely finished, wrought into shape, and polished into brightness. Shakspeare opens a mine which contains gold and diamonds in unexhaustible plenty, though clouded by incrustations, debased by impurities, and mingled with a mass of meaner minerals.'

But, with the motion of all elements,
Courses as swift as thought in every power,
And gives to every power a double power,
Above their functions and their offices.[146]

Sometimes connecting disparate Thoughts merely by means of resemblances in the words expressing them; a thing in character in lighter comedy, especially that kind in which Shakespeare delights, the purposed display of Wit;—sometimes too disfiguring his graver scenes, but more often doubling the natural connection of order of logical consequence in the thoughts by introducing an artificial and sought-for resemblance in word, as in the third line of *Love's Labour's Lost*:

And then grace us in the disgrace of Death—

a figure which often has its force and propriety, as justified by that Law of Passion, which inducing in the mind an unusual activity, seeks for means to waste its superfluity—in the highest and most lyric kind, in passionate repetition of a sublime Tautology (as in the *Song of Debora*),[147] and in lower degrees, in making the words themselves the subjects and materials of that surplus action, the same cause that agitates our very limbs and makes our very gestures tempestuous in states of high excitement. In the *Venus and Adonis*, as if Shakespeare already felt the *necessity* of necessity that impelled him to become a Dramatist, of what interpretation by gesture and look he expected from the Actor, endeavoured to provide by painting the highest degree of which a language is capable, and higher perhaps than any poet ever affected.

The reason why I consider *Love's Labour's Lost* as the first of Shakespeare's plays is that it affords the strongest possible presumption that Shakespeare was not an ignorant man, and that the former part of his life had been passed in scholastic pursuits;—because when a man begins to write, his first work will bear a colour or tincture of his past life, provided he be a man of genius. The earliest plays of Lessing, the German dramatist, were drawn from the university—from prizes bestowed, or other similar incidents and feelings as were natural to young students.[148] Ben Jonson, who had served as a soldier in Flanders, in his excellent works depicted the manners of soldiers,

---

[146] *Love's Labour's Lost*, IV, iii, 321–9.
[147] Judges 5: 7.
[148] The first plays of Gotthold Ephraim Lessing (1729–81) were indeed on scholarly themes: *Der junge Gelehrte* ('The Young Scholar' 1748) and *Der Freigeist* ('The Freethinker' 1749).

and one of his most popular characters, his *Captain Bobadil*,[149] was the mockery of an officer.

What is the *Love's Labour's Lost*? Is it the production of a person accustomed to stroll as a Vagabond about the streets, or to hold horses at a Play-house door, and who had contented himself with making observations on human nature? No such thing! There is scarcely a trace of any observation of nature in Shakespeare's earliest works. The dialogue consists, either of remarks upon what is grotesque in language, or mistaken in literature—all bears the appearance of being written by a man of reading and learning; and the force of genius early saw what was excellent, or what was ridiculous. Hence the wonderful activity of this kind in the first scene of *Love's Labour's Lost*. Such thoughts would never have occurred to a man ignorant and merely an observer of nature. The King says to Biron

> These be the stops that hinder study quite,
> And train our intellects to vain delight.

Biron replies—

> Why! all delights are vain;—and that most vain,
> Which with pain purchased, doth inherit pain:
> As painfully to pore upon a book
> To seek the light of Truth; while Truth the while
> Doth falsely blind the eye-sight of his look
> Light seeking light doth light of light beguile.[150]

I would venture to say that the two first lines of Biron's answer contain a complete confutation of Malthus's theory.[151] Truly we have delights which pain alone could purchase, the continuance of pain without giving the most distant prospect of good to be obtained from it. The concluding sentiment also merits the highest eulogium, comparing the light of Truth to the light of the Sun, the gazing at which destroys the sight.

The play in reality contains in itself very little character. The *dramatis personae* are only the embryos of characters. Biron is afterwards seen more perfectly in Benedict and Mercutio, and Rosaline in Beatrice, the beloved of Benedict. The old man Boyet comes forward afterwards in

---

[149] The boastful military man from *Every Man in His Humour* (1598).

[150] *Love's Labour's Lost*, I, i, 70–7.

[151] The theory expressed in Malthus's *An Essay on the Principle of Population* (1798) that population increase inevitably outstripped the means of subsistence, and that therefore periodic wars and famines were necessary to reduce population to a level that could be supported. Coleridge considered this view profoundly immoral.

Lafeu in *All's Well that Ends Well.* The *poet* in this play is always upper-most and little is drawn from real life. His judgment only is shown in placing the scenes at such a period when we can imagine the transactions of the play natural.

In former ages the Courts of Love flourished, and all that lighter Drapery of Chivalry, which engaged mighty Kings with a sort of serio-comic Interest, and may well be supposed to have engaged more deeply the smaller Princes, at a time when the Nobles' or Princes' Court contained the only Theatre of the Domain or Princedom;— which are now entirely forgotten and appear in themselves improbable. But in Shakespeare's time they were not so far removed, and it was only a pleasing effort on his part to revive the recollection of something not far distant.

The play is most interesting as it exemplifies Shakespeare's mind, when one of the characters, *Longueville*, objects to Biron—

Biron is like an envious sneaping frost,
That bites the first-born infants of the spring.[152]

A thousand times has the answer of Biron occurred to me in this age of prodigies, when the young Roscii are followed as superior beings, wonderment always taking the place of sense.[153] Nothing is valued according to the moral feeling it produces, but only according to its strangeness, just as if a rose could have no sweetness unless it grew upon a thorn, or a bunch of grapes could afford no delight to the taste unless it grew by some miracle from a mushroom. Biron's reply is:—

Well! say I am; why should proud summer boast
Before the birds have any power to sing?
Why should I joy in any abortive birth?
At Christmas I no more desire a rose
Than wish a snow in May's newfangled shows;
But like of each thing that in season grows.[154]

---

[152] I, i, 100–1.
[153] The name of Roscius, a renowned Ancient Roman actor, was often appropriated by actors and other performers in the eighteenth and nineteenth centuries. Coleridge, here, is thinking in particular of the contemporary vogue for 'Young Prodigies': very young actors performing Shakespeare, or other dramatic set-pieces. The debut of William Henry Betty, aged thirteen, was advertised at the Drury Lane theatre in 1804 as 'Young Roscius'. A notebook entry of Coleridge's in 1809 complains of 'the Rosciuses and young Prodigies, in verse or on the stage' and quotes this couplet from *Love's Labour's Lost* (Kathleen Coburn (ed.), *Collected Notebooks* (5 vols, Princeton: Princeton University Press, 1957–2002), 3:3488).
[154] I, i, 102–7. In the original 'power to sing' is 'cause to sing', and 'newfangled shows' is 'newfangled mirth'.

I wish that the last line might be impressed on every parent in this wonder-loving age:—'*but like of each thing that in season grows*'. If they but attended to it, I should not have seen so many miserable little beings taught to think before they had *means* of thinking—one of them I once saw walking into a room and, enquiring why did she so, she answered: 'I do it for exercise, not for pleasure, but too much study will injure my health.' This young lady was aged about four years!

If parents constantly kept the last line in their view, they would not delight in hearing their infants reason when patience ought to be exercised in listening to their natural infant prattle. 'Children,' a friend of mine[155] has truly said, 'do not consider themselves children—they delight in that which they are not, they take pleasure in the pursuits of men, and all that gratifies their vigorous activity.' Instead of attending to this circumstance, what are the books given to children? Little Fanny is to read the story of Little Billy—a child is to come home and tell its mother, 'the sixpence you gave me I gave to a poor beggar,—did I do right Mamma?' 'O! yes, my dear,' cries the mother, kissing him; 'you did,'— thus blending one of the first virtues, Charity, with one of the basest passions of the human heart, the love of hearing oneself praised.

Give me the works which delighted my youth![156] Give me the *History of St. George and the Seven Champions of Christendom*,[157] which at every leisure moment I used to hide myself in a corner to read. Give me the *Arabian Nights Entertainments*, which I used to watch till the sun shining on the bookcase approached it, and glowing full upon it gave me courage to take it from the shelf. I heard of no little Billies, and sought no praise for giving to beggars, and I trust that my heart is not the worse, or the less inclined to feel sympathy for all men, because I first learnt the powers of my nature, and to reverence that nature—for who can feel and reverence the nature of man and not feel deeply for the afflictions of others possessing like powers and like nature?

I trust that what I have thus said in the ardour of my feelings will not be entirely lost, but will awaken in my audience those sympathies without which it is vain to proceed in my criticisms of Shakespeare.

---

[155] Foakes is probably right that this 'friend' is Coleridge himself: he was fond of using the rhetorical device of passing his comments off under this mild fiction.

[156] Tomalin records that S. T. C. delivered this paragraph 'with enthusiasm'.

[157] There were many versions of the legends associated with these seven worthies—Saints George, Andrew, Patrick, Denis, James, Anthony and David. Coleridge probably read a reprint or adaptation of Richard Johnson's *Famous Historie of the Seaven Champions of Christendom* (1596).

The shifting of the scenes can add nothing to the dramatic illusion[158] and only destroy it, by arousing from that delightful dream of our inner nature which is in truth more than a dream. It is a vision of what we might be hereafter—which is the endeavour of the moral being to exert, and at the same time to express itself in, the infinite.

Above it, it should be recollected that I have taken the great names of Milton and Shakespeare rather for the purpose of illustrating great principles than for any minute examination of their works. In the next lecture, however, I hope to be able to go through the *Love's Labour's Lost*; from thence proceed to *Romeo and Juliet*—and afterwards, if time permit, to all those plays of Shakespeare in which is a gradual growth of character, but in which still, the *Poet* is predominant over the *Dramatist.*

---

[158] Tomalin's notes have 'delusion [?illusion]'. 'Dramatic' is an editorial interpolation.

LECTURE 6

The recollection of what has been said by some on the supposed necessity of corporal punishment at college, induces me to express my entire dissent from the notion. Flogging or caning has a tendency to degrade and debase the minds of boys at school. Those who are subjected to it are well aware that the very highest persons in the realm, and those to whom people are accustomed to look up with most respect and reverence, such as the judges of the land, have quietly submitted to it in their pupilage.

I well remember, about twenty years ago, an advertisement from a schoolmaster,[159] in which he assured tender-hearted parents, that corporal punishment was never inflicted, excepting in cases of absolute necessity; and that even then the rod was composed of lilies and roses, the latter, I conclude, stripped of their thorns. What, let me ask, has been the consequence, in many cases, of the abolition of flogging in schools? It has been claimed that reluctance to remove a pimple has not unfrequently transferred the disease to the vitals: sparing the rod, for the correction of minor faults, has ended in the commission of the highest crimes. A man of great reputation (I should rather say

---

[159] Scottish educationalist Andrew Bell (1753–1832) developed a 'monitor' system whilst teaching in Madras in India, which consisted of older or brighter children helping all the other children learn. On returning to Britain he established a school in Leith on these principles, and published widely, inaugurating a national debate, especially with rival educationalist Joseph Lancaster (1778–1838; the 'man of great reputation' Coleridge mentions below) who advocated a pedagogic system of rewards and punishments, including amongst the latter corporal punishment. Bell opposed corporal punishment: 'So many teachers,' he wrote, 'each having only the tuition of such a number of boys as he can at once have under his-eye, and within his reach, command a constant and perpetual attention on the part of the scholar. In most schools, the want of this perpetual agency on the part of the master is attempted to be supplied by a system of terror. But the fear of punishment has neither so constant nor so certain an operation; and the one mode is as far superior to the other, as the prevention of evils is preferable to the punishment of crimes' (Andrew Bell, *An Experiment in Education, made at the Male Asylum of Madras* (London: Cadell and Davies, 1797), 23). Coleridge in his *Notebooks* and the *Biographia Literaria* expressed his support for Bell's child-based, more humane system, as against Lancaster's more instrumental and punitive approach. Collier's 1856 text here implies that Coleridge endorsed the pedagogic benefits of corporal punishment – an unlikely position for him to take and probably the result of (in Foakes' words) Collier 'becoming muddled in his reporting' (CC 5:1, 285 footnote).

of great notoriety)[160] sometimes punished the pupils under his care by suspending them from the ceiling in baskets, exposed to the derision of their school-fellows; at other times he pinned upon the cloathes of the offender a number of last dying speeches and confessions, and employed another boy to walk before the culprit, making the usual monotonous lamentation and outcry.[161] On one occasion this absurd, and really degrading punishment was inflicted because a boy read with a tone, although, I may observe in passing, that reading with intonation is strictly natural, and therefore truly proper, excepting in the excess.[162] What must a parent of well-regulated and instructed mind think of the exhibition of his son in the manner I have described? Here, indeed, was debasement of the worst and lowest kind; for the feelings of a child were outraged, and made to associate and connect themselves with the sentence on an abandoned and shameless criminal. In a mixed audience not a few are desirous of instruction, and some require it; but placed in my present situation I consider myself, not as a man who carries moveables into an empty house, but as a man who entering a generally well furnished dwelling, exhibits a light which enables the owner to see what is still wanting.

Not long since, when I lectured at the Royal Institution, I had the honour of sitting at the desk so ably occupied by Humphry Davy, who may be said to have elevated the art of chemistry to a science;[163] who has discovered that one common law is applicable to the mind and to the body, and who has enabled us to give a full and perfect Amen to the great axiom of Lord Bacon, that knowledge is power.[164] In the delivery of that course I carefully prepared my first essay, and

[160] Joseph Lancaster: see n106.

[161] Lancaster wrote: 'when a boy gets into a *singing* tone in reading, the best mode of cure that I have hitherto found effectual is by force of ridicule. Decorate the offender with matches, ballads ... and, in this garb send him round the school, with some boys before him, crying matches, exactly imitating the dismal tones with which Such things are hawked about the streets in London' (Joseph Lancaster, *Improvements in Education as it Respects the Industrious Classes* (London: J. Lancaster Freeschool, 1803), 89)

[162] Collier's 1856 edition appends a note here: 'This was the Lecturer's own mode of reading verse, and even in prose there was an approach to intonation. I have heard him read Spenser with such an excess (to use his own word) in this respect, that it almost amounted to a song. In blank verse it was less, but still apparent. Milton's *Liberty of Unlicensed Printing* was a favourite piece of rhetorical writing, and portions of it I have heard Coleridge recite, never without a sort of habitual rise and fall of the voice.'

[163] Humphry Davy (1778–1829) was appointed Professor of Chemistry at the Royal Institution in 1802, where he often lectured. S. T. C. lectured there in 1808 'On the Principles of Poetry'.

[164] The most famous apothegm of Sir Francis Bacon (1561–1626), from *Meditationes Sacræ* in *The Works of Francis Bacon: Baron of Verulam* (10 vols, London: C. and J. Rivington et al., 1803), 10:299: *nam et ipsa Scientia potestas est*, 'knowledge itself is power'.

received for it a cold suffrage of approbation: from accidental causes I was unable to study the exact form and language of my second lecture, and when it was at an end, I obtained universal and heart-felt applause. And may I add a hope, that what I offer will be received in a similar spirit? It is true that my matter may not be so accurately arranged; but you shall have the *whole* skeleton, although the bones may not be put together with the utmost anatomical skill.

The immense advantage possessed by men of genius over men of talents can be illustrated in no stronger manner, than by a comparison of the benefits resulting to mankind from the works of Homer and of Thucydides. The merits and claims of Thucydides, as a historian, are at once admitted; but what care we for the incidents of the Peloponnesian War? But woe to that statesman, or, I may say, woe to that man, who has not availed himself of the wisdom contained in 'the tale of Troy divine!'[165]

Lord Bacon has beautifully expressed this idea, where he talks of the instability and destruction of the monuments of the greatest heroes, and compares them with the everlasting writings of Homer, one word of which has never been lost since the days of Pisistratus.

Lastly, leaving the vulgar arguments, that by learning man excelleth man in that wherein man excelleth beasts; that by learning man ascendeth to the heavens and their motions, where in body he cannot come, and the like; let us conclude with the dignity and excellency of knowledge and learning in that whereunto man's nature doth most aspire, which is, immortality or continuance: for to this tendeth generation, and raising of houses and families; to this buildings, foundations, and monuments; to this tendeth the desire of memory, fame, and celebration, and in effect the strength of all other human desires. We see then how far the monuments of wit and learning are more durable than the monuments of power or of the hands. For have not the verses of Homer continued twenty-five hundred years, or more, without the loss of a syllable or letter; during which time, infinite palaces, temples, castles, cities, have been decayed and demolished? It is not possible to have the true pictures or statues of Cyrus, Alexander, Caesar; no, nor of the kings or great personages of much later years; for the originals cannot last, and the copies cannot but lose of the life and truth. But the images of men's wits and knowledges remain in books, exempted from the

---

[165] Milton, *Il Penseroso* (1645), 100.

wrong of time, and capable of perpetual renovation. Neither are they fitly to be called images, because they generate still, and cast their seeds in the minds of others, provoking and causing infinite actions and opinions in succeeding ages: so that, if the invention of the ship was thought so noble, which carrieth riches and commodities from place to place, and commodities the most remote regions in participation of their fruits, how much more are letters to be magnified, which, as ships, pass through the vast seas of time, and make ages so distant to participate of the wisdom, illuminations, and inventions, the one of the other?[166]

Like a mighty ship, they have passed over the sea of time, not leaving a mere ideal track, which soon altogether disappears, but leaving a train of glory in its wake, present and enduring, daily acting upon our minds, and ennobling us by grand thoughts and images: to this work, perhaps, the bravest of our soldiery may trace and attribute some of their heroic achievements. Just as the body is to the immortal mind, so are the actions of our bodily powers in proportion to those by which, independent of individual continuity, we are governed for ever and ever; by which we call, not only the narrow circle of mankind (narrow comparatively) as they now exist, our brethren, but by which we carry our being into future ages, and call all who shall succeed us our brethren, until at length we arrive at that exalted state, when we shall welcome into Heaven thousands and thousands, who will exclaim–'To you I owe the first development of my imagination; to you I owe the withdrawing of my mind from the low brutal part of my nature, to the lofty, the pure, and the perpetual.'

I have looked at the reign of Elizabeth, interesting on many accounts, with peculiar pleasure and satisfaction, because it furnished circumstances so favourable to the existence, and to the full development of the powers of Shakespeare. The Reformation, just completed, had occasioned unusual activity of mind, a passion, as it were, for thinking, and for the discovery and use of words capable of expressing the objects of thought and invention. It was, consequently, the age of many conceits, and an age when, for a time, the intellect stood superior to the moral sense.

The difference between the state of mind in the reign of Elizabeth, and in that of Charles the First is astonishing. In the former period there was an amazing development of power, but all connected with

---

[166] Francis Bacon, *The Advancement of Learning* (1605), in *The Works of Francis Bacon: Baron of Verulam* (10 vols, London: C. and J. Rivington et al., 1803), 1:64–5. Collier identifies that this was passage S. T. C. quoted, but does not quote it himself.

prudential purposes—an attempt to reconcile the moral feeling with the full exercise of the powers of the mind, and the accomplishment of certain practical ends. Then lived Bacon, Burghley, Sir Walter Raleigh, Sir Philip Sidney, and a galaxy of great men; and it is lamentable that they should have degraded their mighty powers to such base designs and purposes, dissolving the rich pearls of their great faculties in a worthless acid, to be drunken as it were by a harlot.[167] What was seeking the favour of the Queen, to a man like Bacon, but the mere courtship of harlotry?

Compare this age with that of the republicans: that indeed was an awful age, and most important as compared with our own. England may be said to have then overflowed from the fullness of grand principle—from the greatness which men felt in themselves, abstracted from the prudence with which they ought to have considered, whether their principles were, or were not, adapted to mankind at large. Compare this revolution with that of a day not long past,[168] when the bubbling-up and overflowing had been produced by the dregs—where there was a total want of all principle, which had raised from the bottom the dregs to the top, and founded a monarchy to be the poisonous bane and misery of the rest of mankind.

It is absolutely necessary to recollect, that the age in which Shakespeare lived was one of great abilities applied to individual and prudential purposes, and not an age of high moral feeling, which gains a man of genius the power of thinking of all things in reference to all. If, then, we should find that Shakespeare took those materials as they were, and yet to all effectual purposes produced the same grand effect as others had attempted to do in an age so much more favourable, shall we not then feel the holiness of genius;—and that though it shone on a dunghill, still the light was as pure as the divine effluence which produced all the beauty of nature?

One of the results of the idea prevailing in that age—that persons must be men of talents in proportion as they were gentlemen—renders certain characters of Shakespeare's drama natural with reference to the time when they were drawn: when we read them we are aware that they are not of our age, and in one sense they may be said to be

---

[167] Dissolving pearls in wine was an actual practice, and whatever Coleridge's scorn here it was more usually done for reasons for health. In the *Great Instauration* (1620) (in *The Works of Francis Bacon: Baron of Verulam* (10 vols, London: C. and J. Rivington et al., 1803), 7:385), Bacon says 'In summer, a draught of white wine in which a very fine powder of pearls and of the shells of crawfish . . . have been infused, refreshes and strengthens the stomach exceedingly.'

[168] That is, the French Revolution. 'Monarchy' is Coleridge's reference to Napoleon.

of no age. A friend of mine[169] well remarked of Spenser, that he is *out of space*: the reader did not know where he is, but still he knows, from the consciousness within him, that it is *natural.* Shakespeare is as much out of time, as Spenser is out of space; yet we feel conscious, though we never knew that such characters existed, that they *might* exist.

This circumstance enabled Shakespeare to paint truly a vast multiplicity of characters by simple meditation: he had only to imitate such parts of his character, or to exaggerate such as existed in possibility, and they were at once true to nature, and fragments of Shakespeare. It is like men who seeing the great luminary of the world through various optics, some declared it to be square, triangular, or round, when in truth it was still the sun.[170] So with the characters of our great poet: but they are still nature, still Shakespeare, and the creatures of his meditation.

When I use the term meditation, I do not mean that Shakespeare was without observation. Mere observation may be able to produce an accurate copy of a thing, and even furnish to other men's minds more ideas than the copyist professed; but they would only be in parts and fragments. Meditation looks at every character with interest, only as it contains something generally true, and such as might be expressed in a philosophical problem.

Shakespeare's characters may be reduced to a few—that is to say, to a few classes of characters. If you take his gentlemen, for instance, the character of Biron is seen again in Mercutio, in Benedick, and in several others. They are men who combine the politeness of the Courtier with the faculties of intellect;—the powers of combination and severance which only belong to an intellectual mind. The wonder is how Shakespeare can thus disguise himself, and possess such miraculous powers of conveying the Poet, and without even raising in us the consciousness of him.

In the address of Mercutio to Romeo regarding the Fairy Queen

---

[169] Dr John Aikin (1747–1822), physician, Unitarian and writer. In the introduction to his edition of Spenser's poetry, Aikin explores the various topographic and temporal problems and impossibilities of *The Faery Queene*, before concluding that the 'merit' of 'Spenser's great poem . . . consists rather in affording a boundless field for the range of fancy, than in that concentration of the interest upon some one important point' (John Aikin (ed.), *The Poetical Works of Edmund Spenser* (6 vols, London: John Sharpe, 1810), 1:xxviii). Coleridge knew Aikin, and met Aikin's sister, the poet Anna Letitia Barbauld (1743–1825).

[170] 'The earth, according to Epicurus, (who seemed to have no fixed or determinate opinion concerning it,) may be round, oval, or lenticular, triangular, pyramidal, square, hexaedrical, or of any other plain figure' (Thomas Francklin, *The Works of Lucian, from the Greek* (2 vols, London: T. Cadell, 1730), 2:258).

Mab[171]—which is so well known that it is unnecessary to repeat it—is to be noticed all the fancy of the poet; and the language in which it is conveyed possesses such facility and felicity, that one would almost say that it was impossible for it to be thought, unless it were thought as naturally, and without effort, as Mercutio represents it. This is the great art by which Shakespeare combines the Poet and the gentleman, throughout borrowing from his own most amiable character that which only could combine them, a perfect simplicity of mind, a delight in what was excellent for its own sake, without reference to himself as causing it, and by that which distinguishes Shakespeare from all others, alluded to by one of his admirers[172] in a short poem, where he tells us that while Shakespeare possessed all the powers of a man, and more than a man, yet he had all the feelings and manners which he painted in an affectionate young woman of eighteen.

Before I enter upon the merits of the tragedy of *Romeo and Juliet*, it will be necessary for me to say something of the language of our country. And here I beg leave to observe, that although I have announced these as lectures upon Milton and Shakespeare, they are in reality, as also stated in the prospectus, intended to illustrate the principles of Poetry: therefore, all must not be regarded as mere digression which does not immediately and exclusively refer to those writers. I have chosen them, in order to bring under the notice of my hearers great general truths; in fact, whatever may aid myself, as well as others, in deciding upon the claims of all writers of all countries.

The language, that is to say the particular tongue, in which Shakespeare wrote, cannot be left out of consideration. It will not be disputed, that one language may possess advantages which another does not enjoy; and we may state with confidence, that English excels all other languages in the number of its practical words. The French may bear the palm in the names of trades, and in military and diplomatic terms. Of the German it may be said, that, exclusive of many mineralogical words, it is incomparable in its metaphysical and psychological force: in another respect it nearly rivals the Greek, I mean in its capability of composition—of forming compound words. Italian is the sweetest language; Spanish the most majestic. All these have their peculiar faults; but I never can agree that any language is unfit for poetry, although different languages, from the condition and

---

[171] *Romeo and Juliet* I, iv, 53ff – the speech beginning: 'O, then, I see Queen Mab hath been with you.'

[172] Collier's original notes say 'Drummond' here; but there is no such poem written by him. In 1856 Collier replaced the name with 'one of his admirers'. The specific poem to which Coleridge alludes here remains untraced.

circumstances of the people, may certainly be adapted to one species of poetry more than to another.

Take the French as an example. It is, perhaps, the most perspicuous and pointed language in the world, and therefore best fitted for conversation, for the expression of light and airy passion, attaining its object by peculiar turns of phrase, which are evanescent, and, like the beautifully coloured dust on the wings of a butterfly,[173] must not be judged by the test of touch. It appears to have no substratum, and it constantly most dangerously tampers with morals, without positively offending decency. As the language for what is called modern genteel comedy all others must yield to French.

Italian can only be deemed second to Spanish, and Spanish to Greek, which contains all the excellences of all languages. Italian, though sweet and soft, is not deficient in force and dignity. As a conformation of this I appeal to Ariosto.

But in English I find that which is possessed by no other modern language, and which, as it were, appropriates it to the drama. It is a language made out of many, and it has consequently many words, which originally had the same meaning; but in the progress of society those words have gradually assumed different shades of meaning. Take any homogeneous language, such as German, and try to translate into it the following lines of Gray:–

> But not to one, in this benighted age,
> Is that diviner inspiration given,
> That burns in Shakespeare's or in Milton's page,
> The pomp and prodigality of heaven.[174]

In German it would be necessary to say 'the pomp and *spendthriftness* of heaven,' because the German has not, as we have, one word with two such distinct meanings, one expressing the nobler, the other the baser idea of the same action.

The monosyllabic character of the English Language enables us, besides, to express more meaning in a shorter space than can be done in any other language. In truth, English may be called the harvest of the unconscious wisdom of the whole nations, and was not the formation of particular individuals. Hence arose the number of its

---

[173] In *A History of the Earth*, Oliver Goldsmith talks of 'that beautifully painted dust which adorns the wings of the butterfly' (Oliver Goldsmith, *A History of the Earth and Animated Nature* (8 vols, Dublin: J. Christie, 1774) 6:90).

[174] The actual lines from Gray's 'Stanzas to Mr Bentley' (1752) are: 'But not to one in this benighted age/Is that diviner inspiration given,/That burns in Shakespeare's or in Milton's page,/The pomp and prodigality of heaven.'

passionate phrases—its metaphorical terms, not borrowed from the Poets, but adopted by them. Our commonest people, when excited by passion, constantly employ them: if a mother lose her child she is full of the wildest fancies, and the words she uses assume a tone of dignity; for the constant hearing and reading of the Bible and Liturgy cloathes her thoughts not only in the most natural, but in the most beautiful forms of language.

I have been induced to offer these remarks, in order to obviate the objection made against Shakespeare on the ground of the multitude of his conceits. I do not pretend to justify every conceit, and a vast number have the ground of the multitude of his conceits been most unfairly imputed to him; for I am satisfied that many portions of scenes attributed to Shakespeare were never written by him. I admit, however, that even in those which bear the strongest characteristics of his mind, there are some conceits not strictly to be justified. The notion against which I warn against is, that whenever a conceit is met with it is unnatural. People who entertain this opinion forget, that they should have deemed them natural had they lived in that age. Dryden in his translation of Juvenal has used the words 'Look round the world,' which are a literal version of the original; but Dr Johnson has swelled and expanded this expression into the following couplet:—

> Let observation, with extensive view,
> Survey mankind from China to Peru;[175]

Mere bombast and tautology!—as if to say, 'Let observation with extensive observation observe mankind extensively.'

If people could throw themselves several centuries back, they would find that conceits, and even puns, were very natural. Puns often arise out of a mixture of a sense of injury, and, as it seems to me, it is a natural way of expressing that mingled feeling. I could point out puns in Shakespeare, where they seem as it were the first openings of the mouth of nature—where nothing else could so properly be said. This is not peculiar to puns, but is of much wider application: read any part of the works of our great dramatist, and the conviction comes upon you irresistibly, not only that what he puts

---

[175] The opening lines of Johnson's *The Vanity of Human Wishes: The Tenth Satire of Juvenal Imitated* (1749). The original Latin is: 'Omnibus in terris, quae sunt a Gadibus usque/ Auroram et Gangen, pauci dinoscere possunt/vera bona' ('there are few who can discern true good, though they look through the whole world from Spain to the lands of the Dawn to the Ganges'). Dryden's version of these lines is: 'Look round the Habitable World, how few/Know their own Good; or knowing it, pursue.'

into the mouths of his personages might have been said, but that it must have been said.

In a future lecture I will enter somewhat into the history of conceits, and the wise use that has been made of them, and besides, (which I hope will be received with favour) attempt a defence of conceits and puns. I admit, of course, that they may be misapplied; but throughout life, I may say, I never have discovered the wrong use of a thing, without having previously discovered the right use of it. To the young I would remark, that it is always unwise to judge of any thing by its defects: the first attempt ought to be to discover its excellences. If a man come into my company and immediately begin to abuse a book, his invectives coming down like water from a shower bath, he tells me no news, because all works of course have defects; but if he show me beauties, he tells me news indeed, because, in my time, I have read so many volumes that have had little or nothing that was good. Always begin with the good–*á Jove principium.*[176]

I will proceed to speak of Shakespeare's wit because an excellent writer,[177] who has done good service to the public taste by driving out the nonsense of the Italian school, has expressed his surprise, that all the other excellences of Shakespeare were, in a greater or less degree, possessed by his contemporaries: thus, Massinger had such and such a thing, Beaumont and Fletcher had more sublimity and figures with equal knowledge of human nature.[178] The point in which none of them had approached Shakespeare, according to this writer, was his wit. I own, I was somewhat shocked to see it said, that the quality by which Shakespeare was to be individualised from all others was wit. I had read his plays over and over, and it did not strike me that wit was his great and characteristic superiority. In reading Voltaire, or (to take a standard and most witty comedy as an example) in reading *The*

---

[176] Vergil, *Eclogues* 3:60, 'Ab Iove principium, Musae'; 'I begin with Jove, O Muses'.

[177] William Gifford (1756–1826). By the 'Italian School', Coleridge means the writers who self-identified as Della Crucians, and whom Gifford mocked in his *Baviad* (1794) and *Maeviad* (1795).

[178] 'The claims of this great poet [Shakespeare] on the admiration of mankind are innumerable, but rhythmical modulation is not one of them: nor do I think it either wise or just to hold him forth as supereminent in every quality which constitutes genius: Beaumont, is as sublime, Fletcher as pathetick, and Jonson as nervous;–nor let it be accounted poor or niggard praise, to allow him only an equality with these extraordinary men in their peculiar excellencies, while he is admitted to possess many others, to which they make no approaches. Indeed, if I were asked for the discriminating quality of Shakspeare's mind, I that by which he is raised above all competition, above all prospect of rivalry, I should say it was WIT' (William Gifford, 'Introduction: Essay on the Dramatick Writings of Massinger', *The Plays of Philip Massinger* (4 vols, London: G. and W. Nicol et al., 1805), 1:li).

School for Scandal,[179] I never experienced the same sort of feeling as in reading Shakespeare.

That Shakespeare has wit is indisputable, but it is not to be compared to that of other writers. His wit is blended with the other parts of his works, and is, by its nature, capable of being so blended. It appears in all parts of his works, whether tragic or comic: it is not like the wit of Voltaire, and of many modern writers, to whom the epithet 'witty' has been properly applied, whose wit consists in a mere combination of words; but in Shakespeare at least nine times out of ten it is produced by a combination of *images*.

It is not always easy to distinguish between *wit* and *fancy*. When the whole pleasure received is derived from surprise at an unexpected turn of expression, then I call it wit; but when the pleasure is produced not only by surprise, but also by an image which remains with us and gratifies for its own sake, then I call it fancy. I know of no mode so satisfactory of distinguishing the signification of the words. I appeal to the recollection of those who hear me, whether the greater part of what passes for wit in Shakespeare, is not most exquisite humour, heightened by a figure, and attributed to a particular character? For instance when Falstaff saw a flea on Bardolph's nose and compared it to a damned soul suffering in Purgatory.[180] The images themselves, in cases like this, afford a great part of the pleasure.

These remarks are not without importance in forming a judgment of Poets and writers in general. There is a great distinction between that sort of talent which gives a kind of electric surprise by a mere turn of phrase, and that which produces surprise by a permanent medium, and always leaves something behind it, which gratifies the *mind*. The first belongs to men of cleverness and talent, who, having been long in the world, have observed the turns of phrase which please in company, and which, pass away with the moment. Of one of these men, who possessed a vast fund of this sort of talent, I remember saying he was like a man who squandered his estate in farthings, but distributed so many that he must needs have been very rich. This sort of talent by no means constitutes genius, although it has some affinity to it.

The wit of Shakespeare is like the flourishing of a man's stick, when he is walking, in the full flow of animal spirits: it is a sort of overflow of hilarity which disburdens, and seems like a conductor, to distribute a portion of our joy to the surrounding air by carrying it away from

---

[179] Richard Brinsley Sheridan's play, first performed 1777.
[180] The Serving Boy in *Henry V* (II, iii, 41) remembers this witticism of the now-dead Falstaff: 'Do you not remember, a saw a flea stick upon Bardolph's nose, and a said it was a black soul burning in hell-fire?'

us. While too it disburdens, it enables us to appropriate what remains to what was most important and most within our direct aim.

I will now touch upon a very serious charge against Shakespeare— that of indecency and immorality. Many have been those who have endeavoured to exculpate him by saying, that it was the vice of his age; but Shakespeare was too great a man to be exculpated by the accidents of any age. These persons have appealed to Beaumont and Fletcher, to Massinger, and to a variety of other, lesser dramatists, to prove that what is complained of was common to them all. Oh! shame and sorrow to us, if it were so: there is nothing common to Shakespeare and to other writers of his day.

It is absolutely necessary, in order to form a proper judgment upon this point, to make a distinction between *manners* and *morals*; and that distinction being once clearly and distinctly comprehended, Shakespeare will appear as pure a writer, in reference to all that we ought to be, and to all that we ought to feel, as he is wonderful in reference to his intellectual faculties. By manners I mean what is dependent on the particular customs and fashions of the age. Even in a state of comparative barbarism as to manners, there might be, and there is, morality. But we have seen much worse times than those, when the mind was so enervated and degraded, that the most distant associations, that could possibly connect our ideas with the basest feelings, immediately brought forward those base feelings, without reference to the nobler; thus destroying the little remnant of humanity, excluding from the mind what is good, and introducing what is bad to keep the bestial nature company.

On looking through Shakespeare, offences against our decency and our manners may certainly be found; but examine history, and observe if it was not the ordinary language of the time, and there could be no offence? What is most observable is that in Shakespeare, it was always calculated to raise a gust of laughter, that would, as it were, blow away all impure ideas, or excite disgust of them.

Above all, let us compare him with some modern writers, the servile imitators of France, and we shall receive a most instructive lesson. I may take the liberty of reading the following note, written by me after witnessing the performance of a modern play at Malta, about nine years ago:[181]–'I went to the theatre, and came away without waiting for the entertainment. The longer I live, the more I am impressed with the exceeding immorality of modern plays: I can scarcely refrain

---

[181] What follows is an expanded and slightly altered version of a passage Coleridge wrote in his *Notebook* on 8 February 1805 (Coburn, *Collected Notebooks*, 2:2436).

from anger and laughter at the shamelessness, and the absurdity of the presumption which presents itself, when I think of their pretences to superior morality, compared with the plays of Shakespeare.' Here let me pause for one moment; for while reading my note I call to mind a novel, on the sofa or toilet of nearly every woman of quality, in which the author gravely warns parents against the indiscreet communication to their children of the contents of some parts of the Bible, as calculated to injure their morals.[182] Another modern author, who has done his utmost to undermine the innocence of the young of both sexes, has the effrontery to protest against the exhibition of the bare leg of a Corinthian female. My note thus pursues the subject:–

> In Shakespeare there are a few gross speeches, but it is doubtful to me if they would produce any ill effect on an unsullied mind; while in some modern plays, as well as in some modern novels, there is a systematic undermining of all morality: they are written in the true cant of humanity, that has no object but to impose; where virtue is not placed in action, or in the habits that lead to action, but, like the title of a book I have heard of, they are 'a hot huddle of indefinite sensations.'[183] In these the lowest incitements to piety are obtruded upon us; like an impudent rascal at a masquerade, who is well known in spite of his vizor, or known by it, and yet is allowed to be impudent in virtue of his disguise. In short, I appeal to the whole of Shakespeare's writings, whether his grossness is not the mere sport of fancy, dissipating low feelings by exciting the intellect, and only injuring while it offends? Modern dramas injure in consequence of not offending. Shakespeare's worst passages are grossnesses against

---

[182] M. G. Lewis's notorious Gothic novel *The Monk* (1797). It is likely that Coleridge was the author of a hostile anonymous account of this novel in the *Critical Review* 19 (1797), 194–200, a supposition reinforced by the fact that this lecture repeats phrases verbatim from that review. In Lewis's novel, Antonia's mother prevents her daughter from reading the Bible on the grounds that 'no reading more improper could be permitted a young woman. Many of the narratives can only tend to excite ideas the worst calculated for a female breast: every thing is called plainly and roundly by its name; and the annals of a brothel would scarcely furnish a greater choice of indecent expressions.' The *Critical Review* notice took particular exception to this: 'the impiety of this falsehood can be equalled only by its impudence. This is indeed as if a Corinthian harlot, clad from head to foot in the transparent thinness of the Cöan veil, should affect to view with prudish horror the naked knee of a Spartan matron!' (See Derek Roper, 'Coleridge and the *Critical Review*', *The Modern Language Review* 55:1 (1960), 11–16.)

[183] James Beattie talks of sensual perception as 'nothing but a mass, collection, heap or bundle of different perceptions' and 'indefinite sensations' (James Beattie, *An Essay on the Nature and Immutability of Truth, in Opposition to Sophistry and Scepticism* (Edinburgh: William Creech, 1772), 279, 179).

the degradations of our nature: those of our modern plays are too often delicacies directly in favour of them.

In my next lecture I will proceed to an examination of *Romeo and Juliet*; and I take that tragedy, because in it are to be found all the crude materials of future excellence; *there* was seen the poet, the great dramatic and tragic poet, but the various parts of the composition are not blended with such harmony as in some of his after writings;–but still more because it affords me the best opportunity of introducing Shakespeare as a delineator of female character, and of love in all its forms, and with all the emotions which deserve that sweet and man-elevating name.

It has been remarked, I believe by Dryden, that Shakespeare wrote for men only, but Beaumont and Fletcher–or rather 'the gentle Fletcher'–for women.[184] I wish to begin by showing, not only that this is not true, but that, of all writers for the stage, he only has drawn the female character with that mixture of the real and of the ideal which belongs to it; and that there is no one character in any of his contemporaries describing a woman, of whom a man, seriously and truly examining his heart and his good sense combined in one moment, could say 'Let that woman be my companion through life: let her be the aid of pursuit, and the reward of my success.'

---

[184] 'The excellency of that poet [Shakespeare] was, as I have said, in the more manly passions; Fletcher's in the softer: Shakespeare writ better betwixt man and man; Fletcher, betwixt man and woman: consequently, the one described friend-ship better; the other love: yet Shakespeare taught Fletcher to write love: and Juliet and Desdemona are originals' (John Dryden, 'Preface to *Troilus and Cressida*', in Walter Scott (ed.), *Works of John Dryden* (18 vols, London: William Miller, 1808) 6:265). 'The gentle Fletcher' is not from Dryden but rather Collins' 'Epistle to Sir Thomas Hanmer' (1743): 'Of softer mold the gentle Fletcher came,/The next in order, as the next in name./With pleas'd attention midst his scenes we find/Each glowing thought, that warms the female mind'.

LECTURE 7

In a former lecture I endeavoured to point out the union of the Poet and the Philosopher, or rather the warm embrace between them, in the *Venus and Adonis* and *Lucrece* of Shakespeare. From thence I passed on to *Love's Labour's Lost*, as the link between his character as a Poet, and his art as a Dramatist; and I showed that, although in that work the former was still predominant, yet that the germs of his subsequent dramatic power were easily discernible.

I will now, as I promised in my last, proceed to *Romeo and Juliet*, not because it is the earliest, or among the earliest of Shakespeare's works of that kind, but because in it are to be found all his excellences such as they afterwards appeared in his more perfect dramas, but differing from them in being less forcibly evidenced, and less happily combined: all the parts are more or less present, but they are not united with the same harmony. There are, however, in *Romeo and Juliet* passages where the poet's whole excellence is evinced, so that nothing superior to them can be met with in the productions of his after years. The main distinction between this play and others is, as I said, that the parts are less happily combined, or to borrow a phrase from the painter, the whole work is less in keeping;[185] there was the productions of grand portions; there were the limbs of what was excellent; but the production of a whole, in which each part gives delight for itself, and the whole, gives more intellectual delight, is the effect of judgment and taste not to be attained but by painful study, and in which we give up the stronger pleasures derived from the dazzling light which a man of genius throws over every circumstance, and where we are chiefly struck by vivid and distinct images. Taste is a subsequent attainment, after the poet has been disciplined by experience, and has added to

---

[185] As a painterly term 'the keeping' refers to the maintenance of a harmonious balance between nearer and further, or smaller and larger, figures in one's overall composition. 'It is not possible to delineate a story, which demand a large space and a great number of persons, on a canvass that is not of proportionate size. If the painter resolves not to want for room, then will the figures be too small, and lose of their effect: but if he make the figures larger, then must he want room for the proper keeping' (William Tooke, William Beloe and Robert Nares, *A New and General Biographical Dictionary* (London: G. G. and J. Robinson et al., 1798), 152).

genius that talent by which he knows what part of his genius he can make intelligible to the part of mankind for which he writes.

In my mind it would be a hopeless symptom, as regards genius, if I found a young man with perfect taste. In the earlier works of Shakespeare we have a profusion of double epithets,[186] and sometimes even the coarsest words are used, if they convey a more vivid image; but by degrees the associations are connected with the image they are to impress, and the poet descends from the ideal into the real world so far as to conjoin both, to give a sphere of active operations to the ideal, and to elevate and refine the real.

In *Romeo and Juliet* the principal characters may be divided into two classes: in one class *passion*–the passion of love–is drawn and drawn truly, as well as beautifully; but the *persons* are not individualised farther than as the actor appears on the stage. It is a very just description and development of the passion, without giving, if I may so express myself, the philosophical history of it, without knowing how such a man became acted upon by that particular passion, but leading it through all the incidents and making it predominant.

Tybalt is, in himself, a common character. And here allow me to remark upon a great distinction between Shakespeare, and all who have written in imitation of him. I know no character in his plays, (unless indeed it is his Pistol) which can be called mere portraits of Individuals: while the reader feels all the delight arising from the individual, yet that very individual is a sort of class character, which makes Shakespeare the poet of all ages.

Of this kind is the character of Tybalt, a man abandoned to his passions and with all the pride of family, only because he thinks it belongs to him as of such a family, and valuing himself highly, simply because he does not care for death. This indifference to death is perhaps more common than any other feeling: men are apt to consider themselves very great, and flatter themselves highly, merely because

---

[186] In the first chapter of the *Biographia Literaria* Coleridge records 'pruning' the excessive use of double epithets from his own juvenilia. He adds a footnote: 'In the *Comus* and other early poems of Milton there is a superfluity of double epithets; while in the *Paradise Lost* we find very few, in the *Paradise Regained* scarce any. The same remark holds almost equally true of the *Love's Labour Lost, Romeo and Juliet, Venus and Adonis*, and *Lucrece*, compared with the *Lear, Macbeth, Othello*, and *Hamlet* of our great Dramatist. The rule for the admission of double epithets seems to be this: either that they should be already denizens of our language, such as *blood-stained, terror-stricken, self-applauding*: or when a new epithet, or one found in books only, is hazarded, that it, at least, be one word, not two words made one by mere virtue of the printers hyphen. A language which, like the English, is almost without cases, is indeed in its very genius unfitted for compounds.'

they possess that which it is a disgrace not to have, but which a wise man never brings forward, but when it is necessary.

Jeremy Taylor in one part of his voluminous works, speaking of a great man, says that he was in his ordinary feelings a coward, as indeed most men are, knowing the value of life, but the power of his reason enabled him, when required, to conduct himself with uniform courage and hardihood.[187] The good bishop, perhaps, had in his mind a story, told by one of the ancients, of a Philosopher and a Coxcomb, on board the same ship during a storm: the Coxcomb reviled the Philosopher for betraying marks of fear: 'Why are you so frightened? I am not afraid of being drowned: I do not care a farthing for my life.'—'You are perfectly right,' said the Philosopher, 'for your life is not worth a farthing.'[188]

Shakespeare never makes his characters win your esteem, but leaves it to the general command of the passions, and to poetic justice. It is most beautiful in the tragedy of *Romeo and Juliet*, that the characters he has principally in view are preserved innocent from all that could do them injury in our feelings concerning them, and yet the other characters, which deserve little interest in themselves, derive it from being instrumental in those situations in which the more important personages develope their thoughts and passions.

Another character of this kind is Capulet:—a worthy, noble-minded old man of high rank, with all the impatience of character that is likely to accompany it. It is delightful to see the sensibilities of nature always so exquisitely called forth; as if the poet had the hundred arms of the Polypus,[189] thrown out in all directions to catch the predominant feeling. We may see in Capulet the manner in which anger seizes hold of everything that comes in its way, as in the lines where Capulet is reproving Tybalt for his fierceness of behaviour, which led him to wish to insult a Montague, and disturb the merriment

---

[187] 'Every man, when shot with an arrow from God's quiver, must then draw in all the auxiliaries of reason . . . [though] he carries along with him the mark of a coward and a fool, let him set his heart firm on this resolution, *I must bear it inevitably, and I will, by God's grace, do it nobly*' (Jeremy Taylor, *Rules and Exercises of Holy Dying* (1651) in Thomas Smart Hughes (ed.), *The Works of Jeremy Taylor* (5 vols, London: A. J. Valpy, 1831), 5:465–6).

[188] 'It happened once that Aristippus was on a voyage to Corinth and, being overtaken by a tempest, fell into great alarm. Some one said, "We plain men are not scared, and yet you philosophers are become cowards?" To which he replied, "The lives at stake in the two cases are not comparable"' (Diogenes Laertius, 'Life of Aristippus' *Lives of the Eminent Philosophers* (c.350 AD) 2.8.72).

[189] An archaic name for cephalopods such as the octopus.

―――Go to, go to;
You are a saucy boy: is't so, indeed?
This trick may chance to scathe you, I know what:
You must contrary me! marry, 'tis time.
Well said, my hearts! You are a princox; go:
Be quiet, or—More light, more light! For shame!
I'll make you quiet. What, cheerly, my hearts![190]

The line

This trick may chance to scathe you, I know what,

was an allusion to the legacy Tybalt might expect; and then, seeing the lights burn dimly, Capulet turns his anger against the servants. So that no one passion is too predominant, but that it includes all the parts of the character, so that the reader never has a mere abstract of a passion, as of anger or ambition, but the whole man is presented to him—the one predominant passion acting as the leader of the band to the rest.

It would not do to introduce into every piece such characters as Hamlet; but even in the subordinate personages, the passion is made instructive at least, even if it has not been an individual, and it has made the reader to look with a keener eye into human nature than if it had not been pointed out to us.

It is one of the great advantages of Shakespeare that he availed himself of his psychological genius to develope all the minutiae of the human heart:—that he showing us the thing makes visible what we should otherwise not have seen: just as, after looking at distant objects through a Telescope, when we behold them subsequently with the naked eye, we see them with greater distinctness than we should otherwise have done.

Mercutio is one of our poet's truly Shakespearian characters; for throughout the plays of Shakespeare, but especially those of the highest order, it is plain that the characters were drawn rather from meditation than from observation, or rather by observation which was the child of meditation. There is a vast difference between a man going about the world with his Pocket book, noting down what he hears and observes, and by practice obtains a facility of representing what he has heard and observed,—himself frequently unconscious of its bearings. This is entirely different from the observation of that mind, which, having formed a theory and a system in its own nature, has remarked

---

[190] *Romeo and Juliet*, I, v, 82–8.

all things that are examples of the truth, and confirming him in that truth, and, above all, enabling him to convey the truths of philosophy, as mere effects derived from the outward watchings of life.

Hence it is that Shakespeare's favourite characters are full of such lively intellect. Mercutio is a man possessing all the elements of a poet: high fancy; rapid thoughts; the whole world was as it were subject to his law of association. Whenever he wishes to impress any thing, all things become his servants: all things tell the same tale, and sound as it were in unison. This is combined with a perfect gentleman, himself unconscious of his powers. It is by his Death contrived to bring about the whole catastrophe of the Play. It endears him to Romeo, and gives to Mercutio's death an importance which it otherwise could not have acquired.

I say this in answer to an observation, I think by Dryden, (to which indeed Dr Johnson has fully replied) that Shakespeare having carried the character of Mercutio as far as he could, till his genius was exhausted, and then killed him to get him out of the way.[191] In truth, on the death of Mercutio the catastrophe depends; and it is produced by it. It serves to show how indifference and aversion to activity in Romeo may be overcome and roused by any deep feeling that is called forth to the most determined actions. Had not Mercutio been made so amiable and so interesting an object to every reader, we could not have felt so strongly as we do the necessity of Romeo's interference, or connecting it so passionately, with the future fortunes of the lover and the mistress.

But what should I say of the Nurse? We have been told that her character is the mere fruit of observation— that it is like Swift's *Polite Conversation*,[192] certainly the most stupendous work of human

---

[191] Johnson wrote: 'Mr. Dryden mentions a tradition of a declaration made by Shakespeare, that "he was obliged to kill Mercutio in the third act, lest he should have been killed by him." Yet he thinks him "no such formidable person, but that he might have lived through the play, and died in his bed," without danger to the poet. Dryden well knew, had he been in quest of truth, that, in a pointed sentence, more regard is commonly had to the words than the thought, and that it is very seldom to be rigorously understood. Mercutio's wit, gaiety and courage, will always procure him friends that wish him a longer life; but his death is not precipitated, he has lived out the time allotted him in the construction of the play; nor do I doubt the ability of Shakespeare to have continued his existence, though some of his sallies are, perhaps, out of the reach of Dryden; whose genius was not very fertile of merriment, nor ductile to humour' (Samuel Johnson, 'Preface to *Romeo and Juliet*' (1765)). Dryden had made his comments in 'Defence of the Epilogue; or, An Essay on the Dramatic Poetry of the Last Age' (1672). Coleridge had access to both of these works in his edition of Samuel Ayscough (ed.), *The Dramatic Works of William Shakespeare* (2 vols, London: John Stockdale, 1807).

[192] Swift's *A Complete Collection of genteel and ingenious Conversation, according to the most polite mode and method now used at Court, and in the best Companies of England* (London: Motte and

memory, and of unceasingly active attention that exists in human records. The Nurse in *Romeo and Juliet* has sometimes been compared to a portrait by Gerard Dow,[193] in which every hair was so exquisitely painted, that it would bear the test even of the microscope. Now, I appeal confidently to my hearers whether the observation of one or two old nurses would have enabled Shakespeare to draw this character of admirable generalisation? No, surely not. Were any man attempt to paint in his mind all the qualities that could possibly belong to a nurse, and he will find them. It is an effect produced not by mere observation. The great prerogative of genius (and Shakespeare had felt and availed himself of it) is now to swell itself to the dignity of a god, and now to keep dormant some part of that nature, to descend to the lowest character–to become any thing, in fact, but the vicious. Thus, in the Nurse you have all the garrulity of old age, and all its fondness; which is one of the greatest consolations of humanity. I have often thought what a melancholy world this would be without children, and what an inhuman world without the aged.

You have likewise in the Nurse the arrogance of ignorance, with the pride of real meanness at being connected with a great family. The grossness, too, which that situation never removes, though it sometimes suspends it; and, arising from that grossness, the little low vices belonging to it, which, indeed, in such minds are scarcely vices.–Romeo at one time was the delightful man, and she was most willing to assist him; but her disposition soon turns in favour of Paris, of whom she professes the same feelings. How admirably too was this contrasted with a young and pure mind, educated in other circumstances!

Another circumstance which ought to be mentioned is truly characteristic of the ignorance of the Nurse:–it is, that in all her recollections, she entirely assists herself by the remembrance of *visual* circumstances. The great difference between the cultivated and the uncultivated mind is this–that the cultivated mind will be found to recall the past by certain regular trains of cause and effect; whereas, with the uncultivated it was wholly done by a coincidence of images or circumstances which happened at the same time. This position is fully exemplified in the following passage, which is put into the mouth of the ignorant Nurse–it is found in Act 1, Scene 3.

Bathurst, 1731) was often reprinted under the title *Polite Conversation*. It is a satire upon the banality of upper-class conversational idioms.

[193] More usually known as Gerrit Dou (1613–75), Dutch Golden Age painter.

Even or odd, of all days in the year,
Come Lammas-eve at night shall she be fourteen.
Susan and she—God rest all Christian souls!—
Were of an age: well, Susan is with God;
She was too good for me: but, as I said,
On Lammas-eve at night shall she be fourteen;
That shall she, marry; I remember it well.
'Tis since the earthquake now eleven years;
And she was wean'd,—I never shall forget it,—
Of all the days of the year, upon that day:
For I had then laid wormwood to my dug,
Sitting in the sun under the dove-house wall;
My lord and you were then at Mantua:—
Nay, I do bear a brain:—but, as I said,
When it did taste the wormwood on the nipple
Of my dug and felt it bitter, pretty fool,
To see it tetchy and fall out with the dug!
Shake quoth the dove-house: 'twas no need, I trow,
To bid me trudge:
And since that time it is eleven years;
For then she could stand alone;[194]

She still goes on with visual images, so true to the character.—More in fact is brought into one portrait here than any single observation could have given, and nothing incongruous to the whole was introduced.

I honour, I love, the works of Fielding as much, or perhaps more, than those of any other writer of fiction of that kind. Take Fielding in his characters of postilions, landladies, and landlords, or any thing that was before his eye, and nothing can be more happy, or humorous; but take any of his chief characters, Tom Jones for instance, where the writer was deserted by observation, where he could not assist himself by the close copying, where it is necessary that something should take place, that some words should be spoken which could not be dictated by mere observation,—take his soliloquies, or the interview between Tom Jones and Sophia before the reconciliation—[195]and I will venture to say, loving and honouring the man as I do, that nothing can be more unnatural: words without spirit wholly incongruous, and without any psychological truth.

But Shakespeare will ever be found to speak the language of nature. Where did he learn the dialogue of Generals: where has he learnt

[194] *Romeo and Juliet*, I, iii, 16–36.
[195] Henry Fielding, *Tom Jones* (1749) book 18, chapter 12.

from observation only such language as the following, where Othello is speaking to Iago regarding Brabantio?

> Let him do his spite:
> My services, which I have done the signiory,
> Shall out-tongue his complaints. 'Tis yet to know,
> Which, when I know that boasting is an honour,
> I shall promulgate, I fetch my life and being
> From men of royal siege; and my demerits
> May speak, unbonneted, to as proud a fortune
> As this that I have reach'd: for know, Iago,
> But that I love the gentle Desdemona,
> I would not my unhoused free condition
> Put into circumscription and confine
> For the sea's worth.[196]

I ask where did Shakespeare observe such language as this? If he did observe it, it was with the inward eye of meditation upon his own nature. He became Othello, and spoke as Othello, in such circumstances, would have spoken.

Another remark I may make upon *Romeo and Juliet* is, that in it the Poet is not entirely blended with the Dramatist,—at least, not in that degree which is afterwards noticed in *Lear, Hamlet, Othello,* or *Macbeth.* Capulet and Montague frequently talk language only belonging to the poet, and not so characteristic of Passion as of a Faculty;—a mistake, or rather an indistinctness, which many of our later Poets have carried through the whole of their work.

When I read the song of Deborah,[197] I never suppose that she was a poet, although I think the song itself a sublime poem. It is as simple a dithyrambic poem as exists; but it is the proper effusion of a woman highly elevated by triumph, by the natural hatred of oppressors, and resulting from a sense of wrongs: it is an exultation on deliverance from them, and this too accomplished by herself. When she commences, 'I, Deborah, arose, that I arose a mother in Israel,' it is poetry in the highest sense: we have no reason, however, to suppose that if she had not been agitated by passion, and animated by victory, she would have been able to talk in the same way; or that if she had been

---

[196] *Othello,* I, ii, 17–28.
[197] Judges 5: 2–31; a victory hymn sung by the Israelite leader Deborah after the defeat of the Canaanites. It begins 'Praise ye the Lord for the avenging of Israel' and continues (verse 7) 'they ceased in Israel until that I Deborah arose, that I arose a mother in Israel.'

placed under different circumstances, which she was not likely to be placed in, she would still have spoken the language of truth.

On the other hand, there is a language which is not descriptive of passion, yet is poetic, and shows a high and active fancy, as when Capulet says,—

> Such comfort as do lusty young men feel,
> When well-apparell'd April on the heel
> Of limping winter treads, even such delight
> Among fresh female buds, shall you this night
> Inherit at my house[198]

Other passages, more happy in illustrating this, might be adduced, where the Poet forgets the character, and speaks in his own person.

In other parts, Shakespeare's conceits are completely justifiable, as belonging to the state of age, or passion of the person using them. In other parts, where they cannot be so justified, they may be excused from the taste of his own and of the preceding age; as for instance, in Romeo's speech,

> Here's much to do with hate, but more with love:—
> Why then, O brawling love! O loving hate!
> O any thing, of nothing first created!
> O heavy lightness! serious vanity!
> Misshapen chaos of well-seeming forms!
> Feather of lead, bright smoke, cold fire, sick health!
> Still-waking sleep, that is not what it is![199]

I dare not pronounce such passages as these to be absolutely unnatural, because there is an effort of the mind, when it would describe what it cannot satisfy itself with the description of, to reconcile opposites and to leave a middle state of mind more strictly appropriate to the imagination than any other, when it is hovering between two images. As soon as it is fixed on one, it becomes understanding; and when it is waving between them, attaching itself to neither, it is imagination. Such is the fine description of Death in Milton:—

>   The other shape,
> If shape it might be call'd, that shape had none
> Distinguishable in member, joint, or limb,
> Or substance might be call'd, that shadow seem'd,
> For each seem'd either: black it stood as night;

---

[198] *Romeo and Juliet,* I, ii, 26–30.
[199] *Romeo and Juliet,* I, i, 175–81.

Fierce as ten furies, terrible as hell,
And shook a dreadful dart: what seem'd his head
The likeness of a kingly crown had on.[200]

These are the grandest efforts of poetry, where the imagination is called forth, not to produce a distinct form, but a strong working of the mind, still producing what it still repels, and again calling forth what it again negatives; and the result is what the poet wishes to impress, to substitute a grand feeling of the unimaginable for a mere image. I have sometimes thought that the passage from Milton might be quoted as exhibiting a certain limit between the Poet and the Painter. Sundry painters had not so thought, and had made pictures of the meeting between Satan and Death at Hell Gate; and how was Death represented? Not as Milton has described him, but by the most defined thing that can be imagined—A Skeleton, perhaps the dryest image that could be discovered; which reduced the mind to a mere state of inactivity and passivity,—and compared with which a Square or a Triangle, is a luxuriant fancy.

It is a general but mistaken notion that, because certain forms of writing, and combinations of thought, are not in common and daily use, they are unnatural. There is no form of language that may not be introduced by a great Poet with great effect in particular situations because they were true to nature, and without an original they could never have existed. Take punning, for instance, which is the most harmless kind of wit, because it never excites envy. A pun may be a necessary consequence of association: as if one man were attempting to show something resisted by another, that other when agitated by a passion, might employ a term used by his adversary in one sense to directly contrary meaning: it came into his mind to do it as one way, and sometimes the best, of replying. It generally arose from a mixture of anger and contempt, which punning is a natural mode of expressing.

It is my intention not to pass any of the important conceits in Shakespeare, some of which are introduced in his after productions with great propriety. It will be recollected, that at the time this great poet lived there was an attempt at, and an affectation of, quaintness, which emanated even from the Court, and to which satire was directed by Osrick in *Hamlet*. Among the Schoolmen of that age, and earlier, nothing was more common than such conceits as he had

---

[200] John Milton, *Paradise Lost* 2:666–73.

employed: it was aided after the restoration of letters, and the bias thus given was very generally felt.

I have in my possession a Dictionary of Phrases,[201] in which those applied to Love, Hate, Jealousy, and such abstract terms, consisted entirely of phrases taken from Seneca or his imitators, or from the Schoolmen, themselves composed of perpetual antitheses, and describing those passions by conjunction and combination of things absolutely irreconcilable. But I am aware that I am only palliating the practice in Shakespeare because he did not write for his own but for all ages, and so far I admit it to be a defect.

If in these lectures I am able to find what were the peculiar faults, as well as the peculiar beauties of Shakespeare, it would be an additional mode of deciding what authority ought to be attached to parts of what are called his works. If we discovered a Play in which there were neither Shakespeare's defects nor his excellences, we should have strong reason to believe that it was not Shakespeare's, and that they were taken either from the old plays, which, in some instances, he reformed or altered, or that they were inserted afterwards by some under-hand, in order to please the mob, and that they were written and played because such a part of Shakespeare's original was too heavy, where the mob called for the clown to lighten the scene. If we found such to be the case, we might conclude that the play or the scene was not Shakespeare's.

It remains for me to speak of the Hero and Heroine, of the Play *Romeo and Juliet* themselves; and I shall do so with unaffected diffidence, not only from the delicacy, but from the great importance of the subject: because it is impossible to defend Shakespeare from the most cruel of all charges against him,—that he is an immoral writer—without entering fully into his mode of displaying female characters, and love, which he has done with greater perfection than any other writer, with the single exception perhaps of Milton in his delineation of the character of Eve.

When I have heard it said, or seen it stated, that Shakespeare wrote for man, but the gentle Fletcher for woman,[202] it has always given me great pain: when, too, I remember how much our characters are formed from reading, I cannot deem it a slight subject, to be passed

---

[201] Probably Hugh Robinson's *Scholae Wintoniensis* (1682).

[202] Coleridge said this at the end of the preceding lecture; see above for fuller note. 'Shakespeare writ better betwixt man and man; Fletcher, betwixt man and woman' (Dryden, 'Preface to *Troilus and Cressida*', 6:265); 'Of softer mold the gentle Fletcher came . . . midst his scenes we find/Each glowing thought, that warms the female mind' (Collins, 'Epistle to Sir Thomas Hanmer' (1743).

over as a mere amusement, like a game at chess. I never have been able to tame down my mind to think Poetry a sport, or an amusement for idle hours.

Perhaps there is no one more sure criterion of the degree of refinement in a moral character and the purity of the intellectual intention, and the deep conviction and sense of what our own nature is in all its combinations, than the different definitions men would give of love, supposing them to be perfectly serious. I will not state the various definitions that have been given; they are probably well-known to many, and it would be better not to repeat them. I will rather give you one of my own, equally free from the extravagance of pretended Platonism (which, like other things which super-moralise, is sure to demoralise) and kept distinct from its grosser opposite.

Considering myself and my fellow-men as it were a link between heaven and earth, as composed of body and of the soul, to reason and to will, and the perpetual aspiration which tells us that this is ours for a while, but it is not ourselves; considering man in this two-fold character, yet united in one person, I conceive that there can be no correct definition of love which does not correspond with the being, and with that subordination of one part to another which constitutes our perfection. I would say therefore that–

> Love is a perfect desire of the whole being to be united to some thing, or some being, felt necessary to its perfection, by the most perfect means that nature permits, and reason dictates.[203]

It is inevitable to every noble mind, whether man or woman, to feel itself, of itself, imperfect and insufficient, not as an animal merely, but altogether as a moral being. How wonderfully, therefore, has Providence provided for us to make that which is necessary for us, a step of that exaltation to a higher and nobler state! The Creator has ordained that one should possess what the other does not, and the union of both is the most complete ideal of the human character that can be conceived. In everything blending the similar with the dissimilar is the secret of all pure delight. Who shall dare then to stand alone, and vaunt himself, in himself, sufficient? In poetry I have shown that it is the blending of passion with order that constitutes perfection; and still more in morals, and more than all was it (and woe be to us if we do not at some time contemplate in a moral view solely) the exclusive attachment of the Sexes to each other.

---

[203] Based almost word for word on a Notebook entry from 1809: see Coburn, *Collected Notebooks*, 3:3514 and footnote.

True it is, that the world and its business may be carried on without marriage; but it is so evident that Providence meant man to be the master of the world; he is the only animal of all climates, and his reason is so pre-eminent over instinct whose place is supplied, that marriage, or the knitting together of society by the tenderest ties, rendered him able to maintain his superiority over the brutes. Man alone is privileged to cloathe himself, and to do all things so as to make him, as it were, a secondary creator of himself, and of his own happiness or misery: and in this, as in all, the image of his Maker is impressed upon him.

Providence, then, has not left us to Prudence only; for the power of calculation, which prudence implies, cannot have existed, but in a state which pre-supposes the Marriage State. If God has done this, shall we suppose that he has given us no moral sense, no yearning, which is something more than animal, to secure that, without which man might form a herd, but could not be a Society? The very idea seems to breathe absurdity.

From this union arise the filial, maternal, brotherly and sisterly relations of life; and every state is but a family magnified. All the operations of the mind, all that distinguishes us from mere brute animals, arises from the more perfect state of domestic life. One certain criterion in forming an opinion of man is the reverence in which he holds woman. Plato has said,[204] that by this we rise from sensuality to affection, from affection to love, and from love to the pure intellectual delight by which we become worthy to conceive that infinite in ourselves, without which it is impossible for man to believe in a God. In short to sum up all, the most delightful of all promises was expressed to us by this practical state, namely our marriage with the Redeemer of mankind.

I might safely appeal to every gentleman in this room, whether when a young man who has been accustomed to abandon himself to his passions and to have lived with freedom, when he falls in love, the first symptom is not a complete change in his manners,—a contempt and hatred of himself for having asserted that he acted by the dictates of nature, that his vices were the inevitable consequences of youth, and that it was impossible they could be conquered. The surest friend of chastity is love: it leads men not to sink the mind in the body, but to draw the body to the mind—the immortal part of our nature. Contrast this feeling with the works of those writers who have done the direct contrary even by the ebullitions of comic humour, while in

[204] In the *Symposium* (c.380–370 BC).

other parts of the same work from the vile confusion, great purity is displayed, such as the purity of love, which above all other qualities renders us most pure and lovely.

Love is not like hunger. Love is an associative quality. The hungry savage is a mere animal, thinking of nothing but the satisfaction of his appetite. What is the first effect of love, but to associate the feeling with every object in nature? The trees whisper, the roses exhale their perfumes, the nightingales sing, the very sky seems in unison with the feeling of love. It gives to every object in nature a power of the heart, without which it would indeed be spiritless, a mere dead copy.

Shakespeare has described this passion in various states, and had begun as was most natural, with love in the young mind. Does he begin by making Romeo and Juliet in love at first glimpse, as a common and ordinary thinker would do? No. He knew what he was about: he was to develope the whole passion, and he takes it in its first elements—that sense of imperfection, that yearning to combine itself with something lovely. Romeo became enamoured of the ideal he had formed in his own mind, and then, as it were, christened the first real being as that which he desired. He appears to be in love with Rosaline; but, in truth, he is in love only with his own idea. He felt the necessity of being beloved which no noble mind can be without.[205] Shakespeare then introduces Romeo to Juliet, and makes it not only a violent, but permanent love at first sight, which has been so often ridiculed in Shakespeare.

This calls upon me to remark one characteristic of Shakespeare, which I think truly belongs to a man of profound thought and genius. It has been too much the custom, when we could not explain any thing that happened by the few words that were employed to explain everything: we pass it over as beyond our reach. They are looked upon as hints, which philosophy could not explain:—as the terra incognita for future discoveries—the great ocean of unknown things to be afterwards explored, or as the sacred fragments of a ruined temple, every part of which in itself was beautiful, but the particular relation of the parts is unknown. In Shakespeare they were every where introduced with respect, and he had acted upon them, and had drawn his characters as seriously influenced by them.

As I may not again have the opportunity, I will here compare the different manner in which Shakespeare has treated the priestly character, with other writers. In Beaumont and Fletcher priests are described

---

[205] 'To be beloved is all I need,/And whom I love, I love indeed' (Samuel Taylor Coleridge, 'Pains of Sleep' (1803), 51–2).

as a vulgar mockery; and, as in other characters, the errors of a few are mistaken for the character of the many: but in Shakespeare they always bring with them our love and respect. He made no abstracts: no copies from the bad parts of human nature; his characters of priests are drawn from the general.

It is remarkable too that throughout all his works Shakespeare has never introduced the passion of Avarice. It belongs only to particular parts of our nature; it is only prevalent in particular states of society and could not be permanent. *The Miser* of Molière and Plautus is now looked upon as a sort of madman. Elwes was a peculiar individual that partook of insanity;[206] but, as a passion, it has disappeared. And how admirably did Shakespeare foresee that such characters could not be permanent, inasmuch as the passion on which they were founded would soon be lost, depending upon accidental circumstances.

None of the plays of Shakespeare is built upon any thing but what is absolutely necessary for our existence, and consequently must be permanent while we continue men. Take the admirable Tragedy of Orestes, or of the husband of Jocasta:[207] yet whatever might be the genius of Sophocles, they have a fault. In *Oedipus* a man is oppressed by fate for an action of which he was not morally guilty; the crime is taken from the moral actor and given to the action; we are obliged to say to ourselves, that in those days they considered things without reference to the real guilt of the persons.

There is no one character in Shakespeare in which envy is pourtrayed, excepting in Cassius, in *Julius Caesar*;[208] yet even there it is not hateful to us, but he has counterbalanced it by a number of excellent feelings. He leads the reader to suppose that it is rather something constitutional, something derived from his mother which he cannot avoid, throwing the blame from the will of man to some unavoidable circumstance, rather than fix the attention of the reader on one of those passions that actually debase the mind.

Wherever love is described as of a serious nature, and much more when it is to lead to a tragical end, it depends on a law of the mind, which, I believe, I shall hereafter be able to make intelligible, and which will not only justify Shakespeare, but show an analogy to all his other characters. This subject I reserve to my next lecture.

---

[206] John Elwes (1714–89) was MP for Berkshire, and a notorious miser.
[207] That is, the two Sophocles' tragedies *Electra* and *Oedipus Tyrannus*.
[208] In the fifth lecture of the 1818–19 series (below) Coleridge does discuss *Othello*'s Iago in terms of envy.

LECTURE 8

It is impossible to pay a higher compliment to poetry, than to consider the effects it has in common with religion, yet distinct as far as distinct can be, where there is no division in those qualities which religion exercises and diffuses over all mankind, as far as they are subject to its influence. I have often thought that religion (speaking of it only as it accords with poetry, without reference to its more serious impressions) is the Poetry of all mankind, so as both have for their object:—

1. To generalise our notions; to prevent men from confining their attention solely, or chiefly, to their own narrow sphere of action, and to their own individualizing circumstances; but by placing them in awful relations it merges the individual man in the whole, and makes it impossible for any one man to think of his future, or of his present, lot, without at the same time comprising all his fellow-creatures.

2. That it throws the object of deepest interest at a distance from us, and thereby not only aids our imagination, but in a most important way subserves the interest of our virtues; for that man is indeed a slave, who is a slave to his own senses, and whose mind and imagination cannot carry him beyond the narrow sphere which his hand can touch, or even his eye can reach.

3. The grandest point of resemblance between them is, that both have for their object (I hardly know whether the English language supplies an appropriate word) the perfecting, and the pointing out to us the indefinite improvement of our nature, and fixing our attention upon that. It bids us, while we are sitting in the dark round our little fire, still look at the mountain-tops, struggling with the darkness, and which announces that light which shall be common to us all, and in which individual interests shall dissolve into one common interest, and every man shall find in another more than a brother.

Such being the case, we need not wonder that it has pleased Providence, that the divinest truths of religion should be revealed to us in the form of Poetry; and that at all times the Poets, though not the slaves of any particular sectarian opinions, should have joined to support all those delicate sentiments of the heart (often when they were most opposed to the reigning philosophy of the day) which may be called the feeding streams of Religion.

I have heard it said that 'an undevout Astronomer is mad.'[209] In the strict sense of the word, every being capable of understanding must be mad, who remains, as it were, sunk in the ground on which he treads;–who, gifted with the divine faculties of indefinite hope and fear, born with them, yet fixes his faith upon that, in which neither hope nor fear has any proper field to display themselves. Much more truly, however, might it be said that, an undevout Poet is mad: in other words, an undevout poet in the strict sense of the term is an impossibility. I have heard of verse-makers who introduced into their works such questions as these:–Whether the world was made of atoms?[210]–Whether there is a universe?–Whether there is a governing mind that supports it? As I have said, verse-makers are not Poets. In the Poet is comprehended the man who carries the feelings of childhood into the powers of manhood; who, with a soul unsubdued, unshackled by custom, can contemplate all things with the freshness, with the wonder of a child; and, connecting with it the inquisitive powers of his manhood, adds, as far as he can find knowledge, admiration; and, where knowledge no longer permits admiration, gladly sinks back again into the childlike feeling of devout wonder.

The poet is not only the man made to solve the riddle of the Universe, but he is also the man who feels where it is not solved, and which continually awakens his feelings being of the same feeling. What is old and worn out, not in itself, but from the dimness of the intellectual eye, brought on by worldly passions, he makes new: he pours upon it the dew that glistens, and blows round us the breeze that cooled us in childhood.

I hope, therefore, that if but in this single lecture I should make some demand on the attention of my hearers to a most important subject, upon which mainly depends all sense of the worthiness or unworthiness of our nature, I shall obtain a pardon. If there be less amusement, I trust a few thoughts will repay on after reflection.

I have been led to these remarks by the play of *Romeo and Juliet*, and by some, perhaps, indiscreet expressions, certainly not well chosen, concerning falling in love at first sight. I have taken one

---

[209] Edward Young, *Night Thoughts* (1745) 9:771.
[210] Sir Richard Blackmore's famously dull epic *Creation: a Philosophical Poem* (1712) challenges the received wisdom that the cosmos is made of atoms, registering amongst other objections 'those atoms wondrous small must be/Small to an unconceivable degree' (Blackmore, *Creation*, 4:462–3).

of Shakespeare's earliest works, in order to show that he, of all his contemporaries (Sir Philip Sidney alone excepted), entertained a just conception of the female character. Certainly, that 'gentleman of Europe'[211]– that all-accomplished man, and our great Shakespeare, were the only writers of that age, who pitched their ideas of female perfections according to the best researches of philosophy: and compared with all those who followed them, they stand as mighty mountains in a deluge, remaining islands while all the rest have been buried by the flood of oblivion.[212]

I certainly do not mean to justify so foolish a thing as a general maxim, as *love at first sight*. To express myself more accurately, I should say that there is, and has existed, a feeling, a deep emotion of the mind, which could only be called *love momentaneous*–not necessarily love at first sight, nor known by the being itself to be so, but by many years of after experience? Before I enter into this apparent paradox, I must first mention the opinion known throughout Europe by the appellation of the *Judicious Hooker*.[213] This venerable theologian and philosopher far removed from the weak passions of life and sitting in his closet divining out of his own heart what might be, and feeling the greatness of a future race by the greatness of his own mind, which still permitted him to pursue the noble and the permanent, has told us that

> the well-spring of that communion is a natural delight which man hath, to transfuse from himself into others, and to receive from others into himself, especially those things wherein the excellency of his kind doth most consist. The chiefest instrument of human communion therefore is speech, because thereby we impart mutually one to another the conceits of our reasonable understanding.[214]

---

[211] Coleridge is quoting himself. In the seventh *The Friend* (28 September 1809) he wrote: 'Sir Philip Sidney,–the favourite of Queen Elizabeth, the paramount gentleman of Europe, the nephew, and– as far as a good man could be–the confidant of the intriguing and dark-minded Earl of Leicester,– was so deeply convinced that the principles diffused through the majority of a nation are the true oracles from whence statesmen are to learn wisdom.'

[212] Collier adds a footnote here. 'I remember, in conversing on this very point at a subsequent period,–I cannot fix the date,–Coleridge made a willing exception in favour of Spenser; but he added that the notions of the author of the *Faery Queen* were often so romantic and heightened by fancy, that he could not look upon Spenser's females as creatures of our world; whereas the ladies of Shakespeare and Sidney were flesh and blood, with their very defects and qualifications giving evidence of their humanity: hence the lively interest taken regarding them.–J. P. C.'

[213] Richard Hooker (1554–1600), influential English priest, theologian and author. The description 'Judicious Hooker' appears to first been used by James I.

[214] Richard Hooker *Of the Laws of Ecclesiastical Polity* (London: William Stansby, 1594) 1.9.

And the eminence of Love or Marriage Communion, is that this mutual Transfusion can take place more perfectly and totally in this than in any other mode. The same writer had also stated in opposition to the materialists and those who think ignobly of nature this fact, and had called upon them to answer it consistently with their own system:

> For man doth not seem to rest satisfied, either with fruition of that wherewith his life is preserved, or with performance of such actions as advance him most deservedly in estimation; but doth further covet, yea oftentimes manifestly pursue with great sedulity and earnestness, that which cannot stand him in any stead for vital use; that which exceedeth the reach of sense; yea somewhat above capacity of reason, somewhat divine and heavenly, which with hidden exultation it rather surmiseth than conceiveth; somewhat it seeketh, and what that is directly it knoweth not, yet very intentive desire thereof doth so incite it, that all other known delights and pleasures are laid aside, they give place to the search of this but only suspected desire. If the soul of man did serve only to give him being in this life, then things appertaining unto this life would content him, as we see they do other creatures; which creatures enjoying what they live by seek no further, but in this contentation do show a kind of acknowledgment that there is no higher good which doth any way belong unto them. With us it is otherwise. For although the beauties, riches, honours, sciences, virtues, and perfections of all men living, were in the present possession of one; yet somewhat beyond and above all this there would still be sought and earnestly thirsted for.[215]

I have therefore to defend the existence of Love, as a passion in itself fit for and appropriate to human nature;—I say fit for human nature, and not only so, but peculiar to it, unshared either in degree or kind by any other of our fellow creatures: as a passion which it is impossible for any creature to feel, but a being endowed with reason, with

---

This quotation is not included in Collier's *Seven Lectures*; instead Collier appends the following footnote: 'Coleridge here made a reference to, and cited a passage from, Hooker's *Ecclesiastical Polity*; but my note contains only a hint regarding it; and the probability is, that I did not insert more of it, because I thought I should be able, at some future time, to procure the exact words, or a reference to them, from the Lecturer. Whether I did so or not I cannot remember, but I find no trace of any thing of the kind.' Collier's original notes strongly suggest that the passage included above—one Coleridge had copied into his Notebooks in 1809 (Coburn, *Collected Notebooks*, 3.3574) and commented upon—is the quotation omitted.

[215] Hooker's *Ecclesiastical Polity* (1594) 1.11.

the moral sense, and with the strong yearnings, which, like all other powerful effects in nature, prophesy some future effect.

If I were to address myself to the materialist, with reference to the human kind, and (admitting the three great laws common to all beings,–1, the law of self-preservation; 2, that of continuing the race; and 3, the preservation of the offspring till protection is no longer needed),–were to ask him, whether he thought that the simple necessity of preserving the race arose from any motives of prudence or duty? Whether he undertook a course of serious reflection, such as if it would be better that we should have a posterity, or if there were any sense of duty impelling us to seek that as our object?–if, I say, I were to ask a materialist, whether such was the real cause of the preservation of the species, he would laugh me to scorn; the materialist would say that nature was too wise to trust any of her great designs to the mere cold calculations of a fallible mortal.

Then the question comes to a short crisis:–is, or is not, our moral nature a part of the end of Providence? or are we, or are we not, beings meant for society? Is that society, or is it not, meant to be progressive? Not to ask a question which I trust none of my auditors would endure:–Whether, independently of the progression of the race, each individual has it not in his power to be indefinitely progressive?–for, without marriage, without exclusive attachment, there could be no human society; herds there might be, but society there could not be: there could be none of that delightful intercourse between father and child; none of the sacred affections; none of the charities of humanity; none of all those many and complex causes, which have raised us to the state we have already reached, could possibly have existence. All these effects do not arise among the brutes; they do not arise among those savages whom strange accidents have sunk below the class of human beings, inasmuch as a stop seems to have been put to their progressiveness.

We may, therefore, fairly conclude that there is placed within us some element, if I may so say, of our nature; something which is as peculiar to our moral nature, as any other part can be conceived to be, name it what you will,–name it devotion,–name it friendship, or a sense of duty;–that there is something peculiar to the moral nature, which answers the moral end; as we find everywhere in the ends of the moral world, that there are material and bodily means proportioned in them.

We are born, and it is our nature and lot to be, body and mind; but when our heart leaps with joy on hearing of the victories of our country, or of the rescue of the unhappy from the hands of an oppressor;

or when a parent is transported at the restoration of a beloved child from a deadly sickness; when the heart beats and the pulse quickens, do we therefore pretend, because the body interprets the emotions of the mind and as far as it can still strives to maintain its claim to sympathy, that therefore joy is not mental? or that joy is not moral? Do we say, that it was owing to a particular degree of fulness of blood that our heart leaped, and our pulse beat? Or do we not rather say, that the regent, the mind, being glad, its slave the body, its willing slave obeyed it? Or if we are operated upon by a feeling of having done wrong, or by a sense of having had a wrong done to us, and it excites the blush of shame or the glow of anger on our cheek, do we pretend to say that, by some accident, the blood suffused itself into veins unusually small, and therefore that the guilty seemed ashamed, or the indignant patriot recoiled from a charge against his honour? We scorn it in all these things. And shall it be therefore deemed a sufficient excuse to the materialist to degrade that passion, on which not only many of our virtues depend, but upon which the whole frame, the whole structure of human society rests, because our body is so united with our mind, that the mind has been employed by Providence to raise what is the lower to the higher? We should be guilty of an act of moral suicide, to degrade that which on every account is most noble, by merging it in what is most base: as if an Angel held out the welcoming hand of brotherhood, and we turned away to wallow with the sow in the sty.

The first feeling that would strike a reflecting man, who wished to see mankind not only in an amiable but in a just light, would be that beautiful feeling in the moral world,—the brotherly and sisterly affections; the existence of strong affection in the one sex to the other greatly modified by the difference of sex; made more tender, more graceful, more soothing and conciliatory by that circumstance of difference of sex, yet still remaining perfectly pure, perfectly spiritual. It would be a glorious effect of human nature, if the instances were only here and there; but how much more glorious, when they are so frequent as to be only not universal. It is the object of religious veneration to all those who love their fellow men, or who know themselves.

The power of education is herein exemplified, and data for hope are given of yet unrealised excellences, perhaps dormant in our nature. When we see so divine a moral effect spread through all classes, what may we not hope of other excellences, of yet unknown quality?

By dividing the sisterly and fraternal from the conjugal affections, we have, in truth, two loves, each of them as strong as any affection can be, or ought to be, consistently with the performance of our duty, and the love we bear to our neighbour. Then, by the former preceding the latter, the latter is rendered more pure, more even, and more constant: the wife has already learned the discipline of pure love in the character of a sister, she has already benefited by the discipline of private life, how to yield, how to command and how to influence. To all this are to be added the beautiful gradations of attachment which distinguish human nature;—from sister to wife, from wife to child, to uncle, cousin, one of our kin, one of our blood, our mere neighbour, our county-man, or our countryman.

The bad effects of this want of variety of orders, this graceful subordination in the character of attachment, I have often observed in Italy and other countries, where the young are kept secluded, from their neighbours and families— all closely imprisoned within the same wall, til the time when they are let out of their cages, before they have learnt to fly—without experience, aided by no kind feeling, and detesting the control which had kept them from enjoying the 'full hubbub of licence'.[216]

The question is, how have nature and Providence secured these blessings to us? In this way:—that the affections in general become those which urge us to leave the paternal nest. We arrive at a definite time of life, and feel passions which invite us to enter into the world; and that new feeling assuredly coalesces with a new object. Suppose we have a vivid feeling which is new to us: that feeling will more assuredly combine with an external object, which is likewise vivid from novelty, than it would do with a familiar one.

To this may be added the variation which seems to have acted very strongly in rude ages, concerning any thing common to us and to the animal creation. Likewise the desire to keep up the bond of relationship in families which had emigrated from the patriarchal seed. All these circumstances would render the marriage of brother and sister unfrequent, and this would produce in those simple ages an ominous feeling: some tradition might assist this sentiment; and, for aught we know, there might be some law preserved in the Temple of Isis, and from thence obtained by the Patriarchs, from whence arose the horror attached to such connections. This horror once felt, once propagated, the present state of feeling on the subject is easily explained.

Children as early begin to talk of marriage as of death, from attending a wedding, or following a funeral: a new young visitor is introduced to the family, and from association they soon think of the

---

[216] Perhaps a reference to the Satyrs' orgy in the third book of the *Faerie Queene*, characterised by its sexual license and 'shrieking hubbubs' (*Faerie Queene* 3.10.43).

conjugal connection. If a child tell his parent that he wishes to marry his sister, he is immediately checked by the stern look, and he is shown the impossibility of such a union. The controlling glance of the parental eye is often more effectual, than any form of words that could be employed; and in mature years a mere look often prevails where exhortation would have failed. As to infants, they are told that it could not be so; and perhaps the best security of moral feeling arises from a supposed necessity. Thus ignorant persons recoil from the thought of any thing because it never has been done, and has been represented as not to be done.

The individual has by this time learned the greatest and best knowledge of the human mind—that we are in ourselves imperfect; and another truth of perhaps equal importance—that there exists in nature a possibility of uniting two beings, each identified in their nature, but distinguished in their separate qualities, so that each should retain what distinguishes them, and at the same time acquire the qualities of that which is contradistinguished to them. This is perhaps the most beautiful part of our nature:—the man loses not the manly character: he does not become less brave or less determined to go through fire and water, were it necessary, in consequence of love: rather say, he becomes far more so. He then begins to feel the beginnings of his moral nature: he then feels the perfectibility of his nature. All the grand and sublime thoughts of a more improved state of being dawn upon him: he can acquire the patience of woman, which in him becomes fortitude: the beauty of the female character, which in him will become a desire to display what is noble and dignified. In short, he will do what in nature is only done by the blue sky of Heaven: the female will unite the beautiful with the sublime, and the male the sublime with the beautiful.

Shakespeare throughout the whole of his plays has evidently conceived the subject of love in this dignified light: he has conceived it not only with moral grandeur, but with philosophical penetration. The mind of man searches for some object to assist it in its perfection, which shall assist him; and he also shall give his assistance in completing their moral nature. These thoughts will occupy many serious moments: imagination will accumulate on imagination, until at length some object shall attract the notice of his mind, and until at last the whole of the weight of his feelings shall be directed to this object.

Who shall say this is not love? Here is system; here are associations, here are strong feelings natural to us as men, and they are attached to one object:—who shall say it is not love? Assuredly not the being himself; assuredly no other than He who knows all things.

Shakespeare has therefore described Romeo as in love with Rosaline, and so completely in love that he declares,

> When the devout religion of mine eye
> Maintains such falsehood, then turn tears to fires;
> And these, who, often drown'd, could never die,
> Transparent heretics, be burnt for liars.
> One fairer than my love? the all-seeing sun
> Ne'er saw her match since first the world begin.[217]

In this full feeling of confidence Romeo is brought to Capulet's, as it were by accident: he sees Juliet, instantly becomes the heretic, and commences the fulness of attachment which forms the subject of the tragedy. Surely Shakespeare the philosopher, the grand Poet who combined truth with beauty and beauty with truth, never could have dreamed that it was a mode of interesting the affections of his audience, by making his Romeo a mere weathercock, who having seen one woman, became the victim of melancholy, eating away his own heart, *concentering* all his hopes and fears in this form, in an instant changes, and falls as madly in love with another being. Shakespeare surely must have meant something more than this, and Romeo tells us what it was. He says that he had a different feeling towards Juliet from that he had towards Rosaline. He adds that Rosaline was the object to which his overbuilt heart attached itself; that our imperfect nature, in proportion as our ideas are vivid, seeks after something in which they may appear realised.

As men of genius, conscious of their own weakness, are ready to believe persons whom they meet, the modes of perfection, when, in truth, they are worse than themselves: they have formed an ideal in their minds, and they want to see it realised; they want it something more than shadowy thought. Their own consciousness of imperfection makes it impossible for them to attach it to themselves: but in the first man they meet, they only see what is good, and they have no conjecture of his imperfections, and they fall down and adore, almost, one greatly inferior to themselves.

Such is frequently the case in the friendships of men or genius and still more frequently in the first loves of ardent feelings and strong imaginations; but still for a man, having had the experience, without any inward feeling demonstrating the difference, to change one object for another seems without example. But it is perfectly according with life: in a life of such various events, such a shifting of scenes, and such

---

[217] *Romeo and Juliet*, I, ii, 88–93.

a change of personages, we may have mistaken in thinking that he or she was what in truth he or she was not; we may have suffered unnecessary pangs, and have felt idly-directed hopes, and then a being may arise who has more resemblance to our ideal. We know we loved the former with purity, and yet it was not what we now feel. Our own mind tells us that the former was but the yearning after the object; in the latter we have found the object correspondent to the idea we had formed.[218]

The same thing arises in every circumstance of taste. What is meant by taste? The inward faculties make a demand. There is a feeling in every man. There is deviation, and he knows it, between that which is common to all mankind and that which individualizes him. Other passions distort whatever object is presented to them. Lear accused the elements of ingratitude,[219] and the madman imagined the straws on

---

[218] Collier's transcript ends at this point with a footnote: 'Here my original notes abruptly break off: the brochure in which I had inserted them was full, and I took another for the conclusion of the Lecture, which is unfortunately lost.' The remainder of the present account is adapted from the summary of the conclusion of the lecture as reported in the *Morning Chronicle* (13 December 1811), rewritten to make it stylistically coherent with the earlier sections. Foakes (CC 5:1, 337) laments that Collier's lost text constitutes 'a substantial part of the lecture'; but I would estimate probably no more than two pages are irrecoverable from the whole. The original text of the *Morning Chronicle*, upon which this restoration is based, is as follows: 'The Lecturer went on to notice the analogy between the operations of the mind with regard to taste and love, as with the former an ideal had been created which the reason was anxious to realise. Other passions distort whatever object is presented to them. Lear accused the elements of ingratitude, and the madman imagined the straws on which he trampled the golden pavement of a palace; but, with love, every thing was in harmony, and all produced natural and delightful associations. In Mr. Coleridge's opinion the conceits put into the mouths of Romeo and Juliet were perfectly natural to their age and inexperience. It was Shakespeare's intention in this play to represent love as existing rather in the imagination than the feelings, as was shown by the imaginative dialogue between the hero and heroine, in the parting scene in the third act. The passion in the youthful Romeo was wholly different from that of the deliberate Othello, who entered the marriage state with deep moral reflections on its objects and consequences. The Lecturer insisted that love was an act of will, and ridiculed the sickly nonsense of Sterne and his imitators, French and English, who maintained that it was an involuntary emotion. Mr Coleridge concluded by referring to Shakespeare's description of the Apothecary, too often quoted against those of unfortunate physiognomy, or those depressed by poverty. Shakespeare meant much more: he intended to convey that in every man's face there was either to be found a history or a prophecy: a history of struggles past or a prophecy of events to come. In contemplating the face of the most abandoned of mankind, many lineaments of villainy would be seen, yet in the under features (if he might so express himself) would be traced the lines that former sufferings and struggles had impressed, which would always sadden and frequently soften the observer, and raise a determination in him not to despair, but to regard the unfortunate object with the feelings of a brother.'

[219] Rather pointedly, mad Lear does not actually accuse the storm of ingratitude: 'Nor rain, wind, thunder, fire, are my daughters:/I tax not you, you elements, with

which he trampled the golden pavement of a palace; but, with love, every thing was in harmony, and all produced natural and delightful associations. It is my opinion that the conceits put into the mouths of Romeo and Juliet are perfectly natural to their age and inexperience. It was Shakespeare's intention in this play to represent love as existing rather in the *imagination* than the feelings, as was shown by the imaginative dialogue between the hero and heroine, in the parting scene in the third act.

> *Juliet*: Wilt thou be gone? it is not yet near day:
> It was the nightingale, and not the lark,
> That pierced the fearful hollow of thine ear;
> Nightly she sings on yon pomegranate-tree:
> Believe me, love, it was the nightingale.
>
> *Romeo*: It was the lark, the herald of the morn,
> No nightingale: look, love, what envious streaks
> Do lace the severing clouds in yonder east:
> Night's candles are burnt out, and jocund day
> Stands tiptoe on the misty mountain tops.
> I must be gone and live, or stay and die.
>
> *Juliet*: Yon light is not day-light, I know it, I:
> It is some meteor that the sun exhales,
> To be to thee this night a torch-bearer,
> And light thee on thy way to Mantua:
> Therefore stay yet; thou need'st not to be gone.
>
> *Romeo*: Let me be ta'en, let me be put to death;
> I am content, so thou wilt have it so.
> I'll say yon grey is not the morning's eye,
> 'Tis but the pale reflex of Cynthia's brow;
> Nor that is not the lark, whose notes do beat
> The vaulty heaven so high above our heads:
> I have more care to stay than will to go:
> Come, death, and welcome! Juliet wills it so.
> How is't, my soul? let's talk; it is not day.[220]

---

unkindness;/I never gave you kingdom, call'd you children,/You owe me no subscription' (*King Lear*, III, ii, 5–18). Either Coleridge is imprecise here, or his comments have been misreported.
[220] *Romeo and Juliet*, III, v, 1–25.

The passion in the youthful Romeo is wholly different from that of
the deliberate Othello, who enters the marriage state with deep moral
reflections on its objects and consequences.

> Vouch with me, heaven, I therefore beg it not,
> To please the palate of my appetite,
> Nor to comply with heat—the young affects
> In me defunct—and proper satisfaction.
> But to be free and bounteous to her mind.[221]

Love is an act of will, not appetite; the sickly nonsense of Sterne and
his imitators, French and English, who maintain that it is an involuntary emotion merits only ridicule.[222]

I conclude by referring to Shakespeare's description of the
Apothecary, too often quoted against those of unfortunate physiognomy, or those depressed by poverty.

> And hereabouts he dwells,—which late I noted
> In tatter'd weeds, with overwhelming brows,
> Culling of simples; meagre were his looks,
> Sharp misery had worn him to the bones:[223]

Shakespeare meant much more: he intended to convey that in every
man's face there was either to be found a history or a prophecy: a
history of struggles past or a prophecy of events to come. In contemplating the face of the most abandoned of mankind, many lineaments
of villainy will be seen, yet in the under features (if I might so express
myself) will be traced the lines that former sufferings and struggles
have impressed, which will always sadden and frequently soften the
observer, and raise a determination in him not to despair, but to
regard the unfortunate object with the feelings of a brother.

---

[221] *Othello*, I, iii, 262–6.
[222] Probably a reference to Sterne's *Journal to Eliza* (1767), in effect a love letter to the
titular figure: 'Reader, whosoe'er thou art, forgive me this involuntary emotion. Let
my mind dwell upon Eliza!' (This was posthumously published. See for example
The European Magazine and London Review, 5 (1784), 172.) An example of the 'French
school' of which Coleridge disapproved might be Françoise de Graffigny's very popular romance *Lettres d'une Péruvienne* (Paris: Dushesne, 1747), whose protagonist falls
helplessly in love ('How weak am I, my dear Celina! Have I need of your assistance to
fortify my reason against an involuntary passion!' 'Letters of a Peruvian Princess', *The
Novelist's Magazine*, 9 (1782) 56).
[223] *Romeo and Juliet*, V, i, 38–41.

LECTURE 9

It is a known but unexplained phenomenon, that among the ancients statuary rose to such a degree of perfection, as almost to baffle the hope of imitating it, and mingled with despair at excelling it; while painting, at the same period, notwithstanding the admiration bestowed upon the ancient paintings of Apelles by Pliny[224] and others, has been proved to be an excellence of much later growth, and to have fallen far short of Statuary. I remember a man,[225] equally admirable for his talents and his rank, pointing to a sign-post, and saying that had Titian never lived, the richness of representation by colour, even there, could never have been existed. In that mechanical branch of painting, perspective, the ancients were equally deficient, as was proved by the discoveries at Herculaneum and the Palace of Nero,[226] in which such blunders were to be found, as to render plausible the assertions of those who have maintained that the ancients were wholly ignorant of it. That they were not totally destitute of it is proved by Vitruvius in the introduction to his second book.[227]

Something of the same kind appears to have been the case with regard to their dramas. Early in the lectures, I noticed how the Greek Stage has been imitated by the French, and by writers of England since the reign of Charles II. The scheme admits of nothing more than the change of a single note, and excludes that which is the true principle of life–the attaining of the same end by an infinite variety of means.

It is true that the writings of Shakespeare are not likenesses of the Greek: they are analogies, because by very different means they

---

[224] Pliny's praise for the fourth century BC painter Apelles of Cos is to be found in his *Natural History*, 35.

[225] In all likelihood this is Sir George Howland Beaumont 7th Baronet (1753–1827), aristocratic friend of Coleridge and patron of the arts.

[226] The Roman town of Herculaneum was buried in volcanic ash by the eruption of Vesuvius in AD 79. The first modern excavation of the site was in 1738, and several more followed throughout the eighteenth century. Nero's palace was at Rome, and had been demolished by Vespasian, although some of its paintings survive.

[227] Vitruvius's ten-book *De architectura* is the classic account of Roman architecture theory and practice. Book 2 is actually concerned with building materials. The visual arts are covered in book 7.

produce the same end; whereas the greater part of the French tragedies, and the English plays on the same plan cannot be called likenesses, but may be called the failing of the same end by adopting the
same means under most unappropriate circumstances.

I have thus been led to consider, that the ancient drama (meaning
the works of Aeschylus, Euripides, and Sophocles, for the miserable
rhetorical works by the Romans are scarcely to be mentioned as dramatic poems) might be contrasted with the Shakespearean drama.–I
call it Shakespearean, because I know of no other writer who has realised the same idea, although I am told that the Spanish poet Calderon,
has been equally successful.[228] The Shakespearean drama and the
Greek drama may be compared to painting and statuary. In the latter,
as in the Greek drama, the characters must be few, because the very
essence of statuary is a high degree of abstraction, which prevents
a great many figures from being combined in the same effects. In a
grand group of Niobe, or in any other ancient heroic subject, how disgusting it would appear were an old nurse introduced. The numbers
must be circumscribed, and nothing undignified must be brought in
company with what is dignified: no one personage must be brought
but what is abstraction: all must not be presented to the eye but the
effect of multitude must be produced without the introduction of any
thing discordant.

Compare this small group with a picture by Raphael or Titian, in
which an immense number of figures may be introduced, even a dog,
a cat or a beggar; and from the very circumstance of a less degree of
labour, and a less degree of abstraction, an effect is produced equally
harmonious to the mind, more true to nature, and in all respects but
one, superior to statuary,–the perfect satisfaction in a thing as a work
of art. The man of taste feels satisfied with what out of his mixed
nature he cannot produce, and to that which the reason conceives
possible, a momentary reality is given, by the aid of imagination.

I need not here repeat what I have said before, regarding the circumstances which permitted Shakespeare to make an alteration so
suitable to his age, and so necessitated by the condition of the age. I
need not again remind you of the distortion of the human voice by
the size of the ancient theatres, and the attempt introduced of making
everything on the stage appear reality; the difference between an
imitation and a likeness is the mixture of a greater number of circumstances of dissimilarity; an imitation differs from a copy, precisely as

[228] The famous Spanish playwright Pedro Calderón de la Barca (1600–81). Coleridge
probably found the favourable comparison of Calderón with Shakespeare in Schlegel.

sameness differs from likeness, in that sense of the word in which we imply a difference conjoined with that sameness.

Shakespeare had likewise many advantages. The great of that time, instead of throwing round them the *chevaux de frise*[229] of mere manners, endeavoured to distinguish themselves by attainments, by energy of thought, and consequent powers of mind. The stage had nothing but curtains for its scenes, and the actor, as well as the author, were obliged to appeal to the imagination, and not to the senses, which gave the latter a power over space and time, which in an ancient theatre would have been absurd, simply because it was contradictory. The advantage is indeed vastly on the side of the modern: he appeals to the imagination, to the reason, and to the noblest powers of the human heart; he is above the iron compulsion of space and time, he appeals to that which we most wish to be, when we are most worthy of being, while the ancient drama binds us down to the meanest part of our nature, and its chief compensation is a simple acquiescence of the mind, that what the Poet has represented might possibly have taken place—a poor compliment to a Poet, who is to be a creator, to tell him, that he has all the excellencies of a historian.

In dramatic composition the unities of time and place so narrow the space of action, and so impoverish the sources of pleasure, that of all the Athenian dramas there is scarcely one which has not fallen into absurdity by aiming at an object, and failing; or which has not incurred greater absurdity by bringing events into a space of time in which it is impossible for them to have happened; not to mention that the grandest effect of the dramatist—to be the mirror of life—is completely lost.

The limit allowed by the Greeks was twenty-four hours; but we might as well take twenty-four months, because it has already become an object of imagination. The mind is then acted upon by such strong stimulants, that the one and the other are indifferent; when once the limit of possibility is passed, there are no bounds which can be assigned to imagination. We soon find that such effects may arise from other causes. Above all, in reading Shakespeare, we should first consider in what plays he means to appeal to the reason, or imagination, faculties which have no relation to time and place, excepting as in the one case they imply a succession of cause and effect, and in the other they form a harmonious picture, so that the impulse given by the reason is carried on by the imagination.

---

[229] Portable frames, usually of wood, set with many projecting spikes and spears that functioned as anti-cavalry defensive measures on a battlefield.

Shakespeare was often spoken of as a Child of Nature, and many had been his imitators, who attempted to copy real incidents; and some of them had not even genius enough to copy nature, but still they produced a sort of phenomenon of modern times neither tragic nor comic, nor tragicomic, but the sentimental. This sort of writing consists in taking some very affecting incidents, which in its highest excellence only aspired to the genius of an onion,—the power of drawing tears; and in which the author, acting like a ventriloquist, distributes his own insipidity. I have seen plays, some translated and some the growth of our own soil, so well acted, and so ill written, that if I could have produced an artificial deafness, I should have been pleased with that performance as a pantomime.

Shakespeare's characters, from Othello and Macbeth down to Dogberry,[230] are ideal. They are not the things but the abstracts of the things, which a great mind may take into itself, and naturalises to its own heaven. In the character of Dogberry itself some important truths are conveyed, or some admirable allusion is made to some folly reigning at the time, which the poet saw must for ever reign.

The enlightened readers of Shakespeare may be divided into two classes:—

1. Those who read with feeling and understanding;
2. Those who, without affecting to understand or criticise, merely feel, and are recipients of the poet's power.

Between the two no medium can be endured. The reader often feels that some ideal trait of our own is caught, or some nerve has been touched of which he was not before aware, and it is proved that it has been touched by the vibration that we feel a sort of thrilling, which tells us that we know ourselves better for it.

In the plays of Shakespeare every man sees himself, without knowing that he sees himself as in the phenomena of nature, in the mist of the mountain, the traveller beholds his own figure, but the glory round the head distinguishes it from a mere vulgar copy. Or as a man traversing the Brocken, in the north of Germany, at sunrise, when the glorious beams are shot askance, and he sees before him a figure of gigantic proportions, and of such elevated dignity, that he only knows it to be himself by the similarity of action.[231] Or as the the Fata

---

[230] Dogberry is the comically pompous night constable from *Much Ado About Nothing*, much given to malapropism.

[231] Coleridge had visited Brocken in 1799, and observed this phenomenon first hand. His poem 'Constancy to an Ideal Object' (written perhaps in 1801) makes reference to it: 'as when/The woodman winding westward up the glen . . . Sees full before him, gliding

Morgana at Messina, in which all forms, at determined distances, are presented in an invisible mist, dressed in all the gorgeous colours of prismatic imagination and with magic harmony uniting them and producing a beautiful whole in the mind of the spectator.[232]

It is rather humiliating to find that, since Shakespeare's time none of our critics seem to enter into his peculiarities. I will not now dwell upon this point, because it is my intention to devote a lecture more immediately to the prefaces of Pope and Johnson. Some of Shakespeare's contemporaries appear to have understood him, and in a way that does him no small honour; moderns in their prefaces praise him as a great genius, but when they come to their judgements on his plays, they treat him like a schoolboy. Nearly all they can do is to express the most vulgar of all feelings, wonderment. They maintain that Shakespeare is an irregular poet, that he was now above all praise, and now if possible below all contempt; and they reconcile it by saying that he wrote for the mob. But no man of genius ever wrote for the mob. He never would consciously write that which was below himself: careless he might be, or he might write at a time when his better genius did not attend him; but he never wrote any thing that he knew would degrade him. Were it so, as well might a man pride himself on acting the beast, or a Catalani, because she did not feel in the mood to sing, begin to bray![233]

Yesterday afternoon a friend left for me a work by a German writer, of which I have only had time to read a small part;[234] but what I did read I approved, and I should be disposed to praise the book much

without tread,/An image with a glory round its head;/The enamoured rustic worships its fair hues,/Nor knows he makes the shadow, he pursues!'

[232] The 'Fata Morgana' is a species of aerial mirage particularly associated with the Italian Strait of Messina: 'that remarkable aerial phaenomenon, called the *Fata Morgana*, or *Fairy Morgana*, is sometimes observed from the harbour Messina, and adjacent places . . . when the weather is calm, there rises above the great current, a vapour, which acquires a certain density, so as to form in the atmosphere horizontal prisms [that] reflect and represent successively, for some time, like a moveable mirror, the objects on the coast, or in the adjacent country: they exhibit by turns the city and suburbs of Messina, trees, animals, men and mountains ; they are really beautiful aerial moving pictures' ('Plate XI', *Naval Chronicle*, 17 (1807) 311).

[233] Angelica Catalini (1780–1849) was an Italian soprano whose fame was Europe-wide. Collier's shorthand notes are perfectly clear here, but as a puzzled Foakes notes in CC 5:1, 353 footnote, he omitted the reference to Catalini in *Seven Lectures*, garbled the transcription of his own transcription and added a bewildering footnote.

[234] *Über dramatische Kunst und Literatur* (3 vols, 1809–11), the published version of the lectures on drama delivered by August Wilhelm (later: von) Schlegel (1767–1845) at Vienna in 1808. The question of how much Coleridge took from Schlegel has been much discussed; accordingly the date at which he first read these lectures is important. Coleridge wrote to Henry Crabb Robinson on 6 November 1811 expressing a wish to read 'Schlegel's Werke'. The friend, mentioned here, who supplied the volumes, was

more highly, were it not that in truth I should be thereby praising myself, as the sentiments contained in it are so coincident with those I had expressed at the Royal Institution.[235] It is not a little wonderful, that so many ages have elapsed since the time of Shakespeare, and that it should remain for foreigners first to feel truly, and to appreciate properly, his mighty genius. The solution of this fact must be sought in the history of the nation: the English have become a busy commercial people, and have unquestionably derived from this many advantages moral and physical: we have grown into a mighty nation—one of the giant nations of the world, whose moral superiority still enables us to struggle with the other, the evil genius of the planet.[236]

The German nations, on the other hand, unable to act at all, have been driven into speculation: all the feelings have been forced back into the thinking and reasoning mind. To do was impossible for them, but in determining what ought to be done, they perhaps exceed every people of the globe. Incapable of acting outwardly, they have acted internally. They first rationally recalled the ancient philosophy; they acted upon their own spirits to work with an energy of which England produces no parallel, since those truly heroic times in body and soul, the days of Elizabeth.

If all that has been written upon Shakespeare by Englishmen were burned, for want of candles, merely to read half of the works of Shakespeare, we should be gainers. Providence has given us the greatest man that ever lived, and has thrown a sop to Envy by giving us the worst critics upon him. His contemporaries were not so insensible; a poem of the highest merit had been addressed to him, and I know nowhere where a more full description, or contradistinguishing of great genius, could be found than in this poem. It is as follows:—

> A mind reflecting ages past, whose clear
> And equal surface can make things appear,
> Distant a thousand years, and represent
> Them in their lively colours, just extent:
> To outrun hasty time, retrieve the fates,
> Roll back the heavens, blow ope the iron gates
> Of death and Lethe, where confused lie
> Great heaps of ruinous mortality:

the German Bernard Krusve, and the implication here is that they were delivered to S. T. C. the day before this (16 December 1811) lecture.

[235] In 1808.

[236] Napoleon, who defeated Prussia and Saxony at the twin battles of Jena and Auerstedt (1806), afterwards incorporating most of Germany into the French Empire.

In that deep dusky dungeon to discern
A royal ghost from churls; by art to learn
The physiognomy of shades, and give
Them sudden birth, wondering how oft they live;
What story coldly tells, what poets feign
At second hand, and picture without brain,
Senseless and soul-less shows: to give a stage
(Ample and true with life) voice, action, age,
As Plato's year, and new scene of the world,
Them unto us, or us to them had hurl'd:
To raise our ancient sovereigns from their herse,
Make kings his subjects; by exchanging verse,
Enlive their pale trunks; that the present age
Joys at their joy, and trembles at their rage:
Yet so to temper passion, that our ears
Take pleasure in their pain, and eyes in tears
Both weep and smile; fearful at plots so sad,
Then laughing at our fear; abus'd, and glad
To be abus'd; affected with that truth
Which we perceive is false, pleas'd in that ruth
At which we start, and, by elaborate play,
Tortur'd and tickl'd; by a crab-like way
Time past made pastime, and in ugly sort
Disgorging up his ravin for our sport:–
–While the plebeian imp, from lofty throne,
Creates and rules a world, and works upon
Mankind by secret engines; now to move
A chilling pity, then a rigorous love;
To strike up and stroke down, both joy and ire
To steer th' affections; and by heavenly fire
Mold us anew, stol'n from ourselves:–
This, and much more, which cannot be express'd
But by himself, his tongue, and his own breast,
Was Shakespeare's freehold; which his cunning brain
Improv'd by favour of the nine-fold train;
The buskin'd muse, the comick queen, the grand
And louder tone of Clio, nimble hand
And nimbler foot of the melodious pair,
The silver-voiced lady, the most fair
Calliope, whose speaking silence daunts,
And she whose praise the heavenly body chants;
These jointly woo'd him, envying one another;

(Obey'd by all as spouse, but lov'd as brother)
And wrought a curious robe, of sable grave,
Fresh green, and pleasant yellow, red most brave,
And constant blue, rich purple, guiltless white,
The lowly russet, and the scarlet bright;
Branch'd and embroider'd like the painted spring;
Each leaf match'd with a flower, and each string
Of golden wire, each line of silk: there run
Italian works, whose thread the sisters spun;
And these did sing, or seem to sing, the choice
Birds of a foreign note and various voice:
Here hangs a mossy rock; there plays a fair
But chiding fountain, purled: not the air,
Nor clouds, nor thunder, but were living drawn;
Not out of common tiffany or lawn,
But fine materials, which the Muses know,
And only know the countries where they grow.
Now, when they could no longer him enjoy,
In mortal garments pent,—death may destroy,
They say, his body; but his verse shall live,
And more than nature takes our hands shall give:
In a less volume, but more strongly bound,
Shakespeare shall breathe and speak; with laurel crown'd,
Which never fades; fed with ambrosian meat,
In a well-lined vesture, rich, and neat.
So with this robe they cloathe him, bid him wear it;
For time shall never stain, nor envy tear it.[237]

Never was any thing so characteristic of Shakespeare, more happily expressed.

It is a mistake to suppose that any of Shakespeare's characters strike us as portraits: they have the union of reason perceiving, of judgment recording, actual facts, and the imagination diffusing over all a magic glory, and while it records the past, projects in a wonderful degree the future, and makes us feel, however slightly, and see, however dimly, that state of being in which there is neither past nor future, but all is permanent and is the very energy of nature.

---

[237] In *Seven Lectures* Collier adds a note to observe that this dedicatory poem from the Second Folio (1632) was signed with the initials 'J.M.S.', and to speculate that it may have been by 'John Milton, Student'. Modern scholarship assigns it to Jasper Mayne (1694–1772).

Although I have affirmed that all Shakespeare's characters are ideal, and the result of his own meditation, yet a just division may be made of those in which the ideal is most prominent to the mind—where it is brought forward more intentionally—where we are made more conscious of the ideal, though in truth they possess no more nor less reality; and secondly of those which, though equally idealised, the delusion upon the mind is of their being real. Shakespeare's plays may be separated into those where the real is disguised in the ideal, and those where the ideal is hidden from us in the real. The difference is made by the different powers of mind, which the poet chiefly appeals to.

At present I shall only speak of those plays where the ideal is predominant; and chiefly for this reason—that those plays have been objected to with the greatest violence. The objections are not the growth of our own country, but the production of France: the judgment of monkeys, by some wonderful phenomenon, put into the mouths of men.[238] We are told by these creatures that Shakespeare is some wonderful monster, in which many heterogeneous components were thrown together, producing a discordant mass of genius and irregularity of gigantic proportions.

Among the ideal plays, I will take *The Tempest*, by way of example. Many others might be mentioned, but it is impossible to go through every piece, and what I say on *The Tempest* will apply to all.

In this play Shakespeare has appealed to the imagination, and he has constructed a plan according to it: the scheme of his drama does not appeal to any sensuous impression (the word 'sensuous' is authorised by Milton)[239] of time and place, but to the imagination, and it will be recollected that his works were rather recited than acted.

In the first scene was introduced a mere confusion on board a ship. The lowest characters are brought together with the highest, and with what excellence! A great part of the genius of Shakespeare consists of these happy combinations of the highest and the lowest, and of the

---

[238] In the preface to his tragedy *Irène* (1778) Voltaire dismisses Shakespeare as 'ni comme un dieu, ni comme un singe', neither God nor monkey, but a barbarian ('tout barbare'), a drunken savage capable of moments of splendour. Schlegel gives an account of Voltaire's hostility, which may be where Coleridge encountered it.

[239] 'Authorised' in the sense that Milton uses it, which indeed he does, in *Of Education* (1644). In Chapter 10 of the *Biographia Literaria* Coleridge expands upon why he liked this Miltonism: 'Thus to express in one word all that appertains to the perception, considered as passive and merely recipient, I have adopted from our elder classics the word *sensuous*; because *sensual* is not at present used, except in a bad sense, or at least as a moral distinction; while *sensitive* and *sensible* would each convey a different meaning. Thus too have I followed Hooker, Sanderson, Milton and others.'

gayest and the saddest. He is not droll in one scene and melancholy in the other, but both the one and the other in the same scene. Laughter is made to swell the tear of sorrow, and to throw, as it were, a poetic light upon it, and the tear mixes a tenderness with the laughter that succeeds. Shakespeare has shown that power, which above all other men he possessed, that of introducing the profoundest sentiments of wisdom, just where they would be least expected, and yet where they are truly natural; and the admirable secret of his drama is, that the separate speeches do not appear to be produced the one by the former, but to arise out of the peculiar character of the speaker.

Before I go further, I may take the opportunity of explaining what is meant by mechanic and organic regularity. In the former the copy must be made as if it had been formed in the same mould with the original; in the latter there is a law which all the parts obey, conforming themselves to the outward symbols and manifestations of the essential principle. If we look to the growth of trees, which by the peculiar circumstances of soil, air, or position differ in shape even from trees of the same kind; but every man is able to decide at first sight which was an ash, or poplar.

This is the case with Shakespeare: he shows us the life and principle of the being with organic regularity. Thus the Boatswain, in the storm, when a sense of danger impresses all and the bonds of reverence are thrown off, gives a loose to his feelings, and thus to the old Counsellor pours forth his vulgar mind:–'Hence! What care these roarers for the name of King? To cabin: silence! trouble us not.'[240]

Gonzalo observes–'Good; yet remember whom thou hast aboard.' The Boatswain replies–'None that I more love than myself. You are a counsellor: if you can command these elements to silence, and work the peace of the present, we will not hand a rope more; use your authority: if you cannot, give thanks that you have lived so long, and make yourself ready in your cabin for the mischance of the hour, if it so hap.–Cheerly, good hearts!–Out of our way, I say.'

An ordinary dramatist would, after this speech, have introduced Gonzalo moralising, or saying something connected with it; for common dramatists are not men of genius: they connect their ideas by association, or by logical connection; but the vital writer in a moment transports himself into the very being of each character, and, instead of making artificial puppets, he brings the real being before us. Gonzalo replies therefore,–'I have great comfort from this fellow: methinks, he hath no drowning mark upon him; his complexion is

[240]   *The Tempest,* I, i, 16f.

perfect gallows. Stand fast, good fate, to his hanging! make the rope of his destiny our cable, for our own doth little advantage. If he be not born to be hanged, our case is miserable.'

Here is the true sailor proud of his contempt of danger, and the high feeling of the old man, who, instead of condescending to reply to the words addressed to him, turns off and meditates with himself, and draws some feeling of comfort to his own mind, by trifling with his face, founding upon it a hope of safety.

Shakespeare had determined to make the plot of this play such as to involve a certain number of low characters, and at the beginning of the piece pitched the note of the whole. It was evidently brought in as a lively mode of telling a story, and the reader is prepared for something to be developed, and in the next scene he brings forward Prospero and Miranda.

How is it done? By first introducing his favourite character, Miranda by a sentence which at once expresses the vehemence and violence of the storm, such as it might appear to a witness from the land, and at the same time displays the tenderness of her feelings:–the exquisite feelings of a female brought up in a desert, yet with all the advantages of education, all that could be given by a wise, learned and affection- ate father. With all the powers of mind not weakened by the combats of life. Miranda exclaims:–

> O! I have suffered
> With those that I saw suffer: a brave vessel,
> Who had, *no doubt*, some noble creatures in her,
> Dash'd all to pieces.[241]

The doubt here expressed could have occurred to no mind but to that of Miranda, who had been bred up with her father and a Monster only: she did not know, as others do, what sort of creatures were in a ship; they never would have introduced it as a conjecture. This shows, that while Shakespeare is displaying his vast excellence, he never fails to introduce some touch or other, which not only makes the scene characteristic of the peculiar person, but combines two things–the person, and the circumstances that acted upon the person. She proceeds:–

> O–the cry did knock
> Against my very heart. Poor souls! they perish'd.
> Had I been any God of power, I would

---

[241] *The Tempest*, I, ii, 5–8.

Have sunk the sea within the earth, or e'er
It should the good ship so have swallow'd, and
The fraughting souls within her.[242]

Still dwelling on that which was most wanting in her nature—these fellow creatures from whom she appeared banished, with only one relict to keep them alive, not in her memory, but in her imagination.

Another instance of excellent judgment, for I am now principally adverting to that, is the *preparation*. Prospero is introduced, first in his magic robe, which, with the assistance of his daughter, he removes, and it is the first time the reader knows as a being possessing supernatural powers. Then he instructs his daughter in the story of their arrival in the island, and it is done in such a manner, that the reader never conjectures the technical use the poet has made of the relation, viz. informing the audience of the story. The next step is that Prospero gives warning, that he means, for particular purposes, to lull Miranda to sleep; and thus he exhibits his first and mildest proof of his magical power. It is not as in vulgar plays where a person is introduced that nobody knows or cares any thing about, merely to let the audience into the secret. Prospero then lulls his daughter asleep, by the sleep stops the relation at the very moment when it was necessary to break it off, in order to excite curiosity, and yet to give the memory and understanding sufficient to carry on the progress of the fable uninterruptedly.

Here I cannot help noticing a fine touch of Shakespeare's knowledge of human nature, and generally of the great laws of the mind: I mean Miranda's infant remembrance. Prospero asks her

Canst thou remember
A time before we came unto this cell?
I do not think thou canst, for then thou wast not
Out three years old.[243]

Miranda answers,

Certainly, sir, I can.

Prospero inquires,

By what? by any other house or person?
Of any thing the image tell me, that
Hath kept with thy remembrance.

---

[242] *The Tempest*, I, ii, 8–13.
[243] *The Tempest*, I, ii, 38f.

To which Miranda returns,

> 'Tis far off;
> And rather like a dream than an assurance
> That my remembrance warrants. Had I not
> Four or five women once, that tended me?

This is exquisite! In general, our remembrances of life arise from vivid colours, especially if we have seen them in motion: persons when grown up, for instance, will remember a bright green door, seen when they were young; but in Miranda, who was somewhat older, it was by four or five women. She might know men from her father, and her remembrance of the past might be worn out by the present object, but women she only knew by herself, by the contemplation of her own figure in the fountain, and yet she recalled to her mind what had been. It was not, that she saw such and such Grandees, or such and such peeresses, but she remembered to have seen something like the reflection of herself: but it was not herself, and it brought back to her mind what she had seen most like herself. It was a constant yearning of fancy re-producing the past, of what she had only seen in herself, and could only see in herself.

In my opinion the picturesque power displayed by Shakespeare, of all the poets that ever lived, is only equalled by Milton and Dante. The power of genius is not shown in elaborating a picture, of which many specimens are given in poems of modern date, where the work is so *dutchified*[244] by minute touches, that the reader naturally asks why words, and not painting, are used? I know a young lady of much taste, who in reading the versifications of voyages and travels that had been published observed that by a sort of instinct, she always cast her eyes on the opposite page, for coloured prints.

The power of poetry is, by a single word to produce that energy in the mind, as compels the imagination to produce the picture. Thus when Prospero says,

> One midnight,
> Fated to the purpose, did Antonio open
> The gates of Milan; and i' the dead of darkness,
> The ministers for the purpose hurried thence
> Me, and thy crying self.[245]

---

[244] After the manner of Dutch realist painting: Coleridge expanded upon this point in Lecture 3, above.

[245] *The Tempest*, I, ii, 128–32.

Thus, by introducing a simple happy epithet, *crying* in the last line, a complete picture is present to the mind, and in this the power of true poetry consists.

In reference to preparation, it will be observed that the storm, and all that precedes the tale, as well as the tale itself, serve completely to develope the main character and the intention of Prospero. The fact of Miranda being charmed asleep fits us for what goes beyond our ordinary belief, and gradually leads us to the appearance and disclosure of a being gifted with supernatural powers.

Before the introduction of Ariel too, the reader was prepared by what preceded; the moral feeling called forth by the sweet words of Miranda,

> Alack; what trouble
> Was I then to you!

in which she considered only the suffering and sorrows of her parent; the reader was prepared to exert his imagination for an object so interesting. The poet makes him wish that, if supernatural agency were employed, it should be used for a being so lovely. 'The wish is father to the thought.'[246] In this state of mind was comprehended what is called *Poetic Faith*[247] before which our common notions of philosophy give way. This feeling is much stronger than Historic Faith, in as much as by the former the mind is prepared to exercise it. I make this remark, though somewhat digressive, in order to lead to a future subject of these lectures—the poems of Milton.

Many Scriptural poems have been written with so much of Scripture in them, that what is not Scripture appears to be not true; it seemed like mingling lies with the most sacred truth. It was for this reason that Milton has taken for his subject of his work that one point of Scripture of which we have the mere fact recorded. A few facts were only necessary, as in the story of *King Lear*, to put an end to all doubt as to their credibility. It is idle to say then that this or that is improbable, because history says that the fact is so. The story on which Milton has founded his *Paradise Lost* is comprized in the Bible in four or five lines,

---

[246] 'Thy wish was father, Harry, to that thought'; *2 Henry IV*, IV, v, 92.

[247] In Chapter 14 of the *Biographia Literaria* this is more famously defined: 'that willing suspension of disbelief for the moment, which constitutes poetic faith'. Coleridge takes the phrase from *Tom Jones* (1749, Book 18, Chapter 1), where Fielding mocks critics who 'have so little *Historic* or *Poetic Faith*, that they believe nothing to be either possible or probable, the like to which hath not occurred to their own Observation'. Fielding adds: 'I think, it may very reasonably be required of every Writer, that he keeps within the Bounds of Possibility; and still remembers that what it is not possible for Man to perform, it is scarce possible for a Man to *believe* he did perform.'

and the Poet has substituted the faith of the mind to regard as true what would otherwise have appeared absurdity.

But to return to *The Tempest*, and to the wondrous creation of Ariel. If ever there could be a doubt that Shakespeare was a great poet, acting by laws arising out of his own nature, and not acting without law, as had been asserted, it would be removed by the character of Ariel. The very first words spoken by Ariel introduce him not as an Angel, above men; not as a Gnome, or a Fiend; but while the Poet gives him all the advantages, all the faculties of reason, he divests him of all moral character, not positively, but negatively. In air he lives, and from air he derives his being. In air he acts; and all his colours and properties seem to be derived from the clouds. There is nothing in Ariel that cannot be conceived to exist in the atmosphere at sun-rise or at sun-set: hence all that belongs to Ariel is all that belongs to the delight the mind receives from external appearances abstracted from any inborn or individual purpose. His answers to Prospero are either directly to the question, and nothing beyond; or if he expatiates, which he does frequently, it is upon his own delights, and the unnatural situation in which he is placed, though under a kindly power and employed to good ends.

Here Shakespeare has made his very first demand characteristic of him.[248] He is introduced discontented from his confinement, and from being bound to obey any thing that he is commanded. We feel it almost unnatural to him, yet it is delightful that he is so employed.– It is as if we were to command one of the winds to blow otherwise than nature dictates, or one of the waves, now sinking away and now rising, to recede before it bursts upon the shore:–This is the sort of feeling we experience.

But when Shakespeare contrasts the treatment of Prospero with that of Sycorax, instead of producing curses and discontent, Ariel feels his obligation; he immediately assumes the airy being, with a mind in which when one feeling is passed, not a trace is left behind.

If there be any thing in nature from which Shakespeare caught the idea of Ariel, it is from the child to whom supernatural powers are given: he is neither born of Heaven, nor of earth; but between both; it is like a may blossom kept by the fanning breeze from falling to the ground suspended in air, and only by violence of compulsion, touching the earth. This aversion of the sylph is kept up through the whole,

---

[248] 'All hail, great master! grave sir, hail! I come/To answer thy best pleasure; be't to fly,/ To swim, to dive into the fire, to ride/On the curl'd clouds; to thy strong bidding task/ Ariel and all his quality' (*The Tempest*, I, ii, 189–93).

and Shakespeare in his admirable judgment has availed himself of this circumstance, to give Ariel an interest in the event, looking forward to that moment when he was to gain his last and only reward—simple liberty.

Another instance of admirable judgment and preparation is the being contrasted with Ariel—Caliban; who is described in such and such a manner by Prospero, as to lead the reader to expect and look for a monstrous unnatural creature. You do not see Caliban at once:— you first hear his voice; it is a sort of preparation, because in nature we do not receive so much disgust from sound as from sight. Still, Caliban does not appear, but Ariel enters as a water nymph.[249] All the strength of contrast is thus acquired without any of the shock of abruptness, or of the unpleasant feeling, which surprise awakes when the object is a being in any way hateful to our senses. The character of Caliban is wonderfully conceived: he is a sort of creature of the earth, partaking of the qualities of the brute, and distinguished from them in two ways:—1. by having mere understanding without moral reason; 2. by not having the instincts which belong to mere animals. Still, Caliban is a noble being: a man in the sense of the imagination: all the images he utters are drawn from nature, and are all highly poetical. They fit in with the images of Ariel: Caliban gives us images from the earth, Ariel images from the air. Caliban talks of the difficulty of find-ing fresh water, the situation of morasses, and other circumstances which the brute instinct not possessing reason, could comprehend. No mean image is brought forward, and no mean passion but animal passions, and the sense of repugnance at being commanded.

The manner in which the lovers are introduced is equally excellent, and it is the last point I shall now mention in reference to this wonder-ful play. In every scene the same judgment might be pointed out, still preparing, and still recalling, like a lively piece of music. One thing, however, I wish to notice before I conclude: I mean the conspiracy against the life of Alonzo, and how our Poet has so prepared the feelings of his readers for their plot, which was to execute the most detestable of all crimes, and which, in another play, Shakespeare has called 'the murder of sleep.'[250]

These men at first had no such notion: it was suggested only by the magical sleep cast on Alonzo and Gonzalo;[251] but they are previously introduced scoffing and scorning at what was said, without regard to

---

[249] *The Tempest,* I, ii, 316.
[250] *Macbeth,* II, ii, 33.
[251] *The Tempest,* II, i, 191–8.

situation or age:–without any feelings of admiration of the excellent truths but giving themselves up entirely to the malignant and unsocial feeling, that of listening to everything that is said, not to understand and to profit by the learning and experience of others, but to find something that might gratify vanity, by making them believe that the person speaking is inferior to themselves.

This is the grand characteristic of a villain; and it would be not presentiment, but an anticipation of Hell, for men to suppose that all mankind was either as wicked as themselves, or might be so, if they were not too great fools to be so. It is true that Pope objected to this conspiracy;[252] and yet it would leave in my opinion a complete chasm, if it were omitted.

Many, indeed innumerable, beauties might be quoted; particularly the grandeur of the language of Prospero in that divine speech, where he takes leave of his magic art; and were I to repeat them, I should pass from the character of a lecturer into a mere reciter. Before I terminate, however, I will take notice of one passage, which has fallen under the very severe censure of Pope and Arbuthnot, who had declared it to be a piece of the grossest bombast.[253] It was this, Prospero addressing himself to his daughter, directing her attention to Ferdinand:

> The fringed curtains of thine eye advance,
> And say what thou seest yond?[254]

Putting this passage as a paraphrase of 'Look what is coming,' it certainly did appear ridiculous, and seemed to fall under the rule I formerly laid down,–that whatever, without injury, can be translated into a foreign language in simple terms, ought to be so in the original or it is not good; but the different modes of expression, it should be remembered, arise from difference of situation and education. A blackguard would use very different words, to express the same thing, to those a gentleman would employ, and both would be natural and proper; the difference arises from the feeling. The gentleman would speak with all the polished language and regard to his own dignity, which belonged to his rank, while the blackguard, who must be considered almost a half brute, and would speak like a half brute, having respect neither for himself or others.

But I am content to try the lines I have just quoted by the

---

252 Pope's view (in a note on this scene in his edition of Shakespeare) was that it was 'impertinent stuff' consisting of 'most improper and ill-plac'd drollery in the mouths of unhappy, shipwreck people.'

253 Pope's *Peri Bathous, or the Art of Sinking in Poetry* (1727).

254 *The Tempest*, I, ii, 409–10.

introduction. How does Prospero introduce them? He has just told Miranda a story, which deeply affects her, and afterwards for his own purposes lulled her to sleep. And Shakespeare makes her wholly inattentive to the present when she awakes, and dwelling only on the past. An actress, who truly understands the character, should have her eyelids sunk down, and be living, as it were, in her dreams. Prospero then sees Ferdinand, and wishes to point him out to his daughter, not only with great, but almost scenic solemnity, himself always present to her and to the spectator as a magician. Something was to appear on the sudden, which was no more expected than we should look for the hero of a play to be on the stage when the curtain is drawn up. It is under such circumstances that Prospero says:

> The fringed curtains of thine eye advance,
> And say what thou seest yond?–

This solemnity of phraseology is in my opinion completely in character with Prospero, who is assuming the magician, whose very art seems to consider all the objects in nature in a mysterious point of view, and who wishes to produce a strong impression on Miranda at the first view of Ferdinand. It is much easier to find fault with a writer merely by reference to former notions and experience, than to sit down and read him, and to connect the one feeling with the other, and to judge of words and phrases, in proportion as they convey those feelings together.

Miranda possesses in herself all the ideal beauties that could be conceived by the greatest poet; but it is not my object now, so much to point out the high poetic powers of Shakespeare, as his exquisite judgment. But to describe one of the female characters of Shakespeare is almost to describe the whole, for each possesses all the excellencies with which they could be invested.

Shakespeare is the wonder of the ignorant part of mankind, but much more the wonder of the learned, who at the same time as he possesses profundity of thought, can be looked upon as no less than a Prophet. Yet at the same time, with all his wonderful powers, making us feel as if he were unconscious of himself, and of his mighty abilities: disguising the half-god in the simplicity of a child, or the affection of a dear companion.

LECTURE 12

In the last lecture I endeavoured to point out in Shakespeare those characters where pride of intellect, without moral feeling, is supposed to be the ruling impulse, as in Iago, Richard III, and even Falstaff. In Richard III, ambition is, as it were, the channel in which the reigning impulse directs itself; the character is drawn by the Poet with the greatest fullness and perfection; and he has not only given the character, but actually shown its source and generation. The inferiority of his person made him seek consolation in the superiority of his mind; he had endeavoured to counterbalance his deficiency. This was displayed most beautifully by Shakespeare, who made Richard bring forward his very deformities as a boast. To show that this is not unfounded in nature, I may adduce the anecdote of John Wilkes, who said of himself that even in the company of ladies, the handsomest man ever created had but ten minutes' advantage of him.[255] A high compliment to himself; but higher to the female sex!

I will now proceed to offer some remarks upon the tragedy of *Richard II*, from its connection with *Richard III*. As, in the last, Shakespeare has painted a man whose ambition was only the channel in which the ruling impulse runs, so, in the first, he has given under the name of Bolingbroke, or Henry IV, where ambition itself, conjoined with great talents, is the uppermost feeling.

One main object of these lectures is to point out the difference between Shakespeare and other dramatists, and no superiority can be more striking, than that this great man could take two characters, which seem so be the same at first sight, and yet, when minutely examined, are totally distinct.

The popularity of *Richard II* is owing, in a great measure, to the masterly manner in which his characters are portrayed; but were there no other motive, it would deserve it from the fact that it contains the

---

[255] A story often told of the radical politician and wit John Wilkes (1727–97). 'John Wilkes was one of the ugliest of God's creatures. His squint was excessive, and his whole countenance most whimsically ill-favoured. "Such an one is a good-looking fellow," said the bold and able agitator, "and my friends tell me that I am as ugly as the devil, but between the handsomest face and my own, I never found with any woman more than half an hour's difference"' (Samuel Atkinson, *Atkinson's Casket* 8 (1833), 430).

most magnificent, and truest eulogium on our native country, which the English language can boast, or which can be found in any other, not excepting the proud claims of Greece and Rome. When I feel, that upon the morality of Britain depends her safety, and that her morality is supported by our national feelings, I cannot read these lines without triumph. Let it be remembered, that while we are proudly pre-eminent in morals, our enemy has only maintained his station by superiority in mechanical means. The passage is as follows:—

> This royal throne of kings, this scepter'd isle,
> This earth of majesty, this seat of Mars,
> This other Eden, demi-paradise;
> This fortress, built by nature for herself
> Against infection and the hand of war;
> This happy breed of men, this little world,
> This precious stone set in the silver sea,
> Which serves it in the office of a wall,
> Or as a moat defensive to a house,
> Against the envy of less happier lands;
> This blessed plot, this earth, this realm, this England,
> This nurse, this teeming womb of royal kings,
> Feared by their breed, and famous by their birth,
> Renowned for their deeds as far from home,
> For Christian service and true chivalry,
> As is the Sepulchre in stubborn Jewry
> Of the world's ransom, blessed Mary's son:
> This land of such dear souls, this dear, dear land,
> Dear for her reputation through the world,
> Is now leas'd out, I die pronouncing it,
> Like to a tenement, or pelting farm.
> England, bound in with the triumphant sea,
> Whose rocky shore beats back the envious siege
> Of watery Neptune.[256]

Every motive, every cause producing patriotism, is here collected, without any of those cold abstractions which have been substituted by modern poets. If this sentence were properly repeated every man would retire from the theatre secure in his country, if secure in his own virtue.

The three principal personages in this play are Richard II, Bolingbroke, and York. I will speak of the last first, as it is the least

---

[256] *Richard II*, II, i, 40–63.

important. Throughout the *keeping* is most admirable.[257] York is a man of no strong powers of mind, though of earnest wishes to do right, but contented if in himself alone he have acted well: he points out to Richard the effects of his extravagance, and the dangers by which he is encompassed, but having so done he is satisfied: there is no future action; he does nothing but remains passive. When Gaunt is dying, he contents himself with giving his own opinion to the King, and that done he retires, as it were, into himself.

One of great objects of these lectures is to meet and defeat the popular objections to particular points in the works of our great dramatic poet; and I cannot help observing here upon the beauty, and true force of nature, with which *conceits*, as they are called, and sometimes even *puns*, may be introduced. What has been the reigning fault of an age must at some time or other have referred to something beautiful in the human mind; and, however conceits may have been misapplied, we should recollect that there never was an abuse, without there having previously been a use. Old Gaunt, dying, sends for the young Prince, and Richard, entering, insolently and unfeelingly says to him:

What, comfort, man ! how is't with aged Gaunt?

and Gaunt replies:

O, how that name befits my composition!
Old Gaunt, indeed; and *gaunt* in being old:
Within me grief hath kept a tedious fast,
And who abstains from meat, that is not *gaunt?*
For sleeping England long time have I watched;
Watching breeds leanness, leanness is all *gaunt*:
The pleasure that some fathers feed upon
Is my strict fast, I mean my children's looks;
And therein fasting, thou hast made me gaunt.
Gaunt am I for the grave, gaunt as a grave,
Whose hollow womb inherits nought but bones.

Richard inquires,

Can sick men play so nicely with their names?

---

[257] As in Lecture 7 above, Coleridge takes the term 'keeping' from painting, where it refers to the maintenance of a harmonious balance between nearer and further, or smaller and larger, figures in an overall visual composition.

To which Gaunt answers:

> No; misery makes sport to mock itself:
> Since thou dost seek to kill my name in me,
> I mock my name, great king, to flatter thee.[258]

He who knows the state of deep passion must know, that it approaches to that state of madness, which is not frenzy or delirium, but which models all things to one reigning idea; still to stray in complaining from the main subject of complaint, and still to return to it again by a sort of irresistible impulse. The abruptness of thought is true to nature. In a modern poem a mad mother thus complains:

> The breeze I see is in yon tree:
> It comes to cool my babe and me.[259]

This is an instance of that abruptness of thought, so natural to grief; and if it be admired in images, can we say that it is unnatural in words, which are in fact a part of our life and existence? In the Scriptures themselves these plays upon words are to be found, as well as in the best works of the ancients, and in the most beautiful parts of Shakespeare; and because this additional grace has in some instances been converted into a deformity, because it has been used in improper places, should we include it in one general censure? When we find it disgusts, we should enquire whether its conceit has been rightly or wrongly used, whether it is in its right or wrong place. It is necessary to opinion to consider the state of passion of the person using this play upon words. It might be condemned not because it is a play upon words, but because it is a play upon words in a wrong place. I feel the importance of these remarks strongly, because the greater part of the filth heaped upon Shakespeare, originated in this circumstance. Dr Johnson says that Shakespeare loses the world for a toy, and can no more withstand a pun, or a play upon words, than his Anthony could Cleopatra.[260] Shakespeare has gained more admiration by the use of speech in this way, than the moderns have by abandoning them:

---

[258] *Richard II*, II, i, 72–87.

[259] William Wordsworth, 'The Mad Mother' (1798), 39–40. The poem was retitled 'Her Eyes Are Wild' in Wordsworth's 1815 collection.

[260] 'A quibble is to Shakespeare, what luminous vapours are to the traveller; he follows it at all adventures, it is sure to lead him out of his way, and sure to engulf him in the mire. It has some malignant power over his mind, and its fascinations are irresistible . . . A quibble, poor and barren as it is, gave him such delight, that he was content to purchase it, by the sacrifice of reason, propriety and truth. A quibble was to him the fatal Cleopatra for which he lost the world, and was content to lose it' (Johnson, 'Preface to Shakespeare' (1765)).

they have in the rules of art lost the admiration, contemplation and comprehension of nature.

I will now proceed to the character of Richard the Second. He is represented as a man not deficient in immediate courage, as appears at the last assassination;[261] or in powers of mind, as appears by the foresight he exhibits throughout the play: but still, he is weak, and womanish, and possesses feelings, which, though amiable in a female, are misplaced in a man, and altogether unfit for a King. In his prosperity he is insolent and presumptuous, and in adversity, Dr Johnson says he is humane and pious.[262] I cannot assent to the latter epithet, because the same character Richard had shown in the commencement is preserved through the whole. Dr Johnson gives to him rather the virtue of a confessor than that of a king.[263]

I admit it truth that the first misfortune Richard meets overwhelms him; but, so far from his feelings being tamed or subdued by it, the very first glance of the sunshine of hope, exalts his spirits, and lifts the King into as strange degree of elevation, as before of depression of mind, and the mention of those in his misfortunes, who had contributed to his downfall, but who had before been his nearest friends and favourites, calls forth expressions of the bitterest hatred and revenge. Thus, where Richard asks:

> ——Where is Bagot?
> What is become of Bushy? Where is Green?
> That they have let the dangerous enemy
> Measure our confines with such peaceful steps?
> If we prevail, their heads shall pay for it.
> I warrant they have made peace with Bolingbroke.[264]

Scroop answers:

> Peace have they made with him, indeed, my lord.

---

261 Act 5 scene 5, where Richard is assassinated, but manages to kill two of his attackers first.

262 'It seems to be the design of the poet to raise Richard to esteem in his fall, and consequently to interest the reader in his favour. He gives him only passive fortitude, the virtue of a confessor rather than of a king. In his prosperity we saw him imperious and oppressive; but in his distress he is wise, patient, and pious' (Johnson, in his notes to *Richard II*). Coleridge had access to this work in his edition of Ayscough (ed.), *The Dramatic Works of William Shakespeare*.

263 In his notes on *Richard II*, Johnson says that Shakespeare gives Richard 'passive fortitude, the virtue of a confessor rather than of a king. In his prosperity we saw him imperious and oppressive, but in his distress he is wise, patient and pious.'

264 *Richard II*, III, ii, 122f.

Upon which Richard, without hearing more, breaks out:

> O villains! vipers, damn'd without redemption!
> Dogs, easily won to fawn on any man!
> Snakes, in my heart-blood warm'd, that sting my heart!
> Three Judases, each one thrice worse than Judas!
> Would they make peace? terrible hell make war
> Upon their spotted souls for this offence!

Scroop adds:

> Sweet love, I see, changing his property
> Turns to the sourest and most deadly hate.
> Again uncurse their souls: their peace is made
> With heads and not with hands: those whom you curse
> Have felt the worst of death's destroying wound,
> And lie full low, grav'd in the hollow ground.

On receiving an equivocal answer,–'Peace have they made with him, indeed, my lord,'–Richard takes it in the worst sense: his promptness to suspect his friends turns his love of them to detestation, and calls forth the most tremendous execrations.

So in the play from the beginning to the end he pours out all the powers of his mind: he seeks a new hope, anticipates new friends, is disappointed, and at length makes a merit of his resignation. He scatters himself into a multitude of images, and in the conclusion endeavours to shelter himself from that which is around him by a cloud of his own thoughts. Throughout his whole character may be noticed the most rapid transitions–from insolence to despair, from the heights of love to the agonies of resentment, and from pretended resignation to the bitterest reproaches. The whole is joined with the utmost richness and capaciousness of thought, and were there an actor capable of representing it, in the character of Richard II would delight us more than any other of Shakespeare's masterpieces,–with, perhaps, the single exception of King Lear. I know of no character preserved with such unequal chastity as that of Richard II.

Next we come to Henry Bolingbroke, the rival of Richard II. He appears to be a man of great courage, and of ambition equal to that of Richard III; but the difference between the two is most admirably preserved. In the latter all that surrounds him is only dear as it feeds his inward sense of superiority: but he is no vulgar tyrant–no Nero or Caligula: he has always an end in view, and a fertility of means to accomplish that end. In the former, that of Bolingbroke, on the contrary we find a man in the first instance who has been sorely injured:

then encouraged by the grievances of his country, and the strange mismanagement of the government, yet scarcely daring to look at his own views. Coming home under the pretence of claiming his duke-dom, and professing that to be his object almost to the last; but, at the last, letting out his design to the full extent, of which he was himself unconscious in the first stages.

This is shown by so many passages, that I will only select one; and I take it the rather, because out of twenty-one octavo volumes of text and notes on Shakespeare, the page on which this passage is found is, I believe, the only one left naked by the commentators. It is where Bolingbroke approaches the castle in which the unfortunate King has taken shelter; and York is in company—the same York who is still contented with saying the truth, but doing nothing for the sake of the truth,—drawing back and becoming passive. Northumberland says,

> The news is very fair and good, my lord:
> Richard not far from hence hath hid his head.[265]

York rebukes him:

> It would beseem the Lord Northumberland
> To say King Richard:—Alack, the heavy day,
> When such a sacred king should hide his head!

Northumberland replies:

> Your grace mistakes me: only to be *brief*
> I left his title cut.

To which York rejoins:

> The time hath been,
> Would you have been so *brief* with him, he would
> Have been so *brief* with you, to shorten you,
> For taking so the *head*, your whole *head's* length.

Bolingbroke observes,

> *Mistake* not, uncle, farther than you should;

And York answers, with a play upon the words 'take' and 'mistake':

> *Take* not, good cousin, farther than you should,
> Lest you *mistake*. The heavens are o'er our heads.

---

[265] *Richard II*, III, iii, 5f.

There the play upon words is perfectly in character. The answer is in unison with the tone of the passion, and seems connected with some phrase used. Bolingbroke then says:

> I know it, uncle, and oppose not myself
> Against their will.

And afterwards, addressing himself to Northumberland:

> Noble lord,
> Go to the rude ribs of that ancient castle;
> Through brazen trumpet send the breath of parle
> Into his ruin'd ears, and thus deliver.

Here, in the phrase 'into his ruin'd ears,' I have no doubt that Shakespeare purposely used the personal pronoun, 'his' to show, that although Bolingbroke was only speaking of the castle, his thoughts dwelt on Richard the king. In Milton the word *her* is used, in relation to *form*, in a manner somewhat similar.[266] Bolingbroke had an equivocation in his mind, and was thinking of the king. He goes on,– 'Harry of Bolingbroke'–which is almost the only instance in which a name forms the whole line; yet Shakespeare meant it to convey Bolingbroke's opinion of his own importance:

> ——Harry of Bolingbroke
> On both his knees doth kiss King Richard's hand,
> And sends allegiance and true faith of heart
> To his most royal person; hither come
> Even at his feet to lay my arms and power,
> Provided that, my banishment repealed,
> And lands restor'd again, be freely granted.
> If not, I'll use th' advantage of my power,
> And lay the summer's dust with showers of blood,
> Rain'd from the wounds of slaughter'd Englishmen.[267]

Then Bolingbroke seems to have been checked by the eye of York, and proceeds:

> The which, how far off from the mind of Bolingbroke
> It is, such crimson tempest should bedrench
> The fresh green lap of fair King Richard's land,
> My stooping duty tenderly shall show.

---

[266] Foakes argues this a reference to *Paradise Lost* 9:457, where 'her form' is Eve's. It might rather, or also, refer to 7:454–5 where 'her . . . perfect forms' refer to the Earth.
[267] *Richard II*, III, iii, 35f.

Thus checked, Bolingbroke passes suddenly to the very contrary extreme of humility, which would not have taken place, had he been allowed to proceed according to the natural flow of the subject. Let me direct attention to the subsequent lines, for the same reason; they are part of the same speech:

Let's march without the noise of threat'ning drum,
That from the castle's tatter'd battlements
Our fair appointments may be well perused.
Methinks, King Richard and myself should meet
With no less terror than the elements
Of fire and water, when their thundering shock
At meeting tears the cloudy cheeks of heaven.[268]

When he had proceeded thus far, York again checks him, and Bolingbroke adds,

He be the fire, I'll be the yielding water:
The rage be his, while on the earth I rain
My waters; on the earth, and not on him.

Throughout the whole play, with the exception of some of the last scenes (though they have exquisite beauty) Shakespeare seems to have risen to the summit of excellence in the preservation of character.

We will now pass to *Hamlet*, in order to obviate some of the general prejudices against Shakespeare, in reference to the character of the hero. Much has been objected to, which ought to have been praised, and many beauties of the highest kind have been neglected, because they are somewhat hidden.

The first question is:–What did Shakespeare mean when he drew the character of Hamlet? My belief is, that the poet regarded his story, before he began to write, much in the same light as a painter regards his canvas, before he begins to paint. What was the point to which Shakespeare directed himself? He meant to portray a person, in whose view the external world, and all its incidents and objects, were comparatively dim, and of no interest in themselves, and which began to interest only, when they were reflected in the mirror of his mind. Hamlet beheld external objects in the same way that a man of vivid imagination, who shuts his eyes, sees what has previously made an impression on his organs.

Shakespeare places him in the most stimulating circumstances that a human being can be placed in. He is the heir apparent of a throne;

---

[268] *Richard II*, III, iii, 49f.

his father dies suspiciously; his mother excludes him from the throne by marrying his uncle. This is not enough; but the Ghost of the murdered father is introduced, to assure the son that he was put to death by his own brother. What is the result? Endless reasoning and urging—perpetual solicitation of the mind to act, but as constant an escape from action; ceaseless reproaches of himself for his sloth, while the whole energy of his resolution passes away in those reproaches. This, too, not from cowardice, for he is made one of the bravest of his time—not from want of forethought or quickness of apprehension, for he sees through the very souls of all who surround him, but merely from that aversion to action, which prevails among such as have a world in themselves.

How admirable is the judgment of the poet! Hamlet's own fancy has not conjured up the Ghost of his father; it has been seen by others: he is by them prepared to witness its appearance, and when he does see it, he is not brought forward as having long brooded on the subject. The moment before the Ghost enters, Hamlet speaks of other matters in order to relieve the weight on his mind: he speaks of the coldness of the night, and observes that he has not heard the clock strike, adding, in reference to the custom of drinking, that it is

More honour'd in the breach than the observance.[269]

From the tranquil state of his mind, he indulges in moral reflections. Afterwards, the Ghost suddenly enters.

Hor. Look, my lord ! it comes.
Ham. Angels and ministers of grace defend us![270]

The same thing occurs in *Macbeth*: in the dagger scene, the moment before he sees it, he has his mind drawn to some indifferent matters; thus has all the effect of abruptness, and the reader is totally divested of the notion, that the vision is a figure in the highly wrought imagination.

Here Shakespeare adapts himself to the situation so admirably, and as it were puts himself into the situation, that, though poetry, his language is the language of nature: no words, associated with such feeling, can occur to us but those which he has employed, especially on the highest, the most august, and the most awful subjects that can interest a human being in this sentient world. That this is no mere fancy, I can undertake to establish from Shakespeare himself. No

---

[269] *Hamlet*, I, iv, 4.16,
[270] *Hamlet*, I, iv, 38–9.

character he has drawn could so properly express himself, as in the language put into his mouth.

There is no indecision about Hamlet. He knows well what he ought to do, and over and over again he makes up his mind to do it. The moment the players, and the two spies set upon him, have withdrawn, of whom he takes leave with a line so expressive of his contempt,

Ay, so; good bye you.—Now I am alone,[271]

he breaks out into a delirium of rage against himself for neglecting to perform the solemn duty he had undertaken, and contrasts the artificial feeling of the players with his own apparent indifference:

What's Hecuba to him, or he to Hecuba,
That he should weep for her?[272]

Yet the player did weep for her, and was in an agony of grief at her sufferings, while Hamlet could not rouse himself to action, that he might do the bidding of his father, who had come from the grave to incite him to revenge:

This is most brave!
That I, the son of a dear father murder'd,
Prompted to my revenge by heaven and hell,
Must, like a whore, unpack my heart with words,
And fall a cursing, like a very drab,
A scullion.[273]

It is the same feeling, the same conviction of what is his duty, that makes Hamlet exclaim in a subsequent part of the tragedy:

How all occasions do inform against me,
And spur my dull revenge! What is a man,
If his chief good, and market of his time,
Be but to sleep and feed? A beast, no more. . . .
    — I do not know
Why yet I live to say—this thing's to do,
Sith I have cause and will and strength and means
To do't.[274]

Yet with all this strong conviction of duty, this resolution arising out of conviction, nothing is done. This admirable and consistent character,

[271] *Hamlet*, II, ii, 549.
[272] *Hamlet*, II, ii, 559–60.
[273] *Hamlet*, II, ii, 582–7.
[274] *Hamlet*, IV, iv, 32–46.

deeply acquainted with his own feelings, painting them with such wonderful power and accuracy, and just as strongly convinced of the fitness of executing the solemn charge committed to him, still yields to the same retiring from all reality, which is the result of having, what we express by the terms, a world within himself.

Such a mind as this is near akin to madness. Dryden has said,

Great wit to madness *nearly* is allied,[275]

and he was right; for he means by *wit* that greatness of genius, which led Hamlet to the perfect knowledge of his own character, which, with all strength of motive, was so weak as to be unable to carry into act his own most obvious duty.

Still, with all this he has a sense of imperfectness, which becomes obvious when he is moralising on the skull in the churchyard. Something is wanted to make it complete—something is deficient, and he is therefore described as attached to Ophelia. His madness is assumed, when he discovers that witnesses have been placed behind the arras to listen to what passes, and when the heroine has been thrown in his way as a decoy.

Another objection has been taken by Dr Johnson, and has been treated by him very severely. I refer to the scene in the third act where Hamlet enters and finds his Uncle praying, and refuses to assail him, excepting when he is in the height of his iniquity. To take the King's life at such a moment of repentance and confession, Hamlet declares,

Why, this is hire and salary, not revenge.[276]

He therefore forbears, and postpones his uncle's death, until he can catch him in some act 'that has no relish of salvation in't.'[277] This sentiment, Dr Johnson has pronounced to be so atrocious and horrible, as to be unfit to be put into the mouth of a human being.[278] The fact is that the determination to allow the King to escape at such a moment is only part of the same irresoluteness of character. Hamlet seizes hold of a pretext for not acting, when he might have acted so effectually:

---

[275] 'Great Wits are sure to madness near alli'd' (Dryden, *Absalom and Achitophel* (1681), 1:163).

[276] *Hamlet*, III, iii, 79.

[277] *Hamlet*, III, iii, 92.

[278] 'This speech, in which Hamlet, represented as a virtuous character, is not content with taking blood for blood, but contrives damnation for the man that he would punish, is too horrible to be read or to be uttered' (Johnson, notes on *Hamlet*). Coleridge had access to this work in his edition of Ayscough (ed.), *The Dramatic Works of William Shakespeare*.

therefore, he again defers the revenge he sought, and declares his resolution to accomplish it at some time,

> When he is drunk, asleep, or in his rage,
> Or in th' incestuous pleasures of his bed.[279]

This, I repeat, was merely the excuse Hamlet made to himself for
not taking advantage of this particular moment to accomplish his
revenge.

Dr Johnson farther states, that in the voyage to England,
Shakespeare merely followed the novel as he found it, as if he had no
other motive for adhering to his original;[280] but Shakespeare never
followed a novel, but where he saw that the story contributed to tell
or explain some great and general truth inherent in human nature. It
was so unquestionably an incident in the old story, and there it is used
merely as an incident, but Shakespeare saw how it could be applied to
his own great purpose, and how it was consistent with the character
of Hamlet, that after still resolving, and still refusing, still determining
to execute, and still postponing the execution, he should finally give
himself up to his destiny, and in the infirmity of his nature hopelessly
place himself in the power, and at the mercy of his enemies.

Even after the scene with Osrick, we see Hamlet still indulging in
reflections, and thinking little of the new task he has just undertaken:
he is all meditation, all resolution as far as words are concerned, but
all hesitation and irresolution, when called upon to act; so that, resolving to do everything, he in fact does nothing. He is full of purpose, but
void of that quality of mind which would lead him at the proper time
to carry his purpose into effect.

Any thing finer than this conception, and working out of a character, is merely impossible. Shakespeare wished to impress upon us
the truth that action is the great end of existence;–that no faculties of
intellect, however brilliant, can be considered valuable, or otherwise
than as misfortunes, if they withdraw us from, or render us repug-
nant to action, and lead us to think and think of doing, until the time
has escaped when we ought to have acted. In enforcing this truth,
Shakespeare has shown the fullness and force of his powers: all that

---

[279] *Hamlet*, III, iii, 89–90.

[280] Johnson doesn't say this, but the edition of *Hamlet* Coleridge was working from,
which included notes from Johnson, Malone and many others, includes this footnote: 'Shakespeare probably had here the following passage in *The History of Hamblett*
book 1 in his thoughts' (quoted CC 5:1, 390) as explanation for why he makes the
prince 'minister of his [the king's] massacrous resolution'. The note is attributed to
Malone.

is amiable and excellent in nature is combined in Hamlet, with the exception of this one quality. He is a man living in meditation, called upon to act by every motive human and divine, but the great purpose of his life is defeated by continually resolving to do, yet doing nothing but resolve.

Lectures on Shakespeare 1818–1819

Samuel Taylor Coleridge

Venue: the Crown and Anchor Tavern, off the Strand.

Lecture 1: Thursday, 17 December 1818 (*The Tempest*)
[Lecture 2: Thursday, 31 December 1818]
Lecture 3: Thursday, 7 January 1819 (*Hamlet*)
Lecture 4: Thursday, 14 January 1819 (*Macbeth*)
Lecture 5: Thursday, 21 January 1819 (*Othello*)
Lecture 6: Thursday, 28 January 1819 (*King Lear*)

LECTURE 1

Once more, though in a somewhat different and I would fain believe, in a more instructive form, I have undertaken the task of criticizing the works of that great dramatist whose own name has become their best and most expressive epithet. The task will be genial in proportion as the criticism is reverential. Assuredly the Englishman, who without reverence, who without proud and affectionate reverence, can utter the name of William Shakespeare, stands disqualified for the office. He wants one at least of the very senses, the language of which he is to employ, and will discourse at best, but as a blind man, while the whole harmonious creation of light and shade with all its subtle interchange of deepening and dissolving colours rises in silence to the silent fiat of the uprising Apollo.[281] However inferior in ability I may be to some who have followed me, I am proud that I was the first in time who publicly demonstrated to the full extent of the position, that the supposed Irregularity and extravagancies of Shakespeare were the mere dreams of a pedantry that arraigned the eagle because it had not the dimensions of the swan. In all the successive Courses delivered by me, since my first attempt at the Royal Institution, it still remains, my object, to prove that in all points from the most important to the most minute, the Judgment of Shakespeare is commensurate with his Genius,—nay, that his Genius reveals itself in his Judgment, as in its most exalted form. And the more gladly do I recur to the subject from the clear conviction, that to judge aright, and with distinct consciousness of the grounds of our Judgment, concerning the works of Shakespeare, implies the power and the means of judging rightly of all other works of intellect, those of abstract science alone excepted.

We commence with *The Tempest*, as a specimen of the Romantic Drama. But whatever play of Shakespeare's we had selected, there is one preliminary point to be first settled, as the indispensable condition not only of just and genial criticism, but of all consistency in our opinions—This point is contained in the words, *probable, natural*. We are all in the habit of praising Shakespeare or of hearing him extolled

---

[281] Apollo as god of Poetry. 'Uprising Apollo' (in Latin, *Ortus Apollo*) was a votive figure at the oracle of Delos.

for his fidelity to Nature. Now what are we to understand by these words in their application to the Drama? Assuredly, not the ordinary meaning of them. Farquhar[282] most ably and if we except a few sentences in one of Dryden's Prefaces (written for a particular purpose and in contradiction to the opinions elsewhere supported by him)[283] first exposed the ludicrous absurdities involved in the supposition, and demolished as with the single sweep of a careless hand the whole edifice of French Criticism respecting the so-called Unities of Time and Place. But a moment's reflection suffices to make every man conscious of what every man must have before felt, that the drama is an imitation of reality not a copy—and that Imitation is contra-distinguished from copy by this, that a certain quantum of difference is essential to the former, and an indispensable condition and cause of the pleasure, we derive from it; while in a copy it is a defect, contravening its name and purpose. If illustration were needed, it would be sufficient to ask— why we prefer a fruit piece of Vanhuysen's to a marble Peach on a mantle piece[284] – or why we prefer an historical picture of West's to Mrs Salmon's Wax-figure Gallery.[285]

Not only that we ought, but that we actually do, all of us judge of the Drama under this impression, we need no other proof than the impassive slumber of our sense of probability when we hear an actor announce himself a Greek, Roman, Venetian or Persian in good Mother English. And how little our great Dramatist feared awakening on it, we have a lively instance in proof in Portia's answer to Neaera's[286] question, What say you then to Falconbridge, the young baron of England?

Portia: You know I say nothing to him, for he understands not me, nor I him: he hath neither Latin, French, nor Italian, and

---

282 George Farquhar (1677–1707), Irish dramatist, whose *A Discourse upon Comedy* (London: John Rivington, 1702) mocks the way theorists of the drama 'lugg'd down' Aristotle 'from the high Shelf' in a fruitless attempt to impose the 'ancient Model' including the dramatic unities on modern drama.

283 Dryden generally advocated that plays follow the Unities, although he made an exception for Shakespeare: 'in most of the irregular Playes of Shakespeare or Fletcher (for Ben Johnson's are for the most part regular) there is a more masculine fancy and greater spirit in all the writing, then [sic] there is in any of the French' (John Dryden, *An Essay of Dramatick Poesie* (London: Henry Herringman, 1668), § 84).

284 Jan van Huijsum (1682–1749), Dutch artist famous for his detailed paintings of flowers and fruit.

285 Benjamin West (1738–1820), Anglo-American painter of historical scenes, most famously of events and figures from immediately before and during the American War of Independence. Mrs Salmon's gallery of wax figures was on Fleet Street.

286 The character is more usually called 'Nerissa'.

you will come into the court and swear that I have a poor penny-worth in the English.[287]

Still, however, there is a sort of Improbability with which we are shocked in dramatic representation, not less than in a narrative of real Life. Consequently, there must be rules respecting it; and as rules are nothing but means to an end previously ascertained (inattention to which simple truth has been the occasion of all the pedantry of the French school) we must first determine what the immediate end or object of the Drama is. And here, as I have previously remarked, I find two extremes of critical decision;–the French, which evidently presupposes that a perfect delusion is to be aimed at,–an opinion which needs no fresh confutation;–The exact opposite to it, brought forward by Dr Johnson, who supposes the auditors throughout in the full reflective knowledge of the contrary. In evincing the impossibility of delusion, he makes no sufficient allowance for an intermediate state, which I have before distinguished by the term, illusion. In what this consists, I cannot better explain, than by referring to the highest state of it, dreaming. It is laxly said that during sleep, we take our dreams for realities, but this is irreconcilable with the nature of sleep, which consists in a suspension of the voluntary and therefore of the comparative power. The fact is, that we pass no judgment either way–we simply do not judge them to be (un)real– in consequence of which the Images act on our minds, as far as they act at all, by their own force as images. Our state while we are dreaming differs from that in which we are in the perusal of a deeply interesting novel, in the degree rather than in the kind, and from three causes – First, from the exclusion of all outward impressions on our senses the images in sleep become proportionally more vivid than they can be when the organs of sense are in their active state. Secondly, in sleep the sensations, and with these the emotions & passions which they counterfeit, are the causes of our dream-images, while in our waking hours our emotions are the effects of images presented to us–(apparitions so detectable). Lastly, in sleep we pass at once by a sudden collapse into this suspension of will and comparative power: whereas in an interesting play, read or represented, we *chuse* to be deceived–The rule therefore may be easily inferred. Whatever tends to prevent the mind from placing itself or from being gradually placed, in this state in which the Images have a negative reality, must be a defect, and consequently any thing that must force itself on the auditors' minds as improbable–not because it

---

[287] *The Merchant of Venice*, I, ii, 66f.

is improbable (for *that* the whole play is foreknown to be) but because it can not but *appear* as such.

But this again depends on the degree of excitement in which the mind is supposed to be. Many things would be intolerable in the first scene of a play, that would not at all interrupt our enjoyment in the height of the interest, when the narrow cockpit may hold

> The vasty field of France, or we may cram
> Within its wooden O the very casques,
> That did affright the air at Agincourt.[288]

And again, on the other hand, many obvious improbabilities will be endured, as belonging to the groundwork of the story rather than to the Drama, in the first scenes, which would disturb or disentrance us from all illusion in the acme of our excitement;—as for instance, Lear's division of his kingdom, and the banishment of Cordelia.

But besides this dramatic probability, all the other excellencies of the Drama, as unity of Interest, with distinctness and subordination of the characters, appropriateness of style, nay and the charm of language and sentiment for their own sakes, yet still as far as they tend to increase the inward excitement, are all means to this chief end,—that of producing and supporting this willing Illusion.

I have but one point more to add – namely, that though the excellencies above mentioned are means to this end, they do not therefore cease to be themselves *ends*,—and as such carry their own justification with them as long as they do not contravene or interrupt the Illusion. It is not even always, or of necessity, an objection to them, that they prevent it from rising to as great a height as it might otherwise have attained; – it is enough, if they are simply compatible with as high a degree of it as is requisite. If the Panorama[289] been invented in the time of Pope Leo X., Raphael would still have smiled in contempt at the regret, that the broom-twigs and so on at the back of some of his grand pictures were not as probable trees as those in the Panorama.

Let me venture to affirm, that certain obvious, if not palpable, improbabilities may be hazarded in order to keep down a scene, to keep it merely instrumental, and to preserve it in its due proportion of interest.–

I now quit this subject for the time—with less regret, because in my next lecture I shall have occasion to take it up again, in application to

---

[288] *Henry V*, Prologue, 11–14.
[289] The term (from the Greek for 'all-seeing') was invented in 1788 by English painter Robert Barker (1739–1806) to describe his huge paintings of Edinburgh, displayed on the inside surface of a cylindrical room into which viewers would walk.

Shakespeare's *historical* dramas. *The Tempest*, I repeat, has been selected as a specimen of the Romantic drama, that is a drama, the interests of which are independent of all historical facts and associations, and arise from their fitness to that faculty of our nature, the Imagination I mean, which owns no allegiance to Time and Place,—a species of drama, therefore, in which errors in Chronology and Geography, no mortal sins in any species, are venial, or count for nothing. It addresses itself entirely to the imaginative faculty; and although the illusion may be assisted by the effect on the senses of the complicated scenery and decorations of modern times, yet this sort of assistance is dangerous. For the principal and only genuine excitement ought to come from within,—from the moved and sympathetic imagination; whereas, where so much is addressed to the mere external senses of seeing and hearing, the spiritual vision is apt to languish, and the attraction from without will withdraw the mind from the proper and only legitimate interest which is intended to spring from within.

The Romance opens with a busy lively scene, admirably appropriate to the *kind* of drama, giving as it were the keynote to the whole harmony. It prepares and initiates the excitement required for the entire piece, and yet does not demand any thing from the spectators, which their previous habits had not fitted them to understand. It is the bustle of a tempest, from which the real horrors are abstracted;—therefore it is poetical, though not in strictness natural—(the distinction to which I have so often alluded)—and is purposely restrained from *concentering* the interest on itself, but used merely as an induction or tuning for what is to follow.

In the second scene, Prospero's speeches, till the entrance of Ariel, contain the finest example, I remember, of retrospective narration for the purpose of exciting immediate interest, and putting the audience in possession of all the information necessary for the understanding of the plot. Observe, too the perfect probability of the moment chosen by Prospero (the very Shakespeare himself, as it were, of the tempest) to open out the truth to his daughter, his own romantic bearing, and how completely any thing that might have been disagreeable to us in the magician, is reconciled and shaded in the humanity and natural feelings of the father. In the very first speech of Miranda the simplicity and tenderness of her character are at once laid open;—it would have been lost in direct contact with the agitation of the first scene. The opinion once prevailed, but, happily, is now abandoned, that Fletcher alone wrote for women;[290]—the truth is, that with very

[290] Dryden's opinion was that Shakespeare's 'excellency' inhered 'in the more manly

few, and those partial, exceptions, the female characters in the plays of Beaumont and Fletcher are, when of the light kind, not decent; when heroic, complete viragos. But in Shakespeare all the elements of womanhood are holy, and there is the sweet, yet dignified feeling of all that *continuates* society, as sense of ancestry and of sex, with a purity unassailable by sophistry, because it rests not in the analytic processes, but in that sane equipoise of the faculties, during which the feelings are representative of all past experience,–not of the individual only, but of all those by whom she has been educated, and their predecessors even up to the first mother that lived. Shakespeare saw that the want of prominence, which Pope notices for sarcasm,[291] was the blessed beauty of the woman's character, and knew that it arose not from any deficiency, but from the more exquisite harmony of all the parts of the moral being constituting one living total of head and heart. He has drawn it, indeed, in all its distinctive energies of faith, patience, constancy, fortitude,–shown in all of them as following the heart, which gives its results by a nice tact and happy intuition, without the intervention of the discursive faculty, sees all things in and by the light of the affections, and errs, if it ever err, in the exaggerations of love alone. In all the Shakespearian women there is essentially the same foundation and principle; the distinct individuality and variety are merely the result of the modification of circumstances, whether in Miranda the maiden, in Imogen the wife, or in Katherine the queen.

But to return. The appearance and characters of the super or ultra-natural servants are finely contrasted. Ariel has in every thing the airy tint which gives the name; and it is worthy of remark that Miranda is never directly brought into comparison with Ariel, lest the natural and human of the one and the supernatural of the other should tend to neutralize each other; Caliban, on the other hand, is all earth, all condensed and gross in feelings and images; he has the dawnings of understanding without reason or the moral sense, and in him, as in some brute animals, this advance to the intellectual faculties, without the moral sense, is marked by the appearance of vice. For it is in the primacy of the moral being only that man is truly human; in his intellectual powers he is certainly approached by the brutes,

---

passions; Fletcher's in the softer: Shakespeare writ better betwixt man and man; Fletcher, betwixt man and woman' (Dryden, 'Preface to *Troilus and Cressida*', 6:265). Coleridge had cited this, and disagreed with it, in the sixth lecture of his 1811–12 series (above).

291 'Most Women have no Characters at all' (Alexander Pope, 'Of the Characters of Women', in *Moral Essays: Epistle II, To a Lady* (London: W. Lewis, 1735), 2).

and, man's whole system duly considered, those powers cannot be considered other than means to an end, that is, to morality.

In this scene, as it proceeds, is displayed the impression made by Ferdinand and Miranda on each other; —it is love at first sight;—

> at the first sight
> They have chang'd eyes:—[292]

and it appears to me, that in all cases of real love, it is at one moment that it takes place. That moment may have been prepared by previous esteem, admiration, or even affection,—yet love seems to require a momentary act of volition, by which a tacit bond of devotion is imposed,—a bond not to be thereafter broken without violating what should be sacred in our nature. How finely is the true Shakespearian scene contrasted with Dryden's vulgar alteration of it,[293] in which a mere ludicrous psychological experiment, as it were, is tried—displaying nothing but indelicacy without passion. Prospero's interruption of the courtship has often seemed to me to have no sufficient motive; still his alleged reason—

> lest too light winning
> Make the prize light—[294]

is enough for the ethereal connections of the romantic imagination, although it would not be so for the historical. The whole courting scene, indeed, in the beginning of the third act, between the lovers, is a masterpiece; and the first dawn of disobedience in the mind of Miranda to the command of her father is very finely drawn, so as to seem the working of the Scriptural command *Thou shalt leave father and mother, &c.*[295] O! with what exquisite purity this scene is conceived and executed! Shakespeare may sometimes be gross, but I boldly say that he is always moral and modest. Alas! in this our day decency of manners is preserved at the expense of morality of heart, and delicacies

---

292   *The Tempest*, I, ii, 441–2.
293   Dryden and Davenport wrote a reworked version of the play, called *The Tempest, or The Enchanted Island* (London: J. Debrett, 1699), in which Miranda has a sister on the island, Dorinda, and a new character is introduced—a youth called Hippolito, who has never seen a women until he falls for Dorinda. Ferdinand believes Hippolito a rival in his wooing of Miranda, although she (at Prospero's prompting) begs him to love the youth anyway.
294   *The Tempest*, I, ii, 452–3.
295   'Therefore shall a man leave his father and his mother, and shall cleave unto his wife: and they shall be one flesh' (Genesis 2: 24).

for vice are allowed, whilst grossness against it is hypocritically, or at least morbidly, condemned.

In this play are admirably sketched the vices generally accompanying a low degree of civilization; and in the first scene of the second act Shakespeare has, as in many other places, shown the tendency in bad men to indulge in scorn and contemptuous expressions, as a mode of getting rid of their own uneasy feelings of inferiority to the good, and also, by making the good ridiculous, of rendering the transition of others to wickedness easy. Shakespeare never puts habitual scorn into the mouths of other than bad men, as here in the instances of Antonio and Sebastian. The scene of the intended assassination of Alonzo and Gonzalo is an exact counterpart of the scene between Macbeth and his lady,[296] only pitched in a lower key throughout, as designed to be frustrated and concealed, and exhibiting the same profound management in the manner of familiarizing a mind, not immediately recipient, to the suggestion of guilt, by associating the proposed crime with something ludicrous or out of place,–something not habitually a matter of reverence. By this kind of sophistry the imagination and fancy are first bribed to contemplate the suggested act, and at length to become acquainted with it. Observe how the effect of this scene is heightened by contrast with another counterpart of it in low life,–that between the conspirators Stephano, Caliban, and Trinculo in the second scene of the third act, in which there are the same essential characteristics.

In this play and in this scene of it are also shown the springs of the vulgar in politics,–of that kind of politics which is inwoven with human nature. In his treatment of this subject, wherever it occurs, Shakespeare is quite peculiar. In other writers we find the particular opinions of the individual; in Massinger it is rank republicanism; in Beaumont and Fletcher even *jure divino* principles[297] are carried to excess;–but Shakespeare never promulgates any party tenets. He is always the philosopher and the moralist, but at the same time with a profound veneration for all the established institutions of society, and for those classes which form the permanent elements of the state–especially never introducing a professional character, as such, otherwise than as respectable. If he must have any name, he should be styled a *Philosophical Aristocrat*, delighting in those hereditary institutions which have a tendency to bind one age to another, and in that distinction of ranks, of which, although few may be in possession, all enjoy the advantages. Hence, again, you will observe the good nature

---

[296] Comparing *The Tempest* Act 2 scene 1 with *Macbeth* Act 1 scene 7.
[297] The divine right of monarchs.

with which he seems always to make sport with the passions and follies of a mob, as with an irrational animal. He is never angry with it, but hugely content with holding up its absurdities to its face; and sometimes you may trace a tone of almost affectionate superiority, something like that in which a father speaks of the rogueries of a child. See the good-humoured way in which he describes Stephano passing from the most licentious freedom to absolute despotism over Trinculo and Caliban. The truth is, Shakespeare's characters are all *genera* intensely individualized; the results of meditation, of which observation supplied the drapery and the colours necessary to combine them with each other. He had virtually surveyed all the great component powers and impulses of human nature,—had seen that their different combinations and subordinations were in fact the individualizers of men, and showed how their harmony was produced by reciprocal disproportions of excess or deficiency. The language in which these truths are expressed was not drawn from any set fashion, but from the profoundest depths of his moral being, and is therefore for all ages.

LECTURE 3

Hamlet was the Play, or rather Hamlet himself was the character, in the intuition and exposition of which I first made my turn for philosophical criticism, and especially for insight into the genius of Shakespeare, *noticed* first among my acquaintances, as Sir G. Beaumont[298] will bear witness, and as Mr Wordsworth knows, though from motives which I do not know or impulses which I *cannot* know, he has thought proper to assert that Schlegel and the German critics *first* taught Englishmen to admire their own great countryman intelligently[299]–and secondly, long before Schlegel had given at Vienna the Lectures on Shakespeare, which he afterwards published, I had given eighteen lectures on the same subject *substantially* the same, proceeding from the same, the *very* same, point of view, and deducing the same conclusions, as far as I either then or now agree with him.

I gave them at the Royal Institution, before from six or seven hundred auditors of rank and eminence, in the spring of the same year, in which Sir H. Davy, a fellow lecturer, made his great revolutionary discoveries in Chemistry. Even in detail the coincidence of Schlegel with my Lectures was so extra-ordinary, that all at a later period who heard the same *words* (taken from my Royal Institution Notes) concluded a borrowing on my part from Schlegel–Mr. Hazlitt, whose hatred of me is in such an inverse ratio to my zealous kindness towards him, as to be defended by his warmest admirer, C. Lamb[300] who (besides his characteristic obstinacy of adherence to old friends, as long at least as

---

[298] Sir George Beaumont, 7th Baronet (1753–1827), patron of the arts, instrumental in founding the National Gallery in London.

[299] Wordsworth's *Poems* (2 vols (London: Hurst, Rees, Orne and Brown, 1815), 1:352) contained an 'Essay, Supplementary to the Preface', that amongst other things said 'The Germans only, of foreign nations, are approaching towards a knowledge and feeling of what he is. In some respects they have acquired a superiority over the fellow-countrymen of the Poet: for among us it is a current, I might say, an established opinion, that Shakespeare is justly praised when he is pronounced to be a wild irregular genius, in whom great faults are compensated by great beauties.'

[300] Hazlitt was lecturing on Shakespeare, from a more politically radical perspective, at the Surrey Institution at the same time that Coleridge was delivering these lectures off the Strand. The friendship between the two men had soured since, as Hazlitt saw it, Coleridge had abandoned his youthful radicalism. A report of S. T. C.'s first lecture in *The Champion* (10 January 1819) suggested he had 'availed himself of the opinions

they are at all down in the world) is linked as by a charm to Hazlitt's conversation, only under the epithet *frantic*–Mr Hazlitt himself replied to an assertion of my plagiarism from Schlegel in these words;–'That is a Lie; for I myself heard the very same character of Hamlet from Coleridge before he went to Germany, and when he had neither read nor could read a page of German.' Now Hazlitt was on a visit to my Cottage at Nether Stowey, Somerset, in the summer of the year 1798, in the September of which (see my *Literary Life*) I first was out of sight of the Shores of Great Britain.[301]

The seeming inconsistencies in the conduct and character of Hamlet have long exercised the conjectural ingenuity of critics; and, as we are always loth to suppose that the cause of defective apprehension is in ourselves, the mystery has been too commonly explained by the very easy process of setting it down as in fact inexplicable, and by resolving the phenomenon into a misgrowth or *lusus* of the capricious and irregular genius of Shakespeare. The shallow and stupid arrogance of these vulgar and indolent decisions I would fain do my best to expose. I believe the character of Hamlet may be traced to Shakespeare's deep and accurate science in mental philosophy. Indeed, that this character must have some connection with the common fundamental laws of our nature may be assumed from the fact, that Hamlet has been the darling of every country in which the literature of England has been fostered. In order to understand him, it is essential that we should reflect on the constitution of our own minds. Man is distinguished from the brute animals in proportion as thought prevails over sense: but in the healthy processes of the mind, a balance is constantly maintained between the impressions from outward objects and the inward operations of the intellect;–for if there be an overbalance in the contemplative faculty, man thereby becomes the creature of mere meditation, and loses his natural power of action.

Now one of Shakespeare's modes of creating characters is, to conceive any one intellectual or moral faculty in morbid excess, and then to place himself, Shakespeare, thus mutilated or diseased, under given circumstances. In Hamlet he seems to have wished to exemplify the moral necessity of a due balance between our attention to the objects

of Hazlitt and of 'another Lecturer', charges that clearly angered Coleridge. Charles Lamb (1775–1834) was a friend of both men.

[301] This opening passage was probably not delivered as part of the lecture, at least not as phrased here. It is written in the edition of Shakespeare (Ayscough, *The Dramatic Works of William Shakespeare*, 2:999–1000) and dated 'Recorded by me, S. T. Coleridge, Jan 7, 1819, Highgate'. It reflects Coleridge's anger at a report carried in the *Morning Chronicle* (29 December 1819) that implied the plagiary he here repudiates.

of our senses, and our meditation on the workings of our minds,–an equilibrium between the real and the imaginary worlds. In *Hamlet* this balance is disturbed: his thoughts, and the images of his fancy, are far more vivid than his actual perceptions, and his very perceptions, instantly passing through the medium of his contemplations, acquire, as they pass, a form and a colour not naturally their own. Hence we see a great, an almost enormous, intellectual activity, and a proportionate aversion to real action consequent upon it, with all its symptoms and accompanying qualities. This character Shakespeare places in circumstances, under which it is obliged to act on the spur of the moment:–Hamlet is brave and careless of death; but he vacillates from sensibility, and procrastinates from thought, and loses the power of action in the energy of resolve. Thus it is that this tragedy presents a direct contrast to that of Macbeth; the one proceeds with the utmost slowness, the other with a crowded and breathless rapidity.

The effect of this overbalance of the imaginative power is beautifully illustrated in the everlasting broodings and superfluous activities of Hamlet's mind, which, unseated from its healthy relation, is constantly occupied with the world within, and abstracted from the world without,–giving substance to shadows, and throwing a mist over all common-place actualities. It is the nature of thought to be indefinite;–definiteness belongs to external imagery alone. Hence it is that the sense of sublimity arises, not from the sight of an outward object, but from the beholder's reflection upon it;–not from the sensuous impression, but from the imaginative reflex. Few have seen a celebrated waterfall without feeling something akin to disappointment: it is only subsequently that the image comes back full into the mind, and brings with it a train of grand or beautiful associations. Hamlet feels this; his senses are in a state of trance, and he looks upon external things as hieroglyphics. His soliloquy:

O! that this too too solid flesh would melt, &c.[302]

springs from that craving after the indefinite–for that which is not–which most easily besets men of genius; and the self-delusion common to this temper of mind is finely exemplified in the character which Hamlet gives of himself:

–It cannot be
But I am pigeon-livered, and lack gall
To make oppression bitter.[303]

[302] *Hamlet*, I, ii, 129f.
[303] *Hamlet*, II, ii, 553–5.

He mistakes the seeing his chains for the breaking them, delays action till action is of no use, and dies the victim of mere circumstance and accident.

There is a great significancy in the names of Shakespeare's plays. In the *Twelfth Night, Midsummer Night's Dream, As You Like It,* and *Winter's Tale,* the total effect is produced by a co-ordination of the characters as in a wreath of flowers. But in *Coriolanus, Lear, Romeo and Juliet, Hamlet, Othello,* &c. the effect arises from the subordination of all to one, either as the prominent person, or the principal object. *Cymbeline* is the only exception; and even that has its advantages in preparing the audience for the chaos of time, place, and costume, by throwing the date back into a fabulous king's reign.

But as of more importance, so more striking, is the judgment displayed by our truly dramatic poet, as well as poet of the drama, in the management of his first scenes. With the single exception of *Cymbeline,* they either place before us at one glance both the past and the future in some effect, which implies the continuance and full agency of its cause, as in the feuds and party-spirit of the servants of the two houses in the first scene of *Romeo and Juliet;* or in the degrading passion for shows and public spectacles, and the overwhelming attachment for the newest successful war-chief in the Roman people, already become a populace, contrasted with the jealousy of the nobles in *Julius Caesar;*—or they at once commence the action so as to excite a curiosity for the explanation in the following scenes, as in the storm of wind and waves, and the boatswain in *The Tempest,* instead of anticipating our curiosity, as in most other first scenes, and in too many other first acts;—or they act, by contrast of diction suited to the characters, at once to heighten the effect, and yet to give a naturalness to the language and rhythm of the principal personages, either as that of Prospero and Miranda by the appropriate lowness of the style,— or as in King John, by the equally appropriate stateliness of official harangues or narratives, so that the after blank verse seems to belong to the rank and quality of the speakers, and not to the poet;—or they strike at once the key-note, and give the predominant spirit of the play, as in the *Twelfth Night* and in *Macbeth;*—or finally, the first scene comprizes all these advantages at once, as in *Hamlet.*

Compare the easy language of common life, in which this drama commences, with the wild wayward Lyric of the opening of *Macbeth.* The tone is quite familiar;—there is no poetic description of night, no elaborate information conveyed by one speaker to another of what both had immediately before their senses—(such as the first distich in Addison's *Cato,* which is a translation into poetry of 'Past four o'clock and a dark morning!');[304]—and yet nothing bordering on the comic on the one hand, nor any striving of the intellect on the other. It is precisely the language of *sensation* among men who feared no charge of effeminacy for feeling, what they had no want of resolution to bear. Yet the armour, the dead silence, the watchfulness that first interrupts it, the welcome relief of the guard, the cold, the broken expressions of compelled attention to bodily feelings still under control—all excellently accord with, and prepare for, the after gradual rise into tragedy;—but, above all, into a tragedy, the interest of which is as eminently ad et apud *intra*,[305] as that of Macbeth is directly *ad extra*.[306]

In all the best attested stories of ghosts and visions, as in that of Brutus, of Archbishop Cranmer, that of Benvenuto Cellini recorded by himself, and the vision of Galileo communicated by him to his favourite pupil Tassoni,[307] the ghost-seers were in a state of cold or chilling damp from without, and of anxiety inwardly. It has been with all of them as with Francisco on his guard,—alone, in the depth and silence of the night;—'twas bitter cold, and they were sick at heart, and *not a mouse stirring.*'[308] The attention to minute sounds,—naturally associated with the recollection of minute objects, and the more familiar and trifling, the more impressive from the unusualness of their producing any impression at all—gives a philosophic pertinency to this last image; but it has likewise its dramatic use and purpose. For its commonness in ordinary conversation tends to produce the sense of reality, and at once hides the poet, and yet approximates the reader or spectator to that state in which the highest poetry will appear, and in its component parts, though not in the whole composition, really is, the language of nature. If I should not speak it, I feel that I should be

---

[304] Addison's influential tragedy *Cato* (Joseph Addison, *Cato: a Tragedy* (London: Printed for the Company, 1712)) begins: 'The dawn is overcast, the morning lowers/And heavily in clouds brings on the day.'

[305] 'Directed towards that which is *inside*'.

[306] 'To the *outside*'.

[307] Brutus (in Shakespeare's *Julius Caesar*) is haunted by the ghost of the emperor he murdered. According to popular legend Archbishop Cranmer (1489–1556) appeared *as* a ghost to a soldier on a winter battlefield, inspiring him to abandon sin and do his duty (see, for instance, 'Cranmer's Ghost', in *Sunday School Tracts, Religious Moral and Entertaining* (London: F. C. and J. Rivington, 1811) which Coleridge may have read). Cellini (1500–71), Italian goldsmith and sculptor, wrote about his life in his famously revealing *Autobiography* (1565), including the story that his castle was haunted by a ghost called 'Lemmonio Boreñ'. Alessandro Tassoni (1565–1635), Italian poet and writer, wrote about his friendship with Galileo in his memoirs, including reports that Galileo had seen a ghost. Coleridge may have read Joseph C. Walker's recent translation of these, *Memoirs of Alessandro Tassoni, Author of La secchia rapita* (translated by Samuel Walker. London: Longman, 1815).

[308] Referring to *Hamlet*, I, i, 8–10.

thinking it;—the voice only is the poet's,—the words are my own. That Shakespeare meant to put an effect in the actor's power in the very first words—'Who's there?'—is evident from the impatience expressed by the startled Francisco in the words that follow—'Nay, answer me: stand and unfold yourself.' A brave man is never so peremptory, as when he fears that he is afraid. Observe the gradual transition from the silence and the still recent habit of listening in Francisco's—'I think I hear them'—to the more cheerful call out, which a good actor would observe, in the—'Stand ho! Who is there?' Bernardo's inquiry after Horatio, and the repetition of his name and in his own presence indicate a respect or an eagerness that implies him as one of the persons who are in the foreground; and the scepticism attributed to him,—

> Horatio says, 'tis but our fantasy;
> And will not let belief take hold of him—[309]

prepares us for Hamlet's after eulogy on him as one whose blood and judgment were happily commingled. The actor should also be careful to distinguish the expectation and gladness of Bernardo's 'Welcome, Horatio!' from the mere courtesy of his 'Welcome, good Marcellus!'

Now observe the admirable indefiniteness of the first opening out of the occasion of all this anxiety. The preparation informative of the audience is just as much as was precisely necessary, and no more;—it begins with the uncertainty appertaining to a question:—

> *Mar*. What, has *this thing* appear'd again to-night?

Even the word 'again' has its *credibilizing* effect. Then Horatio, the representative of the ignorance of the audience, not himself, but by Marcellus to Bernardo, anticipates the common solution— ''tis but our fantasy!' upon which Marcellus rises into

> This dreaded sight, twice seen of us—[310]

which immediately afterwards becomes 'this apparition,' and that, too, an intelligent spirit, that is, to be spoken to! Then comes the confirmation of Horatio's disbelief;—

> Tush! tush! 'twill not appear!—

and the silence, with which the scene opened, is again restored in the shivering feeling of Horatio sitting down, at such a time, and with the two eye-witnesses, to hear a story of a ghost, and that, too, of a ghost

---

[309] *Hamlet*, I, i, 20–1.
[310] *Hamlet*, I, i, 25.

which had appeared twice before at the very same hour. In the deep feeling which Bernardo has of the solemn nature of what he is about to relate, he makes an effort to master his own imaginative terrors by an elevation of style,—itself a continuation of the effort,—and by turning off from the apparition, as from something which would force him too deeply into himself, to the outward objects, the realities of nature, which had accompanied it:—

> *Ber.* Last night of all,
> When yon same star, that's westward from the pole,
> Had made his course to illume that part of heaven
> Where now it burns, Marcellus and myself,
> The bell then beating one.[311]

This passage seems to contradict the critical law that what is told, makes a faint impression compared with what is beheld; for it does indeed convey to the mind more than the eye can see; whilst the interruption of the narrative at the very moment, when we are most intensely listening for the sequel, and have our thoughts diverted from the dreaded Sight in expectation of the desired, yet almost dreaded, Tale—thus giving all the suddenness and surprize of the original appearance;—

> *Mar.* Peace, break thee off; look, where it comes again!—[312]

Note the judgment displayed in having the two persons present, who, as having seen the Ghost before, are naturally eager in confirming their former opinions,—whilst the sceptic is silent, and after having been twice addressed by his friends, answers with two hasty syllables—'Most like,'—and a confession of horror:— 'It harrows me with fear and wonder'.[313]

'Of mine own eyes.'[314] Hume himself could not but have had faith in this Ghost dramatically, let his anti-ghostism have been as strong as Samson against other Ghosts less powerfully raised![315] And observe, upon the Ghost's reappearance, how much Horatio's courage

---

311 *Hamlet*, I, i, 35–9.
312 *Hamlet*, I, i, 40.
313 *Hamlet*, I, i, 44.
314 Horatio's 'I might this not believe/Without the sensible and true avouch/Of mine own eyes' (*Hamlet*, I, i, 54–6).
315 In 'Of Miracles' (Section 10 of *An Enquiry concerning Human Understanding*, 1748) Scottish philosopher David Hume (1711–76) declares that he has an argument against ghosts that 'will, with the wise and learned, be an everlasting check to all kinds of superstitious delusion'.

is increased by having translated the late individual spectrum[316] into thought and past experience,—and the sympathy of Marcellus and Bernardo in daring to strike at the Ghost; whilst in a moment, upon its vanishing, the former solemn awe-stricken feeling returns upon them:—

> We do it wrong, being so majestical,
> To offer it the show of violence.—[317]

Horatio's speech:—

> I have heard,
> The cock, that is the trumpet to the morn,
> Doth with his lofty and shrill-sounding throat
> Awake the god of day, &c.[318]

No Addison could be more careful to be poetical in diction than Shakespeare in providing the grounds and sources of its propriety. But how to elevate a thing almost mean by its familiarity, young poets may learn in this treatment of the cock-crow. Horatio's speech:—

> And, by my advice,
> Let us impart what we have seen to-night
> Unto young Hamlet; for, upon my life,
> The spirit, dumb to us, will speak to him.[319]

Note the inobtrusive and yet fully adequate mode of introducing the main character, *Young* Hamlet, upon whom is transferred all the interest excited for the acts and concerns of the king his father.

The audience are now relieved by a change of scene to the Royal Court, in order that Hamlet may not have to take up the leavings of exhaustion. Observe the set pedantically antithetic form of the King's speech—yet though in the concerns that galled the heels of conscience,—rhetoric below a King, yet in what follows concerning the public weal, not without majesty. Indeed was he not a royal brother?—

> And now, Laertes, what's the news with you? &c.[320]

Thus with great art Shakespeare introduces a most important, but still subordinate character first—as Milton with Beelzebub[321]—So Laertes,

---

[316] Spectre, or ghost.
[317] *Hamlet*, I, i, 142–3.
[318] *Hamlet*, I, i, 149–52.
[319] *Hamlet*, I, i, 167–70.
[320] *Hamlet*, I, ii, 42f.
[321] Milton's *Paradise Lost* opens with Satan in Hell; God and Christ do not appear until Book 2.

who is yet thus graciously treated in consequence of the assistance given to the election of the late king's brother instead of his son by Polonius.

> *Ham.* A little more than kin, and less than kind.
> *King.* How is it that the clouds still hang on you?
> *Ham.* Not so, my lord, I am too much i' the sun.[322]

Hamlet opens his mouth with a playing on words, the complete absence of which throughout characterizes *Macbeth*. This playing on words may be attributed to many causes or motives, as either to an exuberant activity of mind, as in the higher comedy of Shakespeare generally;–or to an imitation of it as a mere fashion, as if it were said–'Is not this better than groaning?'–or to a contemptuous exultation in minds vulgarized and overset by their success, as in the poetic instance of Milton's devils in the battle;[323]–or it is the language of resentment, as is familiar to every one who has witnessed the quarrels of the lower orders, where there is invariably a profusion of punning invective, whence, perhaps, nicknames have in a considerable degree sprung up;–or it is the language of suppressed passion, and especially of a hardly smothered personal dislike. The first, and last of these combine in Hamlet's case; and I have little doubt that Farmer is right in supposing the equivocation carried on in the expression 'too much i' the sun,' or *son*.[324]

> *Ham.* Ay, madam, it is common.

Here Hamlet's suppression prepares him for the overflow in the next speech, in which his character is more developed by bringing forward his aversion to externals, and which betrays his habit of brooding over the world within him, coupled with a prodigality of beautiful words, which are the half embodyings of thought, and are more than thought, and have an outness, a reality *sui generis,* and yet retain their correspondence and shadowy affinity to the images and movements within. Note also Hamlet's silence to the long speech of the king which follows, and his respectful, but general, answer to his mother. Hamlet's first soliloquy:–

---

[322] *Hamlet*, I, ii, 65–7.
[323] A reference to the 'ambiguous words' Satan and Belial call at their angelic enemies before opening fire on them in the battle for heaven (*Paradise Lost*, 6:558–629).
[324] Richard Farmer (1735–97), author of *Essay on the Learning of Shakespeare* (London: Longman, 1767). The edition S. T. C. was working from contained a footnote on this line: 'Mr Farmer questions whether a quibble between *sun* and *son* be not here intended'.

O, that this too too solid flesh would melt,
Thaw, and resolve itself into a dew! &c.[325]

This *taedium vita* is a common oppression on minds cast in the Hamlet mould, and is caused by disproportionate mental exertion, which necessitates exhaustion of bodily feeling. Where there is a just coincidence of external and internal action, pleasure is always the result; but where the former is deficient, and the mind's appetency of the ideal is unchecked, realities will seem cold and unmoving. In such cases, passion combines itself with the indefinite alone. In this mood of his mind the relation of the appearance of his father's spirit in arms is made all at once to Hamlet:—it is— Horatio's speech, in particular—a perfect model of the true style of dramatic narrative;—the purest poetry, and yet in the most natural language, equally remote from the ink-horn and the plough.[326]

Of Polonius's line:—

How prodigal the soul
Lends the tongue vows:—these blazes, daughter, &c.[327]

A spondee has, I doubt not, dropped out of the text. After 'vows', insert either 'Go tō' or 'Mārk you!';—if the latter be preferred, it might end the line: 'Lends the tongue vows:—*Go to*, these blazes, daughter'— or 'Lends the tongue vows:—These blazes, daughter, *mark you*—' Shakespeare never introduces a catalectic line without intending an equivalent to the foot omitted in the pauses, or the dwelling emphasis, or the diffused retardation. I do not, however, deny that a good actor might by employing the last mentioned means, namely, the retardation, or solemn knowing drawl, supply the missing spondee with good effect. But I do not believe that in this or any other of the foregoing speeches, Shakespeare meant to bring out the *senility* or *weakness* of Polonius's mind. In the great ever-recurring dangers and duties of Life, where to distinguish the fit objects for the application of the maxims collected by the experience of a long life, requires no fineness of tact, as in the admonitions to his son and daughter, Polonius is always made respectable. But if the actor were capable of catching these shades in the character, the pit and the gallery would be malcontent.

It is to Hamlet that Polonius is, and is meant to be, contemptible,

---

[325] *Hamlet*, I, ii, 129f.
[326] This paragraph derives from notes Coleridge made for Lecture 3 of his 1813 Lectures on Shakespeare and Education; a note in the edition he used for the 1818 lecture seems to refer him back to his ('See and Transcribe from MSS', CC 5:2, 298) presumably for use on this later occasion.
[327] *Hamlet*, I, iii, 116f.

because in inwardness and uncontrollable activity of movement, Hamlet's mind is the logical contrary to that of Polonius, and besides, as I have observed before, Hamlet dislikes the man as false to his true allegiance in the matter of the succession to the crown.

In addition to the other excellencies of Hamlet's speech concerning the *Wassel*-music[328]—so finely revealing the predominant idealism, the ratiocinative meditativeness, of his character—it has the advantage of giving nature and probability to the impassioned continuity of the speech instantly directed to the Ghost. The momentum had been given to his mental activity; the full current of the thoughts and words had set in, and the very forgetfulness, in the fervour of his argumentation, of the purpose for which he was there, aided in preventing the appearance from benumbing the mind. Consequently, it acted as a new impulse,—a sudden stroke which increased the velocity of the body already in motion, whilst it altered the direction. The co-presence of Horatio, Marcellus, and Bernardo[329] is most judiciously contrived; for it renders the courage of Hamlet and his impetuous eloquence perfectly intelligible. The knowledge,—the unthought of consciousness,—the sensation,—of human auditors,—of flesh and blood sympathists—acts as a support and a stimulation *a tergo*,[330] while the front of the mind, the whole consciousness of the speaker is filled, by the apparition. Add too, that the apparition itself has by its frequent previous appearances been brought nearer to a Thing of this World. This accrescence[331] of objectivity in a Ghost that yet retains all its ghostly attributes and fearful subjectivity, is truly wonderful. In scene 5 we have Hamlet's speech:—

> O all you host of heaven! O earth! What else?
> And shall I couple hell? Oh, fie! Hold, hold, my heart,
> And you, my sinews, grow not instant old,
> But bear me stiffly up. Remember thee!
> Ay, thou poor ghost, whiles memory holds a seat
> In this distracted globe. Remember thee!
> Yea, from the table of my memory
> I'll wipe away all trivial fond records,
> All saws of books, all forms, all pressures past
> That youth and observation copied there,
> And thy commandment all alone shall live

---

[328] *Hamlet*, I, iv, 8-57.
[329] Bernardo is not actually present in *Hamlet* I, iv.
[330] 'From behind'.
[331] A variant of 'accretion', apparently Coleridge's own coinage here.

Within the book and volume of my brain,
Unmixed with baser matter. Yes, by heaven!
O most pernicious woman!
O villain, villain, smiling, damnèd villain!
My tables!–Meet it is I set it down
That one may smile, and smile, and be a villain.[332]

I remember nothing equal to this burst unless it be the first speech of
Prometheus in the Greek drama, after the exit of Vulcan and the two
Afrites.[333] But Shakespeare alone could have produced the vow of
Hamlet to make his memory a blank of all maxims and generalized
truths, that 'observation had copied there,'– followed immediately by
the speaker noting down the generalized fact,

That one may smile, and smile, and be a villain!

In Act the Second, Polonius and Reynaldo converse. In all things
dependent on, or rather made up of, fine address, the *manner* is no
more or otherwise rememberable than the light motions, steps, and
gestures of youth and health. But this is almost every thing:–no
wonder, therefore, if that which can be put down by rule in the
memory should appear to us as mere poring, maudlin, cunning,
–slyness blinking through the watery eye of superannuation. So in
this admirable scene, Polonius, who is throughout the skeleton of
his own former skill and statecraft, hunts the trail of policy at a dead
scent, supplied by the weak fever-smell in his own nostrils.

Ham. Excellent well;
You are a fishmonger.[334]

That is, you are sent to fish out this secret. This is Hamlet's own
meaning. The purposely obscure lines–

Ham. For if the sun breeds maggots in a dead dog,
Being a god, kissing carrion–[335]

–I rather think refer to some thought in Hamlet's mind, contrasting
the lovely daughter with such a tedious old fool, her father, as *he* represents Polonius to himself:–'Why, fool as he is, he is some degrees

---

[332] *Hamlet*, I, v, 92–109.
[333] An 'afrite' or 'afreet' is a monster or demon. Coleridge is talking about Aeschylus's
Prometheus Bound (89f), when Hephaestos (Greek god of smiths and craftsmen), Kratos
('Strength') and Bia ('Force'), having pinned the protagonist to a rock, leave.
[334] *Hamlet*, II, ii, 174.
[335] *Hamlet*, II, ii, 181.

in rank above a dead dog's carcase; and if the sun, being a god that kisses carrion, can raise life out of a dead dog,—why may not good fortune, that favours fools, have raised a lovely girl out of this dead-alive old fool?'

The rugged Pyrrhus—he whose sable arms, &c.[336]

This admirable substitution of the epic for the dramatic, giving such a reality to the impassioned dramatic diction of Shakespeare's own dialogue, and authorized, too, by the actual style of the tragedies before his time (*Porrex and Ferrex*,[337] *Titus Andronicus*, &c.)—is well worthy of notice. The fancy, that a burlesque was intended, sinks below criticism: the lines, as epic narrative, are superb.

In the thoughts, and even in the separate parts of the diction, this description is highly poetical: in truth, taken by itself, this is its fault that it is too poetical!—the language of lyric vehemence and epic pomp, and not of the drama. But if Shakespeare had made the diction truly dramatic, where would have been the contrast between Hamlet and the play in Hamlet?

> The spirit that I have seen,
> May be a devil: and the devil hath power
> To assume a pleasing shape; yea, and, perhaps
> Out of my weakness, and my melancholy,
> (As he is very potent with such spirits)
> Abuses me to damn me.[338]

I here quote Sir Thomas Brown:

> I believe that those apparitions and ghosts of departed persons are not the wandering souls of men, but the unquiet walks of devils, prompting and suggesting us unto mischief, blood and villainy; instilling and stealing into our hearts that the blessed spirits are not at rest in their graves, but wander, solicitous of the affairs of the world. But that those phantasms appear often, and do frequent cemeteries, charnel-houses, and churches, it is because those are the dormitories of the dead, where the devil, like an insolent champion, beholds with pride the spoils and trophies of his victory in *Adam*.[339]

---

[336] *Hamlet*, II, ii, 451f.

[337] Thomas Sackville and Thomas Norton's stiff and stylistically mannered tragedy *Ferrex and Porrex, or Gorboduc* (London: William Griffith, 1562).

[338] *Hamlet*, II, ii, 598–603.

[339] Thomas Browne, *Religio Medici* (London: Robert Scot, 1643) 1 § 37.

LECTURE 4

The opening of *Macbeth* stands in contrast with that of *Hamlet*. In the latter, there is a gradual ascent from the simplest forms of conversation to the language of impassioned Intellect,—yet still the Intellect remaining the *seat* of passion: in the *Macbeth*, the invocation is at once made to the Imagination and the emotions connected therewith.

Hence the movement throughout is the most rapid of all Shakespeare's plays; and hence also, with the exception of the disgusting passage of the Porter (Act ii. sc. 3.), which I dare pledge myself to demonstrate to be an interpolation of the actors, there is not, to the best of my remembrance, a single pun or play on words in the whole drama. I have previously given an answer to the thousand times repeated charge against Shakespeare upon the subject of his punning, and I here merely mention the fact of the absence of any puns in *Macbeth*, as justifying a candid doubt at least, whether even in these figures of speech and fanciful modifications of language, Shakespeare may not have followed rules and principles that merit and would stand the test of philosophic examination. And hence, also, there is an entire absence of comedy, nay, even of irony and philosophic contemplation in *Macbeth*,—the play being wholly and purely tragic. For the same cause, there are no reasonings of equivocal morality, which would have required a more leisurely state and a consequently greater activity of mind;—no sophistry of self-delusion,—except only that previously to the dreadful act, Macbeth mistranslates the recoilings and ominous whispers of conscience into prudential and selfish reasonings, and, after the deed done, the terrors of remorse into fear from external dangers,—like delirious men who run away from the phantoms of their own brains, or, raised by terror to rage, stab the real object that is within their reach :—whilst Lady Macbeth merely endeavours to reconcile his and her own sinkings of heart by anticipations of the worst, and an affected bravado in confronting them. In all the rest, Macbeth's language is the grave utterance of the very heart, conscience-sick, even to the last faintings of moral death. It is the same in all the other characters. The variety arises from rage, caused ever and anon by disruption of anxious thought, and the quick transition of fear into it.

In *Hamlet* and *Macbeth* the scene opens with superstition; but, in each it is not merely different, but opposite. In the first it is connected with the best and holiest feelings; in the second with the shadowy, turbulent, and unsanctified cravings of the individual will. Nor is the purpose the same; in the one the object is to excite, whilst in the other it is to mark a mind already excited. Superstition, of one sort or another, is natural to victorious generals; the instances are too notorious to need mentioning. There is so much of chance in warfare, and such vast events are connected with the acts of a single individual, –the representative, in truth, of the efforts of myriads, and yet to the public and, doubtless, to his own feelings, the aggregate of all, – that the proper temperament for generating or receiving superstitious impressions is naturally produced. Hope, the master element of a commanding genius, meeting with an active and combining intellect, and an imagination of just that degree of vividness which disquiets and impels the soul to try to realize its images, greatly increases the creative power of the mind; and hence the images become a satisfying world of themselves, as is the case in every poet and original philosopher:–but hope fully gratified, and yet the elementary basis of the passion remaining, becomes fear; and, indeed, the general, who must often feel, even though he may hide it from his own consciousness, how large a share chance had in his successes, may very naturally be irresolute in a new scene, where he knows that all will depend on his own act and election.

The Weird Sisters are as true a *Creation* of Shakespeare's, as his Ariel and Caliban,–the Fates, the Furies, and the *materializing* Witches being the elements. They are wholly different from any representation of witches in the contemporary writers, and yet presented a sufficient external resemblance to the creatures of vulgar prejudice to act immediately on the audience. Their character consists in the imaginative disconnected from the good; they are the shadowy obscure and fearfully anomalous of physical nature, the lawless of human nature, –elemental avengers without sex or kin:

Fair is foul, and foul is fair;
Hover thro' the fog and filthy air.[340]

How might we wish in playing Macbeth, that an attempt should be made to introduce the flexile character-mask of the ancient pantomime;–that a Flaxman would contribute his genius to the embodying and making sensuously perceptible that of Shakespeare!

[340] *Macbeth*, I, i, 12–13

The style and rhythm of the Captain's speeches in the second scene should be illustrated by reference to the interlude in *Hamlet*, in which the epic is substituted for the tragic, in order to make the latter be felt as the real life diction. In *Macbeth*, the poet's object was to raise the mind at once to the high tragic tone, that the audience might be ready for the precipitate consummation of guilt in the early part of the play. The true reason for the first appearance of the Witches is to strike the key-note of the character of the whole drama, as is proved by their re-appearance in the third scene, after such an order of the king's as establishes their supernatural power of information. I say information,—for so it only is as to Glamis and Cawdor; the *King hereafter* was still contingent,—[341] still in Macbeth's moral will; although, if he should yield to the temptation, and thus forfeit his free agency, the link of cause and effect *more physico*[342] would then commence. I need not say, that the general idea is all that can be required from the poet,—not a scholastic logical consistency in all the parts so as to meet metaphysical objectors. But O! how truly Shakespearian is the opening of Macbeth's character given in the *unpossessedness* of Banquo's mind, wholly present to the present object,—an unsullied, unscarified mirror!—And how strictly true to nature it is, that Banquo, and not Macbeth himself, directs our notice to the effect produced on Macbeth's mind, rendered *temptible* by previous dalliance of the fancy with ambitious thoughts.

> Good Sir, why do you start; and seem to fear
> Things that do sound so fair?[343]

We might compare the soliloquy of Wallenstein (Act 1 scene iv):

> Is it possible?
> Is't so? I can no longer what I would?
> No longer draw back at my liking? I
> Must do the deed, because I thought of it?
> And fed this heart here with a dream?[344]

And then, again, still unintroitive,[345] addresses the Witches:—

---

[341] *Macbeth*, I, iii, 50. This is the Witches' prophetic promise: 'All hail, Macbeth! that shalt be king hereafter!'

[342] 'In a physical mode' or 'manner'.

[343] *Macbeth*, I, iii, 51–2. Banquo is speaking to Macbeth.

[344] Schiller's *Wallenstein* (1800); these lines are Coleridge's own translation, from the same year (Friedrich Schiller, *The Death of Wallenstein: A Tragedy in Five Acts* (translated by S. T. Coleridge. London: Longman, 1800)).

[345] 'Introitive' is one of Coleridge's coinages (along with related words: 'unintroitive', 'extroitive' and 'retroitive') derived from the Latin *introitus*, which means the

> I' the name of truth,
> Are ye fantastical, or that indeed
> Which outwardly ye show?[346]

The questions of Banquo are those of natural Curiosity,—such as a Girl would make after she had heard a Gypsey tell her School-fellow's Fortune;—all perfectly general, or rather *planless*. But Macbeth, lost in thought, raises himself to speech only by the Witches being about to depart:—

> STAY, you imperfect speakers, tell me more:—[347]

and all that follows is reasoning on a problem already discussed in his mind,—on a hope which he welcomes, and the doubts concerning its attainment he wishes to have cleared up. Compare his eagerness,—the keen eye with which he has pursued the Witches' evanishing—with the easily satisfied mind of the self-uninterested Banquo:—

> The air hath bubbles, as the water has,
> And these are of them:—Whither are they vanish'd?

and then Macbeth's earnest reply,—

> Into the air; and what seem'd corporal, melted
> As breath into the wind.—WOULD THEY HAD STAY'D![348]

Is it too minute to notice the appropriateness of the simile 'as Breath,' in a Cold climate?

Still again Banquo goes on wondering like any common spectator, 'Were such things here as we do speak about?'[349] whilst Macbeth persists in recurring to the *self-concerning*:—'Your children shall be kings'. So surely is the guilt in its Germ anterior to the supposed cause and immediate temptation! Before he can cool, the *confirmation* of the tempting half of the prophecy arrives, and the *catenating* tendency of the imagination is fostered by the sudden coincidence:—

> Glamis, and thane of Cawdor:
> The greatest is behind.[350]

---

entrance to something hollow, like a cave or a womb. Accordingly it means, roughly, 'introductive'.

[346] *Macbeth*, I, iii, 52–4.
[347] *Macbeth*, I, iii, 70.
[348] *Macbeth*, I, iii, 79–82.
[349] *Macbeth*, I, iii, 83. The next line quoted is 86.
[350] *Macbeth*, I, iii, 116–17.

Oppose this to Banquo's simple surprise:–

What, can the devil speak true?[351]

When Banquo speaks:–

> That, trusted home,
> Might yet enkindle you unto the crown,
> Besides the thane of Cawdor.[352]

I doubt whether 'enkindle' has not another sense than that of 'stimulating;' whether of 'kind' and 'kin,' as when rabbits are said to *kindle*.[353] However Macbeth hears no more ab extra:–

> Two truths are told,
> As happy prologues to the swelling act–[354]
> Of the imperial theme.

Then in the necessity of recollecting himself–

> I thank you, gentlemen.

Then he relapses into himself again, and every word of his soliloquy shows the early birthdate of his guilt. He is all-powerful without strength; he wishes the end, but is irresolute as to the means; conscience distinctly warns him, and he lulls it imperfectly:–

> If chance will have me king, why, chance may crown me
> Without my stir.

Lost in the prospective of his guilt, he turns round alarmed lest others may suspect what is passing in his own mind, and instantly vents the lie of ambition:

> My dull brain was wrought
> With things forgotten;–

And immediately after pours forth the *promising courtesies* of a usurper in intention:–

> Kind gentlemen, your pains
> Are register'd where every day I turn
> The leaf to read them.

---

[351] *Macbeth*, I, iii, 107.
[352] *Macbeth*, I, iii, 122.
[353] To give birth.
[354] This and the next quotations are all from the same monologue, I, iii, 27f.

O! the affecting beauty of the death of Cawdor, and the King's pre-sentimental speech—

> There's no art
> To find the mind's construction in the face:
> He was a gentleman on whom I built
> An absolute trust—[355]

Interrupted by—

> O worthiest cousin!

on the entrance of the deeper traitor for whom Cawdor had made way! And here in contrast with Duncan's 'plenteous joys,' Macbeth has nothing but the common-places of loyalty, in which he hides himself with 'our duties.'[356] Note the exceeding effort of Macbeth's addresses to the king, his reasoning on his allegiance, and then especially when a new difficulty, the designation of a successor, suggests a new crime. This, however, seems the first distinct notion, as to the plan of realizing his wishes; and here, therefore, with great propriety, Macbeth's cowardice of his own conscience discloses itself.

In the fifth scene Macbeth is described by Lady Macbeth so as at the same time to reveal her own character. Intellectually considered, he is powerful in all, but has strength in none—morally *selfish*, that is as far as his weakness will permit him. Could he have every thing he wanted, he would rather have it innocently;— ignorant, as alas! how many of us are, that he who wishes a temporal end for itself, does in truth will the *means*; and hence the danger of indulging fancies.

Lady Macbeth's 'with the valor of my Tongue'[357] is a day-dreamer's valiance. All the false efforts of a mind accustomed only to the Shadows of the Imagination, vivid enough to throw the every-day realities into shadows, but not yet compared with their own correspondent realities. She evinces no womanly, no wifely joy, at the return of her husband, no retrospection on the dangers he had escaped. Macbeth bursts forth naturally—'My dearest love'[358]—and shrinks from the boldness with which she presents his own thoughts to him—'We will speak further'.[359] In Macbeth's speech:

---

[355] *Macbeth*, I, iv, 13–16.
[356] 'Your highness' part/Is to receive our duties: and our duties/Are to your throne and state, children and servants' (*Macbeth*, I, iv, 23–5).
[357] *Macbeth*, I, v, 27.
[358] *Macbeth*, I, v, 58.
[359] *Macbeth*, I, v, 71.

If it were done when 'tis done, then 'twere well
It were done quickly;—[360]

We note the inward pangs and warnings of conscience interpreted into *prudential* reasonings. Once the deed is done or doing—now that the first reality commences, Lady Macbeth shrinks. The most simple sound strikes terror, the most natural consequences are horrible, whilst previously every thing, however awful, appeared a mere trifle; conscience, which before had been hidden to Macbeth in selfish and prudential fears, now rushes in upon him in her own veritable person.—'We have scotch'd the snake, not kill'd it'[361]—Ever and ever mistaking the anguish of conscience for fears of selfishness, and thus as a punishment of that selfishness, plunging still deeper in guilt and ruin.

By contrast, how admirably Macduff's grief[362] is in harmony with the whole play! It rends, not dissolves, the heart. 'The tune of it goes manly.'[363] Thus is Shakespeare always master of himself and of his subject,—a genuine Proteus:—we see all things in him, as images in a calm lake, most distinct, most accurate,— only more splendid, more glorified. This is correctness in the only philosophical sense. But he requires your sympathy and your submission; you must have that recipiency of moral impression without which the purposes and ends of the drama would be frustrated, and the absence of which demonstrates an utter want of all imagination, a deadness to that necessary pleasure of being innocently—shall I say, deluded?—or rather, drawn away from ourselves to the music of noblest thought in harmonious sounds. Happy he, who not only in the public theatre, but in the labours of a profession, and round the light of his own hearth, still carries a heart so pleasure-fraught!

Alas for Macbeth! Now all is inward with him; he has no more prudential prospective reasonings. His wife, the only being who could have had any seat in his affections, dies; he puts on despondency, the final heart-armour of the wretched, and would fain think every thing shadowy and unsubstantial, as indeed all things are to those who cannot regard them as symbols of goodness:—

> Out, out, brief candle!
> Life's but a walking shadow; a poor player,

---

[360] *Macbeth*, I, vii, 1f.
[361] *Macbeth*, III, ii, 13.
[362] When he hears the news his family has been murdered (*Macbeth*, IV, iii).
[363] Malcolm, marching with his army against Macbeth, declares: 'this tune goes manly' (*Macbeth*, IV, iii, 235).

That struts and frets his hour upon the stage,
And then is heard no more: it is a tale
Told by an idiot, full of sound and fury,
Signifying nothing.[364]

---

[364] From Macbeth's 'To-morrow, and to-morrow, and to-morrow' soliloquy (*Macbeth*, V, v, 19–28).

A PORTION OF LECTURE 5

Admirable is the preparation, so truly and peculiarly Shakespearian, in the introduction of Roderigo, as the dupe on whom Iago shall first exercise his art, and in so doing display his own character.–Roderigo, already fitted and predisposed by his own passions–without any fixed principle or strength of character (the want of character and power of the passion, like the wind loudest in empty houses, *forms* his character), but yet not without the moral notions and sympathies with honour, which his rank and connections had hung upon him. The first three lines happily state the nature and foundation of the friendship between him and Iago,–the purse,–as well as the contrast of Roderigo's intemperance of mind with Iago's coolness,–the coolness of a preconceiving *Experimenter*. The mere language of protestation–

> If ever I did dream
> Of such a matter, abhor me,–[365]

which fixing the associative link that determines Roderigo's continuation of complaint–

> Thou told'st me
> Thou didst hold him in thy hate–

elicits at length a true feeling of Iago's, the dread of contempt fatal to those who encourage in themselves, and have their keenest pleasure in the feeling and expression of contempt for others. His high self-opinion, and how a wicked man employs his real feelings as well as assumes those most alien from his own, as instruments of his purposes:–

> And, by the faith of man,
> I know my place, I am worth no worse a place.[366]

I think Tyrwhitt's reading of 'life' for 'wife'–

> A fellow almost damn'd in a fair wife–[367]

---

[365] Iago says this (*Othello*, I, i, 4–5); the next quotation follows straight on, lines 5–6.
[366] *Othello*, I, i, 10–11.
[367] Iago's assessment of Cassio (*Othello*, I, i, 20). Thomas Tyrwhitt proposed the

the true one, as fitting to Iago's contempt for whatever did not display power, and that intellectual power. In what follows, let the reader *feel*–how by and through the glass of two passions, disappointed Passion and Envy, the very vices he is complaining of are made to act upon him as if they were so many excellences,–and the more appropriately, because cunning is always admired and wished for by minds conscious of inward weakness;–and yet it is but *half*, it acts like music on an inattentive auditor, *swelling* the thoughts which prevented him from listening to it.

> *Rod.* What a full fortune does the thick-lips owe,
> If he can carry't thus.[368]

Roderigo turns off to Othello; and here comes the one if not the only justification of the Blackamoor Othello, namely as a Negro–who is not a *Moor* at all. Even if we supposed this an uninterrupted Tradition of the Theatre, and that Shakespeare himself, from want of scenes, and the experience that nothing could be made too *marked* for the senses of his audience,–would this prove aught concerning his own intention as a poet for all ages? Can we suppose him so utterly ignorant as to make a barbarous *Negro* plead royal birth,–where Negros then known but as slaves?–On the contrary were not the *Moors* the warriors? Iago's speech to Brabantio implies merely that he was *a Moor*, that is, black. Though I think the rivalry of Roderigo sufficient to account for his wilful confusion of Moor and Negro,–yet, even if compelled to give this up, I should think it only adapted for the acting of the day, and should complain of an enormity built on a single word, in direct contradiction to Iago's 'Barbary horse.'[369] If we could in good earnest believe Shakespeare ignorant of the distinction, still why take one disagreeable possibility instead of a ten times greater and more pleasing probability, as Othello cannot be both?[370]

---

emendation in his *Observations and Conjectures upon Some Passages of Shakespeare* (Oxford: Clarendon, 1766); it was reported in a footnote of the edition of Othello from which Coleridge was working.

[368] *Othello*, I, i, 68–9.

[369] Iago mocks Brabantio with 'you'll have your daughter covered with a Barbary horse' (*Othello*, I, i, 111).

[370] At this point in *Literary Remains* occurs the following passage: 'It is a common error to mistake the epithets applied by the *dramatis personae* to each other, as truly descriptive of what the audience ought to see or know. No doubt Desdemona saw Othello's visage in his mind; yet, as we are constituted, and most surely as an English audience was disposed in the beginning of the seventeenth century, it would be something monstrous to conceive this beautiful Venetian girl falling in love with a veritable negro. It would argue a disproportionateness, a want of balance, in Desdemona, which Shakespeare does not appear to have in the least contemplated.' Foakes (CC 5:2, 314) demonstrates

Brabantio's speech:—

This accident is not unlike my dream:—[371]

The old *careful* Senator, who caught careless, transfers his caution to his *dreaming* power at least. The forced praise of Othello followed by the bitter hatred of him in his speech! And observe how Brabantio's dream prepares for his recurrence to the notion of philtres, and how both prepare for carrying on the plot of the arraignment of Othello *on this ground.*

> *Bra.* Look to her, Moor; have a quick eye to see;
> She has deceiv'd her father, and may thee.
> *Oth.* My life upon her faith.

In real life, how do we look back to little speeches as presentimental of, or contrasted with, an affecting event! Even so, Shakespeare, as secure of being read over and over, of becoming a family friend, provides this passage for his readers, and leaves it to them.
Iago's speech:—

Virtue? a fig! 'tis in ourselves, that we are thus, or thus, &c.[372]

Iago's passionless character! It is all *will* in intellect; and therefore he is here a bold partisan of a truth, but yet of a truth converted into a falsehood by the absence of all the modifications by the frail nature of man. And then comes the *last sentiment,*—

> Seek thou rather to be hang'd in compassing thy joy than to be
> drown'd and go without her.[373]

And the repetition, Go, make money!—a pride in it, of an anticipated Dupe, stronger than the love of Lucre. The remainder, Iago's soliloquy—

> Go to; farewell; put money enough in your purse!
> Thus do I ever make my fool my purse &c.[374]

---

this is not based on Coleridge's notes for this lecture. Indeed it is not clear if this is a passage Henry Nelson Coleridge interpolated from a separate, now lost, S. T. C. note, or whether he concocted it himself. It is cited here since it has been often quoted by critics discussing Coleridge's supposed racism.

[371] *Othello,* I, i, 42f. Coleridge picks up on Brabantio's later speculation that his daughter has been won over with a love-philtre: 'Is there not charms/By which the property of youth and maidhood/May be abus'd?' (*Othello,* I, i, 171–3).

[372] *Othello,* I, iii, 320f.

[373] *Othello,* I, iii, 360–1.

[374] *Othello,* I, iii, 381f.

The triumph! Again, *put money* after the effect has been fully produced. The last speech: the motive-hunting of a motiveless Malignity—how awful! In itself fiendish—whilst yet he was allowed to bear the divine image, too fiendish for his own steady view,—a being next to devil, only *not* quite devil,—and this Shakespeare has attempted and executed, without disgust, and without scandal!

Dr Johnson has remarked that little or nothing is wanting to render the *Othello* a regular tragedy, but to have opened the play with the arrival of Othello in Cyprus, and to have thrown the preceding act into the form of narration.[375] Here then is the place to determine, whether such a change would or would not be an improvement;—nay, (to throw down the glove with a full challenge) whether the tragedy would or not by such an arrangement become *more regular*,—that is, more consonant with the rules dictated by universal reason, on the true common sense of mankind, in its application to the particular case. For surely we may safely leave it to common sense whether to reply to or laugh at such a remark as, for instance—suppose a man had described a rhomboid or parallelogram and a critic were with great gravity to observe—if the lines had only been in true right-angles, the diagram would have accorded to the strictest rules of geometry. For in all acts of judgment, it can never be too often recollected, and scarcely too often repeated, that rules are means to ends, and, consequently, that the end must be determined and understood before it can be known what the rules are or ought to be. Now from a certain species of drama, proposing to itself the accomplishment of certain ends,— these partly arising from the idea of the species itself, but in part, likewise, forced upon the dramatist by accidental circumstances beyond his power to remove or control three rules have been abstracted;—in other words, the means most conducive to the attainment of the proposed ends have been generalized, and prescribed under the names of the three unities,—the unity of Time, the unity of Place, and the unity of Action,—which last would, perhaps, have been as appropriately, as well as more intelligibly, entitled the unity of Interest. With this last the present question has no immediate concern: in fact, its conjunction with the former two is a mere delusion of *words*. It is not properly *a rule*, but in itself the great end not only of the drama, but of the epic, lyric, even to the candle-flame cone of an epigram,—not only

---

[375] Johnson's and Steevens' very last note on *Othello* reads: 'had the scene opened in Cyprus, and the preceding incidents been occasionally related, there had been little wanting to a drama of the most exact and scrupulous regularity' (Samuel Johnson and George Steevens (eds), *The Plays of Mr Shakespeare Volume X: Romeo and Juliet. Hamlet. Othello. Appendixes* (London: C. Bathurst, 1773), 521).

of poetry, but of poesy in general, as the proper generic term inclusive of all the fine Arts as its species. But of the unities of Time and Place, which alone are entitled to the name of rules, the history of their origin will be their best criterion. You might take the Greek Chorus to a place, but you could not bring a place to them without as palpable an equivoque as bringing Birnam wood to Macbeth at Dunsinane.[376] It was the same, though in a less degree, with regard to the unity of Time:—the positive fact, not for a moment removed from the senses, the presence, I mean, of the very same persons in a continued measure of Time;—and though the imagination may supersede perception, yet it must be granted to be an imperfection to place the two in broad contradiction to each other.

But in truth, it is a mere accident of terms in the first place; for the trilogy of the Greek theatre was a drama in three acts, and notwithstanding this, the strange contrivances as to place, as in the *Frogs*.[377] There is no lack of instances in the Greek tragedies—the allowance extorted of 24 hours—is if, perception once violated, it was more difficult to imagine three hours to be three years than to be a whole day and night. Aeschylus' *Agamemnon* furnishes a fine instance of this.[378]

There is a danger in introducing into a situation of great interest one for whom you had no previous Interest. Φρϛφρρ Ιωαν.[379]

---

[376] *Macbeth*, Act 5.

[377] Aristophanes' comic play starts in the mortal world, and shifts its scene to various locations in the underworld.

[378] Aeschylus' tragedy opens with a Watchman observing the beacon fires lit to signal the fall of Troy; during the course of the play, and without any indication of time passing, Agamemnon arrives back in Greece after what must have been a lengthy voyage.

[379] This opaque cipher has never been explained. Two theories suggest themselves, one less and one perhaps more likely. The less plausible explanation is that the Greek here picks up on the reference to Aristophanes' *Frogs* from earlier in the notes. For this to be the case, the Greek would have to altered, on the understanding that Coleridge's 'ω's might be written so poorly as to be confusable with his 'ρ's. The word could then be read as an abbreviated version of φωσφωρος ('light-bearer, light-carrier'; also the name of the Morning Star). φωσφωρ Ιωαν could conceivably be a mangled jotting-down of Aristophanes' Ἴακχ φωσφόρος from *Frogs* 342-3 ("Ἴακχ᾽ ὦ Ἴακχε,/νυκτέρου τελετῆς φωσφόρος ἀστήρ': 'Iacchus, O Iacchus/Shining star of our night-time rituals!'). It is not immediately clear, however, what this has to do with the rest of Coleridge's point. A second theory is that Ιωαν ('John') refers to the Greek Gospel of Saint John. Φρϛφρρ would presumably be a way of coding a specific passage or phrase in that text, though which passage is hard to decipher. The strange use of a terminal sigma (ϛ) in the middle of the word (instead of the usual σ) suggests it is perhaps meant to be two separate words: Φρϛ and φρρ. Chapter 3 of John's Gospel concerns a doubting Pharisee ('τῶν Φαρισαίων'): might Coleridge's 'Φρϛ' be a shortened version of that word? Is this some oblique reference to the introduction of the Pharisee characters into John's narrative?

LECTURE 6

Of all Shakespeare's plays *Macbeth* is the most rapid, *Hamlet* the slowest, in movement. *Lear* combines length with rapidity,–like the hurricane and the whirlpool, absorbing while it advances. It begins as a stormy day in summer, with brightness; but that brightness is lurid, and anticipates the tempest.

It was not without forethought, nor is it without its due significance, that the division of Lear's kingdom is in the first six lines of the play stated as a thing already determined in all its particulars, previously to the trial of professions, as the relative rewards of which the daughters were to be made to consider their several portions. The strange, yet by no means unnatural, mixture of selfishness, sensibility, and habit of feeling derived from, and fostered by, the particular rank and usages of the Individual;–the intense desire to be intensely beloved, selfish, and yet characteristic of the selfishness of a loving and kindly nature;–the feeble selfishness, self-supportless and leaning for all pleasure on another's breast;–the craving after a sympathy with a prodigal disinterestedness, contradicted by its own ostentation, and the mode and nature of its claims;–the anxiety, the distrust, the jealousy, which more or less accompany all selfish affections, and are amongst the surest contradictions[380] of mere fondness from love, and which originate Lear's eager wish to enjoy his daughter's violent professions, whilst the inveterate habits of sovereignty convert the wish into claim and positive right, and the incompliance with it into crime and treason;– these facts, these passions, these moral verities, on which the whole tragedy is founded, are all prepared for, and will to the retrospect be found implied, in these first four or five lines of the play. They let us know that the trial is but a trick; and that the grossness of the old King's rage is in part the natural result of a silly trick suddenly and most unexpectedly baffled and disappointed.

Here we may notice that the improbability and nursery-tale character of the tale is prefixed as the porch of the edifice, not laid as its foundation–So with Shylock's pound of flesh, based upon the old

---

[380] Henry Nelson Coleridge emends this word to 'contradistinctions', which makes more sense of the sentence, and may have been what Coleridge meant.

popular ballad *Gernutus the Jew of Venice*.[381] With how great judgment Shakespeare has done this, and what still remains of it, is combatable.[382]

Thus having been provided in the fewest words, in a natural reply to as natural a question,—which yet answers a secondary purpose of attracting our attention to the difference or diversity between the characters of Cornwall and Albany,—provided the premises and *data*, as it were, having been thus afforded for our after-insight into the mind and mood of the person, whose character, passions, and sufferings are the main *subject-matter* of the play;—from Lear, the persona *patiens*[383] of his drama, Shakespeare passes without delay to the second in importance, the chief agent and prime mover, and introduces Edmund to our acquaintance, preparing us with the same felicity of judgment, and in the same easy, natural way, for his character in the seemingly casual communication of its origin and occasion. From the first drawing up of the curtain Edmund has stood before us in the united strength and beauty of earliest manhood. Our eyes have been questioning him. Gifted thus with high advantages of *person*, and further endowed by Nature with a powerful intellect and a strong energetic will, even without any concurrence of circumstances and accident, pride will be the sin that most easily besets him. But he is the known and acknowledged son of the princely Gloster:—Edmund therefore has both the germ of pride and the conditions best fitted to evolve and ripen it into a predominant feeling. Yet hitherto no reason appears why it should be other than the not unusual pride of person, talent, and birth, a pride auxiliary, if not akin, to many virtues, and the natural ally of honourable impulses. But alas! in his own presence his own father takes shame to himself for the frank avowal that he is his father,—he has 'blushed so often to acknowledge him that he is now brazed to it.'[384] Edmund hears the circumstances of his birth spoken of with a most degrading and licentious levity,—his mother described as a wanton by her own paramour, and the remembrance of the animal sting, the low criminal gratifications connected with her wantonness and prostituted beauty, assigned as the reason, why 'the

---

[381] A sixteenth-century popular ballad, reprinted in Thomas Percy's *Reliques of Ancient English Poetry* (3 vols (London: Dodslet, 1765), 1:222f.); the poem's subtitle is 'Of the Jews crueltie; setting foorth the mercifulnesse of the Judge towards the Marchant. To the tune of Blacke and Yellow.' Percy's headnote records that 'Mr. Warton, in his ingenious *Observations on the Faerie Queen* [1754]' argues this ballad is the source for 'the scene between Shylock and Antonio in the *Merchant of Venice*.'

[382] A Coleridge coinage, meaning 'arguable'.

[383] That is, the passive or suffering character.

[384] *King Lear*, I, i, 10–11.

whoreson must be acknowledged!'[385] This, and the consciousness of its notoriety; the gnawing conviction that every show of respect is an effort of courtesy which recalls while it represses a contrary feeling;– this is the ever trickling flow of wormwood and gall into the wounds of pride,–the corrosive virus[386] which inoculates pride with a venom not its own, with envy, hatred, a lust of that power which in its blaze of radiance would hide the dark spots on his disc,–with pangs of shame personally undeserved, and therefore felt as wrongs, and with a blind ferment of vindictive workings towards the occasions and causes, especially towards a brother, whose stainless birth and lawful honours were the constant remembrancers of *his* debasement, and were ever in the way to prevent all chance of its being unknown, or overlooked and forgotten. Add to this that with excellent judgment, and provident for the claims of the moral sense,–for that which, relatively to the drama, is called Poetic Justice,[387] and as the fittest means for reconciling the feelings of the spectators to the horrors of Gloster's after sufferings,–at least, of rendering them somewhat less unendurable;–(for I will not disguise my conviction, that in this one point the tragic in this play has been urged beyond the outermost mark and *ne plus ultra* of the dramatic)–Shakespeare has precluded all excuse and palliation of the guilt incurred by both the parents of the base-born Edmund, by Gloster's confession, that he was at the time a married man, and already blest with a lawful heir of his fortunes. The mournful alienation of brotherly love, occasioned by the law of primogeniture in noble families, or rather by the unnecessary distinctions engrafted thereon, and this in children of the same stock, is still almost proverbial on the continent,– especially, as I know from my own observation, in the south of Europe,–and appears to have been scarcely less common in our own island before the revolution of 1688, if we may judge from the characters and sentiments so frequent in our elder comedies. There is the younger brother, for instance, in Beaumont and Fletcher's play of *The Scornful Lady*, on the one side, and Oliver in Shakespeare's *As You Like It*, on the other.[388] Need it be said how heavy an aggravation the stain of bastardy must have been,

---

[385] *King Lear*, I, i, 24.
[386] In the sense of the word's Latin meaning, 'poison, venom'.
[387] The phrase was coined by Thomas Rymer in *The Tragedies of the Last Age Consider'd* (London: Richard Tonson, 1678) to describe how a work should inspire proper moral behaviour in its audience by showing good rewarded and vice punished.
[388] In Beaumont and Fletcher's *The Scornful Ladie: a Comedie* (1616) respectable Elder Loveless hands over his estate to his spendthrift brother Young Loveless; by way of contrast, in *As You Like It* Oliver drives his younger brother Orlando from his house.

were it only that the younger brother was liable to hear his own dis-honour and his mother's infamy related by his father with an excus-ing shrug of the shoulders, and in a tone betwixt waggery and shame!

By the circumstances here enumerated as so many predisposing causes, Edmund's character might well be deemed already sufficiently explained, and prepared for. But in this tragedy the story or fable constrained Shakespeare to introduce wickedness in an outrageous form in the persons of Regan and Gonerill. He had read nature too heedfully not to know, that courage, intellect, and strength of charac-ter are the most impressive forms of power, and that to power in itself, without reference to any moral end, an inevitable admiration and complacency appertains, whether it be displayed in the conquests of a Napoleon or Tamurlane, or in the foam and the thunder of a cataract. But in the display of such a character it was of the highest importance to prevent the guilt from passing into utter *monstrosity*,—which again depends on the presence or absence of causes and temptations suffi-cient to *account* for the wickedness, without the necessity of recurring to a thorough fiendishness of nature for its origination. For such are the appointed relations of intellectual power to truth, and of truth to goodness, that it becomes both morally and poetically unsafe to pres-ent what is admirable,—what our nature compels us to admire —in the mind, and what is most detestable in the heart, as co-existing in the same individual without any apparent connection, or any modification of the one by the other. That Shakespeare has in one instance, that of Iago, approached to this, and that he has done it successfully, is, perhaps, the most astonishing proof of his genius, and the opulence of its resources. But in the present tragedy, in which he was compelled to present a Gonerill and a Regan, it was most carefully to be avoided;— and therefore the only one conceivable addition to the inauspicious influences on the preformation of Edmund's character is given, in the information, that all the kindly counteractions to the mischievous feelings of shame that might have been derived from co-domestication with Edgar and their common father, had been cut off by his absence from home, and foreign education from boyhood to the present time, and the prospect of its continuance, as if to preclude all risk of his inter-ference with the father's views for the elder and legitimate Son:—'He hath been out nine years, and away he shall again'.[389]

Cor. Nothing, my lord.
Lear. Nothing?

[389] *King Lear*, I, i, 32–3.

Cor. Nothing.
Lear. Nothing can come of nothing: speak again.
Cor. Unhappy that I am, I cannot heave
My heart into my mouth: I love your majesty
According to my bond; nor more, nor less.[390]

There is something of disgust at the ruthless hypocrisy of her sisters, and some little faulty admixture of pride and sullenness in Cordelia's 'Nothing;' well contrived to lessen the glaring absurdity of Lear, but the surest plan that of forcing away the attention from the nursery-tale of the moment: it has answered its purpose, that of supplying the canvas to paint on. This is also materially furthered by Kent's opposition, which displays Lear's *moral* incapability of resigning the sovereign power in the very moment of disposing of it. Kent is, perhaps, the nearest to perfect goodness in all Shakespeare's characters, and yet the most *individualized.* His passionate affection and fidelity to Lear acts on our feelings in Lear's own favour. Virtue itself seems to be in company with him.

In Lear old age is itself a character,—its natural imperfections being increased by life-long habits of receiving a prompt obedience. Any addition of individuality would have been unnecessary and painful; for the relations of others to him, of wondrous fidelity and of frightful ingratitude, alone sufficiently distinguish him. Thus Lear becomes the open and ample play-room of nature's passions.

Knight. Since my young lady's going into France, Sir; the fool
       hath much pin'd away.[391]

The Fool is no comic buffoon to make the groundlings laugh,—no forced condescension of Shakespeare's genius to the taste of his audience. Accordingly he is *prepared* for, by bringing him into living connection with the pathos of the play, with the sufferings. He is as wonderful a creation as Caliban;— babbling the food of anguish to the mind of Lear, an inspired ideot.

The monster Goneril prepares what is *necessary,* while the character of Albany renders a still more maddening grievance possible, namely, Regan and Cornwall in perfect sympathy of monstrosity. Not a sentiment, not an image, that can give pleasure on its own account, is admitted; pure horror whenever these creatures are introduced, and they are brought forward as little as possible

In this scene and in all the early speeches of Lear, the one general

---

[390] *King Lear*, I, i, 85–93.
[391] *King Lear*, I, iv, 73.

sentiment of filial ingratitude prevails as the main spring of the feelings;—in this early stage the outward object causing the pressure on the mind, which is not yet sufficiently familiarized with the anguish for the imagination to work upon it.

> *Gon.* Do you mark that, my lord?
> *Alb.* I cannot be so partial, Goneril,
> To the great love I bear you.
> *Gon.* Pray you content, &c.[392]

Observe the baffled endeavour of Goneril to act on the fears of Albany, and yet his passiveness, his inertia; he is not convinced, and yet he is afraid of looking into the thing. Such characters always yield to those who will take the trouble of governing them, or for them.[393] Perhaps, the influence of a princess, whose choice of him had royalized his state, may be some little excuse for Albany's weakness.

> *Lear.* O let me not be mad, not mad, sweet heaven!
> Keep me in temper! I would not be mad!—[394]

The mind's own anticipation of madness! The deepest tragic notes are often struck by a half sense of an impending blow. The Fool's conclusion of this act by a grotesque prattling seems to indicate the dislocation of feeling that has begun and is to be continued.

Edgar's false madness serves the great purpose of taking off part of the shock which would otherwise be caused by the true madness of Lear, as well as displaying the profound difference between the two. In modern dramatic literature, madness is shown as mere lightheadedness, as especially in Otway's fanciful delirium:

> Lutes, Laurels, Seas of Milk and ships of Amber.[395]

The excess of folly is delirium, of imagination mania. In Edgar's ravings Shakespeare all the while lets you see a fixed purpose, a practical end in view;—in Lear's, there is only the brooding of the one anguish, an eddy without progression.

---

[392] *King Lear*, I, iv, 273–6.

[393] At this point in his notes (and presumably, not for the lecture as such) Coleridge wrote 'Σιρ T.B. + Σ.Γ.B', a Greek cipher ('Sir T.B. and S.G.B') for Sir Thomas Betrand and Sir George Beaumont, two noblemen who had befriended Coleridge and were acting as his patrons.

[394] *King Lear*, I, v, 46–7.

[395] Thomas Otway's *Venice Preserv'd, or a Plot Discover'd* (London: T. Johnson, 1682), 5.369. The heroine Belvedere has been driven out of her wits by attempted rape and threats of death. Coleridge returned to this line, and its banality when compared with *Lear*'s representation of madness, in Chapter 4 of the *Biographia Literaria*.

Nothing is so heart-cutting as a cold unexpected defence of a cruelty complained of passionately, or so expressive of thorough hard-heartedness. And feel the excessive horror of Regan's 'O, Sir, you are old!'[396]—and then her drawing from that universal object of reverence and indulgence the very reason for her frightful conclusion—'Say, you have wrong'd her!' All Lear's faults increase our pity for him. We refuse to know them otherwise than as means and aggravations of his sufferings and his daughters' ingratitude. The tranquillity from the first *stun* permits Lear to *reason*—

O, reason not the need! Our basest beggars
Are in the poorest thing superfluous.
Allow not nature more than nature needs,
Man's life's as cheap as beast's. Thou art a lady.
If only to go warm were gorgeous,
Why, nature needs not what thou gorgeous wear'st,
Which scarcely keeps thee warm. But, for true need—
You heavens, give me that patience, patience I need.
You see me here, you gods, a poor old man,
As full of grief as age, wretched in both.
If it be you that stir these daughters' hearts
Against their father, fool me not so much
To bear it tamely. Touch me with noble anger.
And let not women's weapons, water drops,
Stain my man's cheeks![397]

Thence to the fourth scene of the third Act. O, what a world's convention of agonies is here! All external nature in a storm, all moral nature convulsed,—the real madness of Lear, the feigned madness of Edgar, the babbling of the Fool, the desperate fidelity of Kent—surely such a scene was never conceived before or since! Take it but as a picture for the eye only, it is more terrific than any which a Michel Angelo, inspired by a Dante, could have conceived, and which none but a Michel Angelo could have executed. Or let it have been uttered to the blind, the howlings of nature would seem converted into the voice of conscious humanity. This scene ends with the first symptoms of positive derangement; and the intervention of the fifth scene is particularly judicious,—the interruption allowing an interval for Lear to appear in full madness in the sixth scene. Lear's speech:—

---

[396] *King Lear*, II, iv, 139; the following quotation is line 144.
[397] *King Lear*, II, iv, 259–73.

> Ha! Goneril!–with a white beard!–They flattered me like a dog;
> and told me, I had white hairs in my beard, ere the black ones
> were there. To say Ay and No to every thing I said!–Ay and No
> too was no good divinity. When the rain came to wet me once,
> &c.[398]

The thunder recurs, but still at a greater distance from our feelings.
And then in scene seven:–

> Where have I been? Where am I?–Fair daylight?–
> I am mightily abused.–I should even die with pity
> To see another thus, &c.[399]

How beautifully the affecting return of Lear to reason, and the mild
pathos of these speeches prepare the mind for the last sad, yet sweet,
consolation of the aged sufferer's death!

---

[398] *King Lear*, IV, vi, 80f.
[399] *King Lear*, IV, vii, 52f.

Lectures on Shakespeare, Milton, Dante, Spenser, Ariosto and Cervantes, 1819

Samuel Taylor Coleridge

Venue: the Crown and Anchor Tavern, off the Strand.

[Lecture 1: Thursday 11 February 1819]
[Lecture 2: Thursday 18 February 1819]
Lecture 3: Thursday 25 February 1819 (*Troilus and Cressida*)
[Lecture 4: Thursday 4 March 1819]
[Lecture 5: Thursday 11 March 1819]
[Lecture 6: Thursday 18 March 1819]
[Lecture 7: Thursday 25 March 1819]

A PORTION OF LECTURE 3

According to a note in Stockdale's edition: 'Mr. Pope (after Dryden) informs us, that the story of Troilus and Cressida was originally the work of one Lollius, a Lombard: but Dryden goes yet further; he declares it to have been written in Latin verse, and that Chaucer translated it.–Lollius was a historiographer of Urbino in Italy.'[400]

'*Lollius was a historiographer of Urbino in Italy.*' So affirms the notary, to whom the Sieur Stockdale committed the *disfacimento*[401] of Ayscough's excellent edition of Shakespeare. Pity that the researchful notary has not either told us in what century, and of what history, he was a writer, or been simply content to depose, that Lollius, if a writer of that name existed at all, was a somewhat somewhere. The notary speaks of the *Troy Boke* of Lydgate, printed in 1513. I have never seen it; but I deeply regret that Chalmers did not substitute the whole of Lydgate's works from the MSS. extant, for the almost worthless Gower.[402]

The *Troilus and Cressida* of Shakespeare can scarcely be classed with his dramas of Greek and Roman history; but it forms an intermediate link between the fictitious Greek and Roman histories, which we may call legendary dramas, and the proper ancient histories; that is, between the *Pericles* or *Titus Andronicus*, and the *Coriolanus*, or *Julius Caesar*. *Cymbeline* is a congener[403] with *Pericles*, and distinguished from *Lear* by not having any declared prominent object. But where shall we class the *Timon of Athens*? Perhaps immediately below *Lear*. It is a *Lear* of the satirical drama; a *Lear* of domestic or ordinary life;–a local eddy of passion on the high road of society, while all around is the week-day goings on of wind and weather; a *Lear*, therefore, without its soul-searching flashes, its ear-cleaving thunder-claps, its

---

[400] This is Samuel Ayscough's *The Dramatic Works of William Shakespeare with, Explanatory Notes*. The passage quoted here is from 2:857, Ayscough's headnote to *Troilus and Cressida*. It continues: 'Shakspeare received the greatest part of his materials for the structure of this play from the *Troy Boke* of Lydgate, printed in 1513.'

[401] 'Decline' or 'decay'.

[402] In Alexander Chalmers (ed.), *The Plays of William Shakespeare, vol. VI, containing King Henry the Sixth, Part 3, King Richard the Third, King Henry the Eighth, Troilus and Cressida* (London: F. C. and J. Rivington, 1805).

[403] That is, it belongs in the same class as.

meteoric splendours,—without the contagion and the fearful sympathies of nature, the fates, the furies, the frenzied elements, dancing in and out, now breaking through, and scattering, now hand in hand with, the fierce or fantastic group of human passions, crimes, and anguishes, reeling on the unsteady ground, in a wild harmony to the shock and the swell of an earthquake. But my present subject is *Troilus and Cressida*; and I suppose that, scarcely knowing what to say of it, I by a cunning of instinct run off to subjects on which I should find it difficult not to say too much, though certain after all that I should still leave the better part unsaid, and the gleaning for others richer than my own harvest.

Indeed, there is no one of Shakespeare's plays harder to characterize. The name and the remembrances connected with it prepare us for the representation of attachment no less faithful than fervent on the side of the youth, and of sudden and shameless inconstancy on the part of the lady, And this is, indeed, as the gold thread on which the scenes are strung, though often kept out of sight, and out of mind by gems of greater value than itself. But as Shakespeare calls forth nothing from the mausoleum of history, or the catacombs of tradition, without giving, or eliciting, some permanent and general interest, and brings forward no subject which he does not moralize or intellectualize,—so here he has drawn in Cressida the portrait of a vehement passion, that, having its true origin and proper cause in warmth of temperament, fastens on, rather than fixes to, some one object by *liking* and temporary preference.

> Fie, fie upon her!
> There's language in her eye, her cheek, her lip,
> Nay, her foot speaks; her wanton spirits look out
> At every joint and motive of her body. Such set down
> For sluttish spoils of opportunity,
> And daughters of the game[404]

This Shakespeare has contrasted with the profound affection represented in Troilus, and alone worthy the name of love;—affection, passionate indeed, swoln with the confluence of youthful instincts and youthful fancy, and growing in the radiance of hope newly risen, in short enlarged by the collective sympathies of nature;—but still having a depth of calmer element in a will stronger than desire, more entire than choice, and which gives permanence to its own act by converting it into faith and duty. Hence with excellent judgment, and

---

[404] *Troilus and Cressida*, IV, vi, 55–64, omitting lines 59–62.

with an excellence higher than mere judgment can give, at the close of the play, when Cressida has sunk into infamy below retrieval and beneath hope, the same will, which had been the substance and the basis of his love, while the restless pleasures and passionate longings, like sea-waves, had tossed but on its surface,—this same moral energy is represented as snatching him aloof from all neighbourhood with her dishonour, from all lingering fondness and languishing regrets, whilst it rushes with him into other and nobler duties, and deepens the channel, which his heroic brother's death had left empty for its collected flood. Yet another secondary and subordinate purpose Shakespeare has inwoven with his delineation of these two characters,—that of opposing the inferior civilization, but purer morals, of the Trojans to the refinements, deep policy, but duplicity and sensual corruptions of the Greeks.

To all this, however, there is so little comparative projection given,—nay, the masterly group of the Greek warriors and statesmen, Agamemnon, Nestor, and Ulysses, and, still more in advance, Ajax, Achilles, and Thersites, so manifestly occupy the fore-ground, that the moral uppermost of the poet's intentions seems to be the natural vassalage of strength and courage to superior intellect. Nor has Shakespeare taken any pains to connect this truth with the more interesting moral embodied in the titular hero and heroine of the play. In fact, I am half inclined to believe, that in this piece Shakespeare gratified a fancy of his own, that he amused himself by translating the heroes of Greek tradition into the more intellectual, more complex, charactered and more *featurely* Knights of Christian chivalry, the distinct yet lightly-pencilled profiles of the Epic and Homeric muse into the substantial, robust individualities of the romantic drama. I mean that the *Troilus and Cressida* is, and was meant to be, a bold, broad picture, the subject being the Tale of Troy, but the figures all Gothic faces, and in Gothic drapery, each intensely filling the space it occupies, or recalling the wild fig or yew-tree, which, as if by some strange metempsychosis, the spirit of the hero below, had passed into it, splits the solid marble of the ancient tomb out of which it rises. In short, it is a grand history-piece, in the style of Albert Durer.[405]

I regret that I must leave the character of Thersites without more particular notice; for verily he is the Caliban of Demagogues;—who hates all his betters so sincerely, that he needs no end or motive

---

[405] The great German artist Albrecht Dürer (1471–1528). Presumably Coleridge's reference is to one of Dürer's vigorous engravings of Renaissance knights, such as 'Ritter, Tod und Teufel' ('The Knight, Death and the Devil', 1513).

for his malignity, but its own cordial and comforting virulence;—just shrewd enough to detect the weak brain, and sufficiently fool enough to provoke 'the armèd fist' of his superiors;[406]—he will shift at an hour's notice from one faction to its opposite, and enlist for a fresh bounty into a malcontent corps, with no other condition but that he shall be required to do nothing but *abuse*, and be allowed to abuse as much and as *purulently* as he likes, that is, as he can. Briefly, Thersites is—I say *is*, for he is one of the Immortals, and independently of his apotheosis and canonization by Homer and Shakespeare, survives by successive transmigration. Our Thersites is a mule;—quarrelsome by the original discord of his parentage, and contradictory in embryo;—a slave by tenure of his own baseness;—made to kick and be cudgelled, to bray and be brayed, to hate and despise and sink below hatred by being utterly despicable.

Aye, aye! But he is a devilish clever fellow for all that. The handsome Achilles, at the head of his Myrmidons, he who will trust neither party and scorns both Greek and Trojan, yet gave no little credit to his friend Thersites. And even Ajax, the champion of his country in a perilous time, declared publicly, that this very Thersites ought to have a statue of gold raised to his honour. True! and as far as relates to the latter instance, strange; but as true. Since an ass once spoke like an angel,[407] a wise man, and with almost an angel's tongue, may perhaps be forgiven for having once in his life uttered sounds too near to those of an ass.

[406] From Ajax's threat to Achilles: 'with my armèd fist/I'll pash him o'er the face' (*Troilus and Cressida*, II, iii, 191–2).

[407] Balaam's ass, that is, in Numbers 22: 21–8.

Appendix:
A Hitherto Unnoticed Account of
Coleridge's 1811–1812 Lecture Series

Although Foakes' two-volume edition of the *Lectures on Literature*[408] does a remarkable job in locating and collating the various scattered accounts and reports of Coleridge's lecturing, there are a few sources which he happened to miss. One such, a fairly lengthy account of lectures 4 and 7–9 of the 1811–12 series, is printed here, followed by some speculations as to its authorship. It appeared under the title: 'Intelligence–Literary, Philosophical &c' in *The General Chronicle and Literary Magazine* (4 (April 1812), 310–12, and 411–15). The first part of this is as follows:

> Mr. COLERIDGE, a gentleman already well known for his own poetical writings, has lately delivered, in the metropolis, lectures upon the general body of English poetry, not refraining even from the invidious task of delivering public criticisms upon the productions of living writers. Polite criticism is the source of so many elegant enjoyments, that every effort in that department claims the attention of persons of taste, and the present subject is one which strictly belongs to our head of Literary Intelligence.
>
> Mr. Coleridge was naturally led to dwell upon the writings of Shakespear, that well of poetry, the waters of which are continually presented to our lips, and of which we are yet never weary. He commenced his fourth lecture by adverting to the period when Shakespear wrote, and the discouragements of the poet, from the prejudices which prevailed against his sublime art. He conceived, with Mr. Malone, that Shakespear began his public career about 1591, when he was 27 years of age. From the rank his father sustained, he did not credit the stories of the humble situation of the poet, whose earliest productions he considered to be the *Venus and Adonis*, and *Lucrece*, and from these it was easy to

[408] R. A. Foakes, *Samuel Taylor Coleridge Lectures 1808–1819 on Literature* (2 vols, Princeton: Princeton University Press/London: Routledge, 1987).

predict his future greatness: *poeta nascitur non fit.* In these models we could discern that he possessed at least two indications of his genuine character—he was not merely endowed with a thirst for the end, but he enjoyed an ample capability of the means; and in the selection of his subject he distinguished one that was far removed from his private interests, feelings, and circumstances. A third was, that the *Venus and Adonis* is immediate in its impulse on the senses; everything is seen and heard as if represented by the most consummate actors. The poet does not, like Ariosto, or like Wieland, speak to our sensual appetites; but he has by his wonderful powers raised the student to his own level, a thousand exterior images forming his rich drapery, and all tending to profound reflection, so as to overpower and extinguish every thing derogatory and humiliating. As little can the mind, thus agitated, yield to low desire, as the mist can sleep on the surface of our northern Windermere, when the strong wind is driving the lake onward with foam and billows before it. There are three requisites to form the poet:—1, sensibility; 2, imagination; 3, powers of association. The last and least is principally conspicuous in this production; but although the least, it is yet a characteristic and great excellence of the art. The lecturer having read the description of the horse and the hare in the same piece, next proceeded to discuss the merits of the *Lucrece*, in which, he said, we observe impetuous vigour and activity, with a much larger display of profound reflection, and a perfect dominion over the whole of our language, but nothing deeply pathetic, examining the dramatic he should rather pursue the order which had been composed: *Love's Labour Lost—All's Well that Ends Well—Romeo and Juliet—The Midsummer Night's Dream—As You Like It—Twelfth Night*—which were produced when the genius of the poet was ripening. Then he should follow him through *Troilus and Cressida—Cymbeline—The Merchant of Venice*—and *Much Ado about Nothing.* Last, to the grandest efforts of his pen, *Macbeth—Lear—Hamlet*—and *Othello.* These interesting subjects were reserved for the next and ensuing lectures. After some short comparative observations, principally in vindication of the great dramatist, Mr. Coleridge concluded with a simple passage from Burns, to show the capacity of the poet to give novelty and freshness, profundity and wisdom, entertainment and instruction, to the most familiar objects. This is eminently conspicuous, when the transient character of his subject is thus beautifully expressed by the Scottish bard:

Like snow that falls upon a river
A moment white, then gone for ever![409]

The second part follows on pages 411–15:

Mr COLERIDGE having concluded the preliminary discussions
on the nature of the Shakspearian Drama and the genius of the
poet, and briefly noticed *Love's Labour Lost*, as the link which connected together the poet and the dramatist, proceeded in his seventh lecture to an elaborate review of *Romeo and Juliet*, a play in
which are to be found all the individual excellences of the author,
but less happily combined than in his riper productions. This
Mr. C. observed to be the characteristic of genius, that its earliest
works are never inferior in beauties, while the merits which taste
and judgment can confer are of slow growth. Tibalt and Capulet
he showed to be representatives of classes which Shakespear
had observed in society, while in Mercutio he exhibited the first
character of his own conception; a character formed of poetic
elements, which meditation rather than observation had revealed
to him; a man full of high fancy and rapid thought, conscious
of his own powers, careless of life, generous, noble, a perfect
gentleman. On his fate hangs the catastrophe of the tragedy. In
commenting on the character of the Nurse, Mr. C. strenuously
resisted the suggestion, that this was a mere piece of Dutch painting; a portrait in the style of Gerard Dow. On the contrary, her
character is exquisitely generalized, and is subservient to the display of fine moral contrasts. Her fondness for Juliet is delightfully
pathetic: What a melancholy world would this be without children! how inhuman, without old age! Her loquacity is characteristic of a vulgar mind, which recollects merely by coincidence
of time and place, while cultivated minds connect their ideas by
cause and effect. Having admitted that these lower persons might
be suggested to Shakespear by observation, Mr. C. reverted to
his ideal characters, and said, I ask, where Shakespear observed
this? (an heroic sentiment of Othello's) it was with his inward
eye of meditation on his own nature. He became Othello, and
therefore spoke like him. Shakespear became, in fact, all men but
the vicious; but in drawing his characters, he regarded essential,
not accidental relations. Avarice he never pourtrayed, for avarice
is a factitious passion. *The Miser* of Plautus and Moliere is already
obsolete; Mr. C. entered into a discussion of the nature of fancy;

---

[409] Robert Burns, 'Tam o'Shanter' (1791), 61–2.

showed how Shakespear, composing under a feeling of the unimaginable, and endeavouring to reconcile opposites by producing
a strong working of the mind, was led to those earnest conceits
which are consistent with passion, though frigidly imitated by
writers without any. He illustrated this part of his subject by a
reference to Milton's conception of Death, which the painters
absurdly endeavour to strip of its fanciful nature, and render
definite by the figure of a skeleton, the dryest of all images, compared with which, a square or a triangle is a luxuriant fancy.

Mr. C. postponed the examination of the hero and heroine of
the piece, but prefaced his inquiry by remarks on the nature of
love, which he defined to be a perfect desire of the whole being
to be united to some thing or being which is felt necessary to its
perfection, by the most perfect means that nature permits, and
reason dictates; and took occasion, with great delicacy, to contrast this link of our higher and lower nature, this noblest energy
of our human and social beings with what, by gross misnomer,
usurps its name; and asserted, that the criterion of honour and
worth among men is their habit of sentiment on the subject of
love.

Mr. Coleridge commenced his eighth lecture by pointing out
the great similarity in the effects produced by poetry and religion,
the latter of which he had ever deemed the poetry of all mankind,
in which the divinest truths were revealed. He had heard it said,
that 'an undevout astronomer is mad;' much more truly might it
be stated, that an undevout poet is insane; in fact it was an impossibility. After impressing upon his auditors what a poet was, viz.
that he combined all the feelings of the child with the powers of
the man, he proceeded to trace the passion of love from its earliest origin, asserting by the way, that Shakespear and Sir Philip
Sidney only, of all their contemporaries, entertained a fit notion
of the female character. They rose like the heads of two mighty
mountains in a deluge, remaining islands, while all around them
was swallowed up by the oblivious flood. He next entered at
length into a defence of the existence of love as a passion, fitted
only for, and appropriate only to, human nature, during which
he combated with much force the doctrines of the materialists,
maintaining that man was formed of body and of mind, and
that in the heights of joy or the depths of sorrow, although the
former was the willing and sympathising servant, the latter was
mainly acted upon by the delight or by the sorrow. He asserted,
that without marriage, the result of exclusive attachment, which

was dictated by heaven, men might be herds, but could not form
society: without it, all the sacred affections and charities of our
nature could never have existence.

The origin and cause of love was a consciousness of imperfection, and an unceasing desire to remedy it: it was a yearning after
an ideal image, necessary to complete the happiness of man, by
supplying what in him was deficient; and Shakespear, throughout
his works, had viewed the passion in this dignified light: he had
conceived it not only with moral grandeur, but with philosophical penetration. Romeo had formed his ideal image; he imagined
that Rosaline supplied the deficiency; but the moment he beheld
Juliet he discovered his mistake; he felt a nearer affinity to her,
he became perfectly enamoured, and the love he felt formed the
foundation of the tragedy. The feeling of Romeo towards Juliet
was wholly different, as he himself expressed it, from that which
he had experienced toward Rosaline.

The lecturer went on to notice the analogy between the operations of the mind with regard to taste and love, as with the
former an ideal image had been created which the reason was
anxious to realize. Other passions distort whatever object is presented to them. Lear accused the elements of ingratitude, and the
madman imagined the straws on which he trampled to be the
golden pavement of a palace; but, with love, every thing was in
harmony, and all produced natural and delightful associations.
In Mr. C.'s opinion, the conceits put into the mouths of Romeo
and Juliet are perfectly natural to their age and inexperience. It
was Shakespear's intention in this play to represent love as existing rather in the imagination, than in the feelings, as was shown
by the imaginative dialogue between the hero and heroine, in
the parting scene in the third act. The passion in the youthful
Romeo was wholly different from that of the deliberate Othello,
who entered the marriage state with deep moral reflections on its
objects and consequences. The lecturer insisted that love was an
act of the will, and ridiculed the sickly nonsense of Sterne and
his imitators, French and English, who maintained that it was an
involuntary emotion. Having adverted to the trueness to nature
of the tragic parts of Romeo and Juliet, Mr. Coleridge concluded
by referring to Shakespear's description of the Apothecary, too
often quoted against those of unfortunate physiognomy, or
those depressed by poverty. Shakespear meant much more; he
intended to convey, that in every man's face there was either
to be found a history or a prophecy—a history of struggles past,

or a prophecy of events to come. In contemplating the face of the most abandoned of mankind, many lineaments of villainy would be seen; yet, in the under features (if he might so express himself), would be traced the lines that former sufferings and struggles had impressed, lines which would always sadden and frequently soften the observer, and raise a determination in him not to despair of the unfortunate object, but to regard him with the feelings of a brother.

Mr. Coleridge introduced his ninth lecture by some original remarks on the distinction between sculpture and painting, and drew an analogy between them and the ancient and the Shakespearian drama. He noticed the advantages and disadvantages of which our immortal poet had to avail himself or to combat, bestowing some severe censures on what was called the 'Sentimental Drama,' which, in its highest state of perfection, only aspired 'to the genius of an onion, the power of drawing tears.' Shakespear's characters, he observed, from Macbeth down to Dogberry, were ideal, and the reader almost every where sees himself depicted without being conscious of it, but much exalted and improved; as the traveller in the North of Germany, at sunrise, in the mists of morning beholds his own form, of gigantic proportions, only knowing it to be his own by the similarity of action. The lecturer afterward adverted to the defective criticism of the English commentators on Shakespear, and the just conceptions of his talents by the German writers, accounting for it by observing, that Englishmen had been chiefly employed in action, while Germans, incapable of action, had been engaged in reflecting upon action. – Shakespear's plays might be divided, first, into those where the real was disguised in the ideal; 2dly, into those where the ideal was hidden in the real. At present, he should refer to those where the ideal was predominant, and chiefly because many objections had been raised against such performances; not objections the growth of England, but of France; the judgment of monkies, by some wonderful phenomenon, put into the mouths of men. As a specimen of the ideal plays, Mr. Coleridge took the Tempest, of which he entered into an elaborate criticism. In the first scene the author had shown his wonderful power of combination of the gay with the sad; where even laughter added to the tear which grief had drawn. He had there likewise introduced the most profound sentiments of wisdom; and Mr. Coleridge illustrated his position by various quotations. In the succeeding scene, Prospero and

Miranda are introduced, the latter of whom possessed all the exquisite sensibility of a female brought up far from the busy haunts of men, yet with all the advantages of education. Mr. C. dwelt with peculiar felicity on the various delicate traits of her character. The admirable gradations by which the supernatural powers of Prospero were disclosed, were also noticed, as well as the natural developement of the fable in the relation of the father to his daughter; and Shakespear's accurate knowledge of human nature, by the circumstances of the recollection of long past events by Miranda. The great picturesque power of the poet, equalled only by Pindar and Dante, which often consisted in supplying by a mere epithet a picture to the imagination of the reader, and the inimitable preparation for the conclusion by the fine judgment of Shakespear, received much attention. The character of Ariel, which was neither angel, gnome, nor demon, but rather like a child supernaturally gifted, was happily opposed to Caliban, painted with such masterly originality, and introduced by the brutal sound of his inhuman voice before his disgusting shape was exhibited to view. After slightly glancing at the characters of Ferdinand and Alonzo, Mr. C. entered into an eulogy of the scene in which a conspiracy was formed to destroy the latter, and explained his reasons for the praise he bestowed in opposition to the opinions of Pope and Arbuthnot. He concluded, by justifying the expression employed by Prospero to his daughter, 'Advance the fringed curtain of thine eye,' which the two annotators above noticed had asserted to be gross bombast.

There is a good deal of specific detail in this second account which confirms Collier's notes of these later lectures. Burns is quoted in Lecture 4, or rather slightly misquoted here exactly as Tomalin records (the actual line is 'Or like the snow falls in the river . . .') which suggests the misquotation may have been Coleridge's own. Coleridge's repudiation of the idea that the Nurse in *Romeo and Juliet* is like the from-life paintings of Gerard Dow (more usually spelled Dou) and the points about Milton's death are in Lecture 7; the points about Sidney and Lear in Lecture 8 and the rest in Lecture 9. Indeed the close parallels between the phrasing here and the phrasing in Collier's notes, down to multiple specific expressions and sentences, and idiosyncrasies of spelling (from 'Dow' and 'monkies' to 'developement') speaks either to the accuracy of Collier's note-taking, or, surely more likely, to the fact that Collier himself wrote this account of the lectures for *The General Chronicle and Literary Magazine*. The bad news for our purposes is that this account adds nothing to the accounts we already have of these lectures. Still, if this 1812 report is by Collier, there's one small germ of interest: for he later lost his notes on Lecture 4, and so the paragraphs above may constitute his only remaining account of that lecture. The points mentioned are all logged by Tomalin, although the phrasing is subtly different in places. So the account here, perhaps by Collier:

> As little can the mind, thus agitated, yield to low desire, as the mist can sleep on the surface of our northern Windermere, when the strong wind is driving the lake onward with foam and billows before it.

Where the version recorded by Tomalin is:

> The reader's thoughts are forced into too much action to sympathise with what is merely passion in our nature. As little could the noisome mist hang over our northern Windermere, when a strong and invigorating gale was driving the lake in foam and billows before it.

If this is Collier, then it would at least explain why he was so assiduous in taking shorthand notes of these lectures: he was reporting them, and presumably getting paid.

Index